# NOTHING IS WRITTEN IN STONE

*The Notebooks of*

## JUSTIN KEATING

*Edited by* **ANNA KEALY**
*and* **BARBARA HUSSEY**

THE LILLIPUT PRESS
DUBLIN

First published 2017 by
THE LILLIPUT PRESS
62–63 Sitric Road, Arbour Hill
Dublin 7, Ireland
www.lilliputpress.ie

ISBN 978 1 84351 677 4

A CIP record for this title is available from
The British Library.

10 9 8 7 6 5 4 3 2 1

Set in 11 pt on 15 pt Garamond with
Frutiger display by Marsha Swan
Printed in Spain by GraphyCems

# Contents

*Illustrations between pages 142 and 143*

# *Foreword*

It was 1973 and there were problems. I was preparing to shoot *Zardoz* at Ardmore Film Studios. We were building sets. Seán Connery and Charlotte Rampling were on their way.

The carpenters demanded equal pay with the prop men. The prop men insisted on maintaining their differential with the carpenters. It was intractable. We ground to a halt. I needed a lot of rifles for the picture. For a film you hire weapons from Bapty's in London, but there was a war raging in the North and there was a strict prohibition on importing weapons, even ones that couldn't fire bullets. One of the offending carpenters whispered in my ear that the lads from the North could get me all the guns I needed.

Justin Keating was the newly appointed Minister for Industry and Commerce. I sought an audience and listed my woes. He looked stern. At the mention of the IRA offer he bristled with fury. He made notes. I found him intimidating. Oh, by the way, I said, the studio is going broke and threatening to close us down. Would the government consider taking it over? His severe visage broke into a crooked smile. He said, Is there anything else I can do for you?

He acted decisively. We got our weapons. The carpenters and the propmen were shamed at stopping the movie. They kissed and made up. Justin bought the studio.

He became a friend. And on many an occasion, with the help of a couple of jars, I began to realize what an extraordinary man he was. He wanted to root out corruption and cronyism from politics; he was a lapsed Communist but wanted Ireland to become a socialist republic. He believed that the Catholic Church was an oppressive colonial power that had kept the country weak. He planned its demise. Despite (or because of) having a Jewish wife, he was passionately and publically anti-Zionist. He was cultured and well read. He had a grasp of history. He knew all about agriculture and how to feed the world, and about our obligation to nurture the earth. He was so far removed from the tribalism and village pump politics of Ireland of the day that one wondered how on earth he had got into government.

A couple of years later I was shooting at the Warner Brothers Studios in LA. Justin called me to say he was coming over to drum up business. I told the studio how important he was. He came on to the set, where a huge floral tribute awaited him in the colours of the Irish flag. The crew and cast applauded. He was not in the least embarrassed.

What a delightful surprise that Justin speaks to us from beyond the grave, as it were, with all the old brio and wit and wisdom. We owe a debt to those who rescued these notebooks so long after his death.

At his humanist funeral where no priest dared show his face, his son David spoke eloquently of his father's multifaceted life, and as he was lowered into the grave in his cardboard coffin I joined his comrades from the Labour Party in singing 'The Internationale'. Michael D. Higgins was in particularly good voice, I recall.

*John Boorman, Wicklow*

# Preface

After I retired from legal practice, Justin and I were able to spend time in a family house in the Languedoc in France, and most days while we were there he would devote time to writing in his notebook, a simple copybook bought in the local shop. I can see him now, settling down at the table. Once he began to write, the words seemed to flow for him. He left eight notebooks. The earliest is dated July 2006, the final one October 2009, and for one or two there is no date.[1]

He wrote down what he could recall from memory and expected to have time to check details later; he didn't get that time. So I have done that to the best of my ability, but lacking notes to work from, I may have overlooked items he would have checked. For instance, some poetry extracts are educated guesses, with only the poet's name for guidance.

Justin lived his life as though he had forever – a wonderful way to live, considering the dire warning he had been given upon his diagnosis with Paget's disease in the late 1970s. However, on the last day of 2009, with snow on the ground, he went to bed for a rest and never woke up. He was just seven days short of his eightieth birthday.

As he would have said, why am I telling you this? Well, the notebooks were there, of course, uncorrected and unfinished. For a time they remained in a filing cabinet – I found it very painful to open them because his voice comes through so strongly in the writing. Slowly, I started to read them and realized he could make me laugh still, and his ideas were interesting. Using speech dictation

---

1. The original notebooks will reside with the Justin Keating papers in the University College Dublin Archive and will be available once the papers have been catalogued.

software, I read his words aloud and found I had the beginnings of this manuscript. I emailed the first part to my stepchildren, Carla [King], Eilis [Quinlan] and David. They were intrigued and wanted more. I moved house twice in the meantime, but eventually all eight notebooks were transcribed. It seemed to us that much of what he had to say was relevant to today's world.

## THINGS HE DIDN'T WRITE ABOUT

Justin loved his three children deeply, as well as his grandchildren and great-grandchildren. Yet in his notebooks he had not got much beyond the description of their births and the delight he experienced with Laura then. He did not plan to die before finishing his book. He would have regretted not getting the time to write more. But there is also very little about his father Seán, and again, I think he intended to come back to that – a recurring phrase in the notebooks. However, there is a passage in which Justin describes his father as the most honest man he ever met. I suggest that the theme of reworking his paradigm, which lies at the heart of the book, is an attempt by Justin to re-examine and not only correct, but also acknowledge, his mistaken attitudes/stances and actions and take responsibility for them. A phrase he liked was 'If you show me better, then I must change.'

Another surprising omission is that of humanism. He devoted a lot of time and energy to the movement, and yet there is barely a mention of it or the important role he played in attracting people to learn about it. While he wrote with conviction about the teaching of religion and the damage he believed it has caused, it is unfortunate that he didn't get the opportunity to write about the positivity of the humanist ethic for its followers. One of his articles, 'The Greening of Humanism', is included in the book.

He was a gregarious man with a wide circle of friends, and a good storyteller. However, in the last four or five years of his life Justin became less mobile as the Paget's disease took hold, and he endured a lot of pain.[2] One of the crueller twists of fate was that his hearing went; in restaurants or crowded places he struggled to hear the conversation. By happenstance the pitch of my voice is such that he could usually hear me, so at times I took on the role of intermediary.

Justin was widely acknowledged as a brilliant communicator. In tribute, Brendan Halligan wrote: 'Cool, rational and patient in debate, his forensic skills

---

2. Paget's disease of bone accelerates the generation of new bone tissue. Affected bones can become soft and fragile over time, leading to bone pain and deformity.

in assembling and deconstructing a debate were legendary.' He believed that communication was a skill, and it was one he worked at and honed for each lecture and speech until he was satisfied. On television, he had a way of leaning into the camera to better convey his point. He often criticized those who delivered their message 'from above' with this quotation from Oliver Goldsmith's *The Deserted Village*:

> And still they gazed, and still the wonder grew
> That one small head could carry all he knew.

Those expecting an academic's tone might be surprised by his conversational style. My sense is that this was intentional, because Justin wanted to examine complex ideas without distancing any part of an audience.

Along the way I have wavered about publishing the book, but was spurred on by the encouragement I got from David, Eilis and particularly Carla, who has been hugely helpful and endlessly patient. I am pleased that Lilliput Press is publishing the book and I look forward to its launch and its reception. My greatest regret is that Justin is not here to debate the issues with readers.

Finally, I want to thank Anna Kealy, who has done a huge amount of work editing the book with me. It was not an easy task. The family and I wanted to make sure Justin's voice came through in the book and she was most meticulous about this; even when her judgement might have urged her to tweak a bit here and there, she stuck to her brief. Her contribution was enormous and I could not have got the book to publication without her help. It was a pleasure to work with her on the project, particularly when there was time for coffee, chat and the odd piece of chocolate cake.

*Barbara Hussey*

All eight handwritten notebooks. *Courtesy of Anna Kealy.*

# Editorial Preface

When Barbara approached me for help in editing Justin's notebooks, I was intrigued. It has turned out to be a uniquely fascinating project, not only in its wide-ranging, forthright content but also in its complexity as an editorial brief.

In their raw form, the notebooks were a work obviously interrupted. Life episodes, vivid anecdotes and impassioned arguments unfurled in no sequence beyond that in which they had come to Justin with pen in hand. He had composed multiple drafts of many episodes – consistent in fact, but varying in context or intricacy – and these had to be streamlined or merged as seamlessly as possible. The scope of his subject matter was immense, and he had left gaps in the text or notes to himself where he had intended to confirm details, to later expand upon a topic, or to connect it to another theme. Barbara invested long hours of research and consulted individuals to resolve lingering queries. Here and there a word in Justin's script was illegible, and amateur handwriting analysis came into play. Where a glancing reference was made or where additional information would be necessary or illuminating, footnotes were composed. Justin had envisioned a bibliography; this too was compiled and included.

Justin had also jotted down a few notes on his own intentions for the completed manuscript: major themes, a skeleton structure – and some keywords that now tantalize. We can't know what else he might have added (or indeed altered, come revision time). The text in our hands called for a bespoke structure, however. Of several alternatives, we settled on a structure of nine chapters progressing chronologically, each containing a section of personal narrative and a corresponding thematic segment. In this, the idea was to strike a balance between providing accessibility for readers and honouring Justin's firm belief that his own story was of less consequence than his conclusions – but that the path between the two was paramount.

On a personal note: rarely does an editorial project combine all the satisfaction of an intricate puzzle with such a riveting array of topics. In the many months' journey to publication, not a week went by without some national or international event relevant to the notebooks' contents. A great many project meetings began with an overview of these and some musings as to what Justin's thoughts might have been. I have come to admire his intellectual honour and curiosity; it feels strange to bid farewell to a voice I never heard in life, but which now seems very familiar. I hope that those who knew him best and those encountering his thinking for the first time in these pages will be equally absorbed.

*Anna Kealy*

# Acknowledgments

A large number of people have helped us along this journey from the handwritten notebooks Justin left to the finished book, whether with advice, information, permissions, encouragement or some combination of these: our heartfelt thanks go to all, including and beyond those named below.

The National University of Ireland has very generously awarded a grant in respect of the publication of *Nothing Written in Stone: The Notebooks of Justin Keating,* for which we are extremely grateful.

Especial thanks to David Keating, Carla King, Eilis Quinlan and Laura Kleanthous for permission to publish some of their personal photographs in the book, as well as their generosity in answering queries we raised and clarifying matters when the need arose. Thanks too to photographer Stan Shields of Galway, Asta Helleris, Paul Helleris, Helena Mulkerns and Lelia Doolan.

David McConnell, Honorary President of the Humanist Association of Ireland, kindly granted us permission to reproduce the article 'The Greening of Humanism'; thanks also to Billy Hutchinson, Nicolas Johnson, Catherine O'Brien and Brian Whiteside. Brian McClinton, then editor of *Humanism Ireland*, was extremely receptive and helpful.

Our thanks to Trevor White, former editor of *The Dubliner* magazine, who granted permission for the reproduction of the article in Appendix D, and to Rabbi David Goldberg, for permission to cite from his response.

Others whose assistance was much appreciated: Dominic Martella, UCD Faculty of Veterinary Medicine; Kate Manning, UCD Archives; Dr Attracta Halpin; solicitors Linda Scales and Andrea Martin; Caroline Hussey; David Waddell; members of the Labour Party, including Senator Ivana Bacik, Tony Brown, Barry Desmond, Brendan Halligan, Ruairí Quinn, Denise Rogers, Willie Scally and Alex White.

A great deal of research went into identifying and confirming details from the original notebook text, and we received invaluable help in this from many and varied quarters.

Our thanks to those who helped on the topics of farming and television, particularly James Conway and Conal C. Shovlin, who responded to an appeal on the RTÉ radio programme 'Countrywide' by forwarding copies of their *Telefís Feirme* Certificates of Proficiency signed by Justin. Damien O'Reilly, Ian Wilson, Tom Llewelyn, John Holland, Larry Sheedy and Mary O'Hehir also helped us on that quest.

In addition, we are grateful to: Louis Keating and Eimear O'Connor, for their help on Seán Keating; Michael Viney, who was able to identify the 'dally dooker'; Biddy White Lennon, Guild of Foodwriters, Florence Campbell and Nigel Slater for their help with the date of the *Observer* amateur chef competition in which Justin was a finalist; James Harte at the National Library of Ireland; Lizzie MacGregor of the Scottish Poetry Library, who quickly identified Ronald Campbell MacFie's work from the few lines we had; Neil Ward, for his help on figures for spending on education; Ann Butler, who provided information about the works of Úna Troy (Elizabeth Connor); Margaret Quinlan and Owen Lewis for deciphering an illegible energy-related term; Una Keating, for her information on the trial of Charles Kerins; Michael Gorman, for lending us the book *Fallen Order: A History*.

Warm thanks to Maire Bates, Lorna Siggins, Joan Fitzpatrick, Don Buckley, Brid Fanning and Gerard Fanning, Marianne Gorman, Kaye Fanning and John Fanning, Katrina Goldstone, Gemma Hussey and Brian Hussey for their help and support throughout.

Many thanks to David Dickson, Professor of Modern History, Trinity College Dublin for his invaluable advice and guidance on the manuscript, and to pre-readers David Keating, Loughlin Kealy and Tom Hoban.

Lastly, we are most grateful to Antony Farrell and the Lilliput Press team, including Djinn von Noorden and Suzy Freeman; Niall McCormack, who designed the cover; John Boorman, for penning the Foreword; and Bill McCormack, for his voluntary contribution on the index.

# *Chronology*

1930 Born in Dublin to May and Seán Keating (7 January)

1935–38 Primary school at Loreto Rathfarnham

1938–45 Secondary school at Sandford Park School, Ranelagh

1942 Witnessed murder of Det. Sergeant Denis O'Brien (9 September)

1944 Witness at Special Criminal Court trial of Charles Kerins for Denis O'Brien's murder

1945 Passed Intermediate Certificate

1945–46 Dalton Tutorial School, Rathmines

1946 Matriculated and began pre-med at UCD

1946 Joined the Labour Party, founded Rathfarnham branch

1951 Graduated from UCD with MVB;[1] enrolled at University College London

1953 Married Loretta Wine at Caxton Hall, London (9 May)

1955 Returned to Dublin and lived in a flat in Kenilworth Square

1955–60 Worked at UCD Veterinary College, Dublin

1956 Carla born (9 April)

1958 Built house in Bolbrook, Tallaght

1958 Eilis born (18 January)

1959 Research in Sweden, France and Denmark; chose TCD over UCD

1960 Joined TCD as a lecturer in veterinary anatomy

1960 David born (30 May)

Early 1960s Joined the Grassland Association; became veterinary correspondent of *The Irish Farmers Journal*

---

1. *Medicinae Veterinariae Baccalaureus*, or Bachelor's degree in Veterinary Medicine.

1965 Took two-year leave of absence from TCD; became Head of Agricultural Broadcasting in RTÉ; left Labour Party

1965–67 Made *Telefís Feirme* and *On the Land*

1967 Made television documentary *Surrounded by Water*

1967–68 Rejoined Labour Party

1968 Made *Into Europe?*, contributed to *Work*, both documentaries

1969 Elected as Labour Party TD in North County Dublin

1969 Sold Bolbrook and bought Bishopland Farm

1973 Among Ireland's first participants in European parliament: Jan–Feb 1973

1973–77 In government (coalition with Fine Gael): Minister for Industry and Commerce

1975 Set up National Film Studios of Ireland

June 1977 Lost seat as TD – constituency had been reduced by one seat

1977–81 Elected to the Senate from the Agricultural Panel

1977 Elected Dean of the Faculty of Veterinary Medicine (UCD)

1977 Received diagnosis of Paget's disease

1978 Resigned as Dean, and as Associate Professor in Department of Veterinary Anatomy in UCD

1979 Made *A Sense of Excellence* – four programmes on Ireland's manmade cultural heritage

1983 Became Chairman of The Crafts Council of Ireland

1983 Made six-part television programme *Love's Island*, on Cyprus

Sept 1983 Politics programme on RTÉ: *Keating on Sunday*

1984 Member of the European Parliament (February–June)

1984 Appointed Chairman of the National Council for Educational Awards

1987 Finalist in UK Amateur Chef Competition

1992–97 Adjunct Professor of Equine Science at the University of Limerick

1995 Appeared in *Where Do I Begin*, a documentary on Seán Keating directed by David Keating (broadcast in 1996)

1998 Elected President of the Humanist Association of Ireland

July 2004 Finalization of divorce from first wife, Loretta

2005 Married Barbara Hussey (3 February)

2008 Interviewed by Rístéard O'Domhnaill for award-winning documentary *The Pipe* (2010)

2009 Died aged seventy-nine, at Ballymore Eustace (31 December)

# NOTHING IS WRITTEN IN STONE

# *Introduction*

I have been described as an 'opinionated little git', and I think that is fair. I have opinions on almost everything. Perhaps foolishly, I have done many different things in my life, and have therefore inevitably had a complex set of experiences. I don't think the recital of the detail of my life is of much interest, even to me. I have retained poor documentation and have no new revelations. I am not going to reveal or discuss the details of my private life, except in the broadest and most anonymous terms; it is not important (except to myself and those who love me).

Those who want scandal or the making public of things hitherto secret must look somewhere else. There is plenty of politics in it – but for the details, chapter and verse, of what went on during my time in government, a splendid account has been given by my friend Garret FitzGerald. The documentation is enormous. It will all ultimately come into the public domain. And during the last quarter-century I have lost interest in party politics (it is not where the real action is), just as I have in the TV and film industries, in which I used to have a deep interest. I can see no reason to think that my life has been so unique and extraordinary as to merit an autobiography, except that ... something of the politician remains. (There is always an escape clause.)

Since the early 1980s I have been progressively incapacitated, although I was able to do a few useful things of which I am proud, such as chairing the National Council for Educational Awards and, best of all, the establishment of the Faculty of Equine Studies at the University of Limerick. But I was not in continuous employment, and for much of the time I was not in an intense personal relationship. There's a famous question from a questionnaire by the late unloved Senator Joe McCarthy, which asked in its zeal to sniff out subversives: 'Do you read books?' And that was my salvation in the 1980s and later: I read books.

I realized that I had inherited a whole ideas system just by being born in the time and at the place where my consciousness formed. I did not choose it. Part of what I got, I feel lucky about and have retained, but much I have discarded. One might say that since retirement I have been reworking my paradigm. In that reworking I have reached conclusions, but as a humanist with a scientific training, I hold those conclusions lightly. It is a point of honour *not* to remain 'true to my beliefs'. On the contrary: the honour lies – if you show me better – in changing. And I hold these beliefs with various degrees of firmness and subject to continuous revision, so that they almost certainly contain inconsistencies. I have been modifying the software of my brain for all of my conscious life. I hope to be doing so until the day I die.

When I was in my teens I had many passionately held beliefs about almost everything, but they were diffuse, scattered, unconnected. The core of the paradigm was the great narrative of Communism. I also had strong opinions about food, mostly derived from those of my beloved aunt Mary Frances. I was very involved with gardening (here the influence was my mother) and with the countryside in general. I turned away from the city, though it was on my doorstep, to become a vet and a farmer. But the various beliefs, about God or sex or class relationships or food or global arrangements, were separate, not much worked out (though I didn't think this at the time) and held in what across the decades I can only call a 'Catholic way', by which I mean 'certainty received via authority'. The content of my paradigm was quite different, but my method of thinking was much the same as if I had been a Jew or a Muslim or Christian. I had never heard of Cromwell's explosion of exasperation: 'I beseech you in the bowels of Christ, conceive it possible that you may be mistaken!' I did not know enough to realize that I didn't know everything.

But six decades later my beliefs, though all lightly held, are growing together. The particular individual, accidental influences that build our youthful paradigm are mostly worked through, many of them rejected. But what surprises me a little, and gives me pleasure, is that the different bits are becoming reconciled and working their way into a single system. The way that I want to cook and eat and dress are all of a piece with my ideas about global warming, the defence of the ecosphere, Gaia[1] and the threat of nuclear extinction.

What I think is important, not just for me but for all of us, is the understanding that the paradigm received in childhood is a matter of accident: of where it was in the world that one's consciousness came into being. That has no more value as a life guide than any other life guide. Who can claim that the beliefs they inherited – some of which were forced upon them aged five or six or seven – were the best to be had, and that clinging to them through thick and thin is somehow a virtue? To me, the opposite is true. Show me better and I must change.

The faith-based affirmation 'I am right because my God told me' is the road to the destruction of humankind and the rest of our present natural world. I very strongly think that by holding beliefs by 'faith' or 'revelation' or the contents of some old book written in a different age, one does something very wicked which in our current world threatens the survival of our species in a way that it did not prior to the technological advances of the twentieth century. Since the dramatic expansions of chemistry (especially organic) and metallurgy – and subsequently of material science, atomic physics, world population, the science of arms and the rate at which we consume the earth's resources – we have a killing power completely new to human experience, making it more rather than less likely that we will destroy ourselves. If we continue to try to run the world using mainly a Judeo–Christian–Islamic paradigm, our species will become extinct quite quickly. Mayr (a very profound biologist) has estimated that most species last about 100,000 years, and our time is up.[2] Furthermore, I think that those who offer religious certainties to small children when they are at the height of the process of socialization are abusing those children and stealing their autonomy.

But nothing is set in stone; we can survive. Just not with a paradigm based on ignorant and superstitious belief that has its roots almost 3000 years ago. That of most people in most countries is built around a set of religious and nationalist and 'racist' myths (the inverted commas are because, in my view, there is no such thing as a race). This baggage is set fair to kill us. My deep conviction is that if many (if not all) of us do not change our inherited paradigm, then we will not survive the next century. This is our most pressing need.

---

1. The Gaia Hypothesis, formulated by chemist James Lovelock and microbiologist Lynn Margulis in the 1970s and introduced in *Gaia: A New Look at Life on Earth* (Oxford UP, 1979), proposes that organisms interact with their inorganic surroundings on Earth to form a holistic, self-regulating, complex system that helps to maintain conditions for life on the planet.
2. Ernst Walter Mayr (1904–2005) was one of the twentieth century's leading evolutionary biologists.

I see very little point in describing a series of experiences I particularly recall. But without listing the big themes that have taken over my mind, without indicating the evolution of my thought, without offering my conclusions after eight busy decades, a mere description would be worth neither writing nor reading. Some readers may want only the narrative. Some may want only the conclusions. But those who read both will find the connection. They will see where the conclusions are coming from. And *that* they may find interesting.

My justification for writing is this: I wish to record the evolution of my beliefs and then to set out my current conclusions. While I am satisfied that these treat of important questions, they may well be nonsense. So, this book contains a record of the events in my life that caused me to doubt, re-examine and very often change the set of ideas and ideals I grew up with. If it appears self-centred, it is because I have deliberately omitted a great deal: my friendships; the nuanced situations in which I found myself; much about my personal relationships with women; and my dealing with the issue, central to every life, of how we deal with our sexuality. The purpose is to explain the modifications I have made to my paradigm (there is that word again, but I need it) due to my life experiences.

But it is a record of where I am now – as a matter of honour, if you show me better, I must change – and the longer I live, the *more* I should change. I believe each of us has a duty to rework our paradigm till the day we die.

*Justin Keating*

# 1. Acorns to Oaks

## KILLAKEE

The moo-cows were coming up the road; only they weren't moo-cows, but Mr Doyle's bullocks. But the age I was, the distinction was lost on me. They were passing our gate and going on to the twenty-five acres of mountaintop above our house that Mr Doyle had rented from my father. Later on, when there was a drought, barrels of water were brought up on a cart and poured into a trough. Out of a desire to help, I added my little bit of piss, which act I was not allowed to forget for years. And the first horse I ever bestrode was Mr Doyle's carthorse; so flat of back that my short little legs stuck out sideways, so enormous that I was a little bit afraid.

Up the hill at Killakee, at the edge of the Featherbed bog, we lived in the second-last house. The Kellys were at the top, just below what is now the Killakee car park. Our house was a slightly elegant cottage, which was built, I guess, as part of the Massey estate. The ruins of the big house, the ice house which was near our home, the reservoir cottage just at the bend (the reservoir supplied water to the buildings, farm as well as domestic) which constituted the core of the estate; the whole decaying remains of wealthy elegance was part of my childhood playground. And we knew that my father was coming home when we heard the roar of the Harley Davidson as he changed down a gear at the reservoir corner.

Deep snow drifted in front of our house, so deep that it was higher than the front door. My father pulled the frozen door inwards so that there was the vertical face of snow preventing exit. And then a few days later, my father's brother Joe arrived outside in his car, packed with food to sustain his snowbound brother and his family. I have one other strong memory of my father from that time. He had a beautiful shotgun with a long single barrel; a poacher's gun, he used to say with a little pride. He was a splendid shot, though he would not kill for pleasure, only for the pot. But what wonders Killakee brought home! Rabbits, of course, and the odd hare. Also, with great pride, the odd snipe. Someone around us was rearing pheasants, and the odd wanderer got snapped up. And best of all, ah, best of all was the grouse. Colonel Guinness, who lived in Tibradden across the valley, used to keep a grouse moor, burning heather and employing beaters for the great days of the shoot. My father's twenty-five acres shared a boundary with the colonel's land, and the grouse were poached unmercifully. It wasn't just for the pot. There was a degree of redistributive class antagonism as well.

Posy Bevins had bright, bright, almost staring wild blue eyes. She helped my mother in the house. With two small children in a cottage with no running water, or flush toilet, or electricity, or gas for heating and cooking, and of course no telephone, it was almost the reverse of what the young are used to now. No grocery delivery on top of the mountain. And then, even housewives without much money could still have servants. Since the range of things that had to be done by hand was so enormous, there was good reason. Now there is every kind of kitchen equipment at the turn of a switch, and a developed delivery and takeaway system for food, but no help. Women are even more overburdened, since men mostly still refuse to take on their share of housework and cooking even when the women go out to work. Blessed are the ways of helpless men. For lots of men, it is a fine art.

Posy had no children of her own at that time, and to some extent that pert little boy (me) enjoyed the role of her surrogate child. 'Enjoyed' is the word. She knitted me an outfit in red wool. Trousers, top and a knitted cap. All in red, with a white bobble. We had a bad-tempered Bedlington terrier, wherever it came from. And one day, in a mad mood, she put the whole lot, from trousers to cap, onto our terrier, who enjoyed the game as much as I did. Red trousers on its hind legs, red jacket on its chest and forelegs, red knitted cap with a big bobble precariously on its head. My mother must have been out. I loved my mother, but I loved Posy too – she was so much fun.

At three years of age, or perhaps a little less, the red jumpsuit was important in fixing very early memories. Not as much as the 'moo-cows' or Mr Doyle's house, but after them, the red suit features in my earliest memories. Among the most exciting was wading waist-deep or deeper through crackling autumn leaves on the road at the back of Lord Massey's house. Those early memories were mostly very happy and nearly always out of doors, even when the weather was very cold. I grew up hardly noticing bad weather.

My older brother Mike was not an important part of my earliest memories. Posy, my mother, and a rather distant father (he always remained so) were the important people. Apart from that, my memories are of the wonderland on the top of Killakee mountain and the paths, trees and streams of the Massey estate.

But there is one darker memory, which influenced my whole life. There was a tiny mountain torrent behind our house. In winter it was full of very cold water, very narrow but surprisingly deep. I was walking across the hillside one day with my mother. She popped across the stream, turned and held her hand out to me. But I, proud of being able to walk across the field by myself (my wife would say I haven't changed a bit, even though I am crippled by Paget's disease), spurned the proffered hand and jumped – right into the middle of the stream, which swept me away, submerging me and turning me over. I fetched up what must have been eight or ten feet down at a shallow part, and my mother fished me out. It was not the indignity – I was much too frightened for that – but the terror from total submersion in very cold water, which made me afraid of water ever since. I learned to swim late and with difficulty, and I never learned to relax and trust the water. To this day I fight my liquid surroundings, and the only time I ever swam as I would wish was thirty years later, when I was drunk. Not to be advised.

'What was it?' I said to my mother years later. 'It was dark, I was sitting beside your legs, I was hugging a parcel in a brown paper bag, which was warm and slightly greasy, and we were moving. What was that?'

'You were hugging your supper,' she said. 'We stopped in Rathfarnham at the fish and chip shop in Church Lane. You were in the toe of the sidecar of the Harley Davidson and we were going home, up the mountain to Killakee.'

I didn't often get to ride in the sidecar, as my father favoured my older brother (there were just the two of us) in the small routine things that old motorcycles required. Mike became an engineer.

I asked my mother (like with the fish and chips) to tell me what I was looking at. If we looked out from across the road we could see Dublin and the bay spread out in front of us. If we moved a bit, we could see the edge of Dun Laoghaire harbour. A bit the other way and we could see over to Howth, Ireland's Eye and Lambay Island – if the air was clear, up to the mountains of Mourne. That particular day there were a few large ships in the bay, and one of them had a prominent plume of smoke. 'Why?' I asked. 'The Eucharistic Congress,' my mother replied, somewhat acidly. The ships had brought Catholics (pilgrims, I suppose you could call them) and then I noticed it was getting up steam to sail away again.

That was our world. Cold, poor, raw land and bog beyond, the ruins of the Massey estate, the Harley Davidson, Dublin spread out in front of us. To the left as we looked down on the city, there was the long reclining shape of Montpelier Hill like a breast, then crowned with the nipple of the Hellfire Club, in ruins, where a century and a half before the bucks of Dublin had caroused. Now the whole skyline is sanitized. Coniferous trees planted all over the top of Montpelier Hill have grown up to obscure the remains of other declamatory buildings, and all is respectable again.

In the 1920s and into my late teens we lived with the occasional disappearance of friends due to tuberculosis. My father had had a fright with TB before I was born. The family feared it. So my mother, the farmer's daughter from Co. Kildare, kept goats. I never tasted cow's milk till I was about five years old. And the odd surplus kid goat ended up being eaten also. Ever since, the common meats of intensive farming have seemed pale and flavourless in comparison to the game that formed my first palate, with goat's milk, and goat's curd cheese.

There was another strand, later important in my life, which I first became aware of in Killakee. Some IRA men, of whom George Gilmore was the only one I remember well, had built an arms dump towards the bottom of the Massey estate, and I remember the frisson when it was discovered, probably due to a tip-off, and emptied by local guards and detectives. I don't know when it happened. I didn't know what it meant, but I have a vague recollection of the phrase 'arms dump' and perhaps of the Broy Harriers,[1] whoever they were, who found the arms dump. It had been built by IRA men, including our friends the Gilmore brothers. And I remember my parents talking about Jack White, the scion of an eminent British army officer and an officer himself, who had changed sides and trained the Citizen Army. Many years later, in my early teens, I found and devoured a copy of *The Communist Manifesto* with Jack White's initials on it.

So there we were, on the top of our mountain. Not many neighbours. Not many other kids to play with. Just my brother, nearly three years older than me,

---

1. The Auxiliary Special Branch of the Gardaí, founded in 1934 and nicknamed for its founder Police Commissioner Eamon 'Ned' Broy, in a pun on the Bray Harriers hunt.

and myself. Aware of wild land and poor farmland, of domestic and wild animals, of the IRA and the Catholic Church, and very much of our parents. My father could do pretty much anything (except cook – perhaps, like a proper man of his day, it wasn't so much couldn't as wouldn't). He made my mother's gold wedding ring. He was a good carpenter. He made the stained-glass window for the main gable in the house he was just about to build. He was a skilful poacher. He was a brilliant photographer with the new movie cameras. He could take a piece of charcoal and draw a free line at the first try that was unquestionably and unalterably in the right place. About the pictures, at the time I knew and felt nothing.

My mother, I know in retrospect, was a witch. From me, that is high praise. Minding her goats, she could think like a goat. And with fruit and vegetables, it seemed that she could sense what they needed so that they performed with love, evidenced by splendid growth and performance. I have no idea how she knew all these things about the land, the animals and crops. She did not read all that much of instructive texts. But know she did. She was an earth mother. And in a completely non-spiritual way (which she would have mocked), she was in touch with the earth. I hope I learned a little of that from her; at least enough to try.

But the isolated idyll had to end. The land was poor. The house was uncomfortable. My father's work was in the city and we were far from the primary school that we were to attend.

My father bought a couple of acres of land at Ballyboden, just beyond Rathfarnham village, and designed a house. It was close enough to the nuns' primary school at Loreto Rathfarnham for Michael and me to walk there. We were about to be domesticated, though 'civilized' would be too strong a word. But I have never ceased, to this day, to miss the mountain.


### BALLYBODEN

What surprises me most as I write this, more than seventy years later, was that almost all the main currents of my life were already set before we came down off the mountain, what seems to me in retrospect to have been down from paradise.

The love of nature was already deep in me; of horses, cattle, trees and other plants. I learned then the sense of awe and delight and reverence from contact with nature that has served me all my life, in the way that religion serves many people. I learned that guns, physical force, the carryover from 1916, what I later knew as 'the national question', were an important part of life. And I had the first feeling, though very unclearly, that our family was a bit different; that my parents had no great desire to be part of any community, nor had any great respect for the prevailing ideas of our world.

My father was one of the most honest men I have ever met. It was not just that I never knew him to say anything that was not true. But if someone in friendship or admiration said complementary things, which were a bit of an exaggeration, he went back to correct them. Where did it come from, I wonder? Not from his home city of Limerick ('Mind you, I said nothing' … 'Whatever you say, say nothing when you talk about you-know-who' … 'Who told you that?'). Maybe from his 'sceptic' father. Perhaps in personal rejection of the sloppy mess that was the Limerick of his growing-up. He taught me how to use tools, how to sharpen them, most important of all, to love them. But he was austere and distant.

One of the joys of coming down from the mountain to our new house in Ballyboden was that it offered me new land to explore – much better land than Mr Doyle had rented from my father. There I saw my first warbles (almost totally gone now).[2] And there, over the wall from our land, on the edge of a mill stream, was a beautiful oak tree. The cattle loved to shelter under it, and they had mashed the surrounding earth to wonderful fertile mush. Aged about six, I was exploring this. I came on something about the size of the first joint of my thumb. Growing out from one end were two shoots, one going downwards and one up. I had no idea what it was, but I fished it out of the mud, wrapped it in a much-abused handkerchief, and carried it home to my father. What was it? 'An acorn,' he said, 'oak – aik.' I loved him for word explanations like that. And going down was not a shoot, he said, but the root. Going up: what would be the trunk and branches … of a huge tree. This blew my mind. 'What should I do?' I asked. 'Plant it – maybe it will live.' I did, and it did. It is three-quarters of a century growing; it is a huge tree now, scattering acorns of its own. And I love oaks more than any other tree, more even than noble beeches and graceful birch, which give us delicious refreshing drinks when the sap is rising. I've given mine the odd hug.

We moved *pro tem* into a nearby gatelodge two houses up from W.B. Yeats's Riversdale until our house (where my sister-in-law still lives) was finished. I was able, before I was six years old, to go everywhere on the site, and to get the sense of what would be a beautiful house (though not a very practical or comfortable one) in the process of growth. And then the delight of moving in: running water; a flush toilet, rather than the Elsan; a plumbed bath, rather than a tin one on the floor; electricity, with an electric cooker; and, not long after, a telephone.

---

2. The warble fly or cattle grub.

## SCHOOL

Amid this excitement was the greater one of going to school; a new world for me. The Loreto Convent in Rathfarnham had a co-ed primary school attached to its rather snooty girls' secondary school. But the boys had to leave before puberty. On the first day Mike hated it and wanted to go home. I loved it, and took to it without a backward glance. I was always walking on his heels and giving him a hard time. Perhaps recognizing that I had grown up with very few friends (and no girls), I plunged into the social whirl of the playground, so wished for after the mountain.

There is a recollection that I am still ashamed of (though not very). The nun in charge organized a competition in a long classroom free of desks and all furniture. The prize was a set of farm animals and farm workers cast in lead, which was placed on a table at the end of the room. Our class was blindfolded and spread out through the room, turned in various directions. Whoever got to the prize first won it. Even before the word 'Go!' I worked my eyebrows up and down so vigorously that I could just see out under the blindfold. That's not the bit I am ashamed of. I had realized that if I made a beeline for the prize I would be spotted, so – seemingly at random, but relentlessly – I fumbled and turned and struck out in all directions (watching if anybody else was getting close) before I very gently and slowly zeroed in on the prize. Nobody noticed my ruse. I was the winner. The propensity to cheat, even at the age of five, worried me. I was somewhat reassured decades later, when I was reading about the behaviour of higher apes, that they did it too.

I don't know if the precocious development of sexual feelings happens in all children. It certainly happened to me, though it faded again until puberty. Between about three and a half and five I had a brief and very enjoyable period of being sexually aware. I had a sweet and lovely romance with the daughter of the house where my parents rented the gatelodge before our house was finished. We were rumbled by her older brother, who manifested outrage, but I felt no guilt, only warm exciting pleasure. But that was only a tryout for my affair with a nun.

She was a large, strong, cheerful young woman, who did not have the full nun's costume. She must have been in training; a postulant or something. At break time I used to rush out to the playground, which she supervised. Between us we developed a game that I in my six-year-old head called 'walk up and turn over'. She would stretch out her arms straight in front of her with her big strong thumbs sticking upwards. I would jump up and grab the two thumbs and walk up her habit, and when I was up as far as I could go I would turn over and land back on the ground facing towards her. And after a while I began to notice things. She seemed to quite enjoy having me walk on her breasts. As the days passed, I ventured further. One day, when I got to the top of her thighs, greatly daring, I put one foot squarely in her crotch and gave her pubis a good rub. She said nothing. She could have ended all this at any moment. But she was there in the playground the next day, thumbs at the ready.

Was this sexual abuse? Was she, aged I suppose nineteen, abusing me, aged five or six? Was I sexually abusing *her*? I don't believe there was any abuse involved. I know it was very pleasant. I think she enjoyed it. I had no sense of sin or guilt. I can't remember how or when it stopped. My sexual feeling, so clear and strong and nice, waned and did not reappear until I was about thirteen. And I don't remember what became of her. I hope it did not give rise to the terrible guilt feelings, which so plague and destroy so many Catholic lives. If she was ever fully professed, she cannot have found a life of celibacy easy.

Sex was not the only important thing at Loreto. Educationally, I found the work easy and mostly I enjoyed it. A good recollection was of a wonderful German nun, Mother Margaret, who had great hands and taught those who wanted (as I emphatically did) the basics of carpentry in a special woodwork class on a Saturday morning. Marvellous. Michael and I loved it and that buttressed our father's love of tools and manual skill. I have always had that feeling, which forty years later fuelled my interest in the craft movement. As my father used to say in another context, 'How can they hate skill?' I don't hate it, I love it, and Mother Margaret gave us a start.

## THE ARAN ISLANDS

It is a sunny evening. We are going west down Galway Bay towards Aran on the old *Dun Aengus*, which served the islands for so many years, and around the boat, in water made golden by the reflected sunshine, porpoises are playing – circling, running ahead of us and generating the extraordinary sense of lightness and fun that sea mammals seem able to do. I don't remember my mother on the boat. She must have been there somewhere, but the only people that I recall are my father, my brother and Victor Waddington, who was my father's agent and a family friend. Waddington (we always used his surname) had a Voigtländer reflex camera and took the photograph of us three Keatings. He got off on that occasion at Kilronan on Inis Mór and stayed, I think, at Kilmurvey. The details are hazy now, but nothing can ever erase the sense of beauty and wonder, to the point of awe, that I felt out on the water.

Robert Flaherty had made *Man of Aran* there years before and became a fast friend of my father's, as did one of the Aran men in the film, Pat Mullen. He met us on the pier, wearing the traditional Aran clothes. What I remember most about them from that visit was the acrid peat-smoke smell, which I still love and which calls up with great power the islands before the Second World War and the idyllic summers we spent there. I must have picked up enough Irish to play with the local kids on Inis Oírr, as they had no English. The girls had no knickers either and it was there, since I had no sisters, that I discovered the difference between boys and girls. It was a place of innocence then – or at least, if the decay had started I was too young to notice the signals of a dependency culture, or the falseness of the role that romantic myth had given to 'Celtic' islanders. My father went to Aran every year, almost always by himself. But we never went after 1939. In the course of the war Seán Moylan, who was a close friend from 1921 and by then a minister in the Fianna Fáil government, asked my father to go to Aran – where he had been an annual visitor for decades, and therefore innocent-seeming – to keep an eye on a German spy. There was not much doubt which side we were neutral on.

I was not back until 1953 and by then, tourism to Aran (aided by the publicity given by the works of Synge and Flaherty, and to a lesser extent, of my father) was becoming more common and the dependency culture had progressed apace. We (my new wife and myself) came thinking we would spend a few nights on Inis Mór, but on the quayside we were approached by a man clad in the now much rarer traditional clothes. He had the great lean rangy physique of fish, cabbage and potatoes and, though he was not young, he had a full set of excellent teeth. His objective was to sell us sweep tickets, and as a judgmental and impetuous young man I suggested that we get back on the boat, still at the quayside, and go back to Galway, which we did. Later on, we had a house in a deeply Gaeltacht part of Connemara, which I will write about later. It was there I began to dislike the local society and its racist Celtic nationalism.

Years later I was on Inis Meáin, the middle Aran Island, with one of the great friends of my life, a Danish actor and theatre director called Hans-Henrik Krause whose great loves were O'Casey, Synge and Bertolt Brecht. We were out on the shore near the pier, where a man was baiting lobster pots with big beautiful pollock, which he had pulled out of the sea in the space of ten minutes. I decided I would show off my cooking skills by building a driftwood fire on the shore and cooking a pollock on the embers. Pollock is a watery bland fish, but the impro-vised grill dries it out and makes it quite nice. Having said what I intended to do, I walked the hundred yards to the lobster pot man and asked him to sell me a pollock. There were about four on the ground and, friendly, he told me to choose the one I wanted. I did, and said to him, 'How much?' He replied with a set of gestures I used to see a lot as a kid. He dropped his chin on his chest, twisted a bit of his forelock around a finger and scraped the ground with his big toe. And after a moment, he said, 'I'll leave it to yourself, sir.' I must have exploded, because Krause said to me as we cooked the pollock, 'What was that, when you shouted and waved your arms?' I hadn't realized that I did, but I hate those gestures of pretended servitude, and I am very pleased to say that the Irish are coming of age and gaining some self-respect. Success is the best cure. The 'Celtic Tiger' (I hate that racist term) is healing us.

## DETECTIVE SERGEANT DENIS O'BRIEN

Fit-ups were thriving when I was a kid. Drama, recitations, an unrideable mule, jugglers and – for me, best of all – the trapeze. I believed I could do some of those things too. At home there was a row of beautiful beech trees. The perfect one for my purpose was about twenty yards from the entrance drive to the bungalow that our new neighbour had built. He had two daughters but no son, and I surmise that my pert self was to a tiny degree a surrogate son. He allowed me to walk all over the building site of his new bungalow, and taught me (which I partly felt already from our own house) to love a building site and building skills. He rented our front field, which he cut for hay. He taught me, small as I was, how to sharpen a scythe and cut with it; lots of things. He was a friend. Over a low bough in the beech tree near his drive, I constructed a trapeze. And there I would go every morning and do my set: chin-ups, turnovers, hanging by my ankles; that kind of thing.

One day, which started like any other (it must have been in holiday time because I wasn't at school), I went out to my trapeze and was just starting up. I heard the engine of his car in front of his house. He drove towards the road. As he passed over a little bridge on the mill stream, I heard what sounded like one or two shots. He jammed his car against the wall, threw open the driver's door, which he sheltered behind, and with a drawn revolver in his hand faced back towards where the first shot had come from. I was less than twenty yards away and frozen by surprise and fear. And then, across the road towards which he was driving, in the yard of Kyle's builders, behind his back and in my full sight, a man stood up with what I now know was a sub-machine gun. It hadn't a belt for the bullets, but a drum. I could see the bullets hitting my friend. I could see him fall, transformed from the lean, hardy, vigorous man he was into a bundle of crumpled rags.

Who was he, my neighbour? Denis O'Brien, Detective Sgt; Dinny, my friend. His killers? The IRA. Apart from those killers, I was the only witness. For some reason I do not understand, and of which I am ashamed, my family was much less supportive towards his widow and daughters than they should have been. Too late, I can only apologize for that sixty years later. Later on I was to go to court, which was trying one of the people involved in the murder, and for me, not personally involved, that was almost as traumatic as witnessing the murder. And again for reasons I do not understand, my parents, usually so perceptive and supportive, paid almost no attention to my trauma. Over the months and years, I internalized it and repressed the memory. I went on with my life. There was plenty beckoning. Only in the last quarter-century have I learnt to let the memory out, and to talk about it.

I have not written these recollections of childhood in sequence. I was blocked. I had clear (and very happy) recollections, but I could not get them onto paper. It was only when I started this part of the narrative, of the murder of my friend, that I got freed up, and the words started to flow. In my early growing-up, the IRA were all around us: the Gilmores and the arms dump; my father's brother Joe and sister-in-law Mercedes Joyce, who were, I think, still in the IRA prior to World War II; and many others. Ever since, I have hated the IRA and the making of politics with guns and bombs with both passionate and intense anger. Those feelings became important much later in my life.

Later. I am in Collins Barracks, where the Military Court was sitting.[3] I was waiting (for what seemed hours and hours) to give evidence. There was a notice on the wall that read *There is a place to spit and throw your cigarette ends*. I read this over and over, with the emphasis first on 'is' and then on 'place'. And then I was inside, before the soldiers who were the judges, and in the dock was the defendant, on trial for his life: Charles Kerins.[4] He was quite young. He was born

---

3. Not in fact a military court, but a sitting of the Special Criminal Court, established under the Offences Against the State Act 1939. Section 38(3) states that 'an officer of the Defence Forces not below the rank of commandant' may be a member of a Special Criminal Court; the only eligible group not of the legal profession. The Kerins trial documentation shows that the Court consisted of army officers only; to a young boy it would have resembled a military court.

4. Det. Sgt Denis O'Brien's murder occurred on 9 September 1942. The trial took place on 2 September 1944 and Charles Kerins was hanged on 1 December of that year.

of woman. Hopefully was welcomed into the world, and loved. And here he was, an ignorant young man, brainwashed and programmed before he had the power of independent judgment, inheriting a wicked paradigm he did not fashion; a belief he had inherited rather than choosing. Here he was, on trial for the most precious thing that any of us possess – his life. He had participated in the killing of my friend, whom I knew well. But Kerins, whom I did not know, was also a human being. In the words of Shylock, on the school curriculum that year, 'If you prick me, do I not bleed?'[5] He did bleed. In front of me. It was really awful – beyond saying.

I do not believe my parents should have let me go into the court without support. I do not believe that a court should have built so much of the trial for the life of the defendant on the evidence of a sole witness who was then fourteen years old. I know there was other evidence. Though I loathe the death penalty, I do believe the verdict was correct. But when he was executed, I hurt like hell. It was not fair or decent. As I conclude so often now: if one side behaves badly, it does not follow that the other side behaves well. Much later in life, I was to get into serious trouble for saying the same thing about Northern Ireland. Much as I loathe the IRA (about which more anon) it does not mean that I countenance either the Loyalist paramilitaries, the RUC, the British army or more especially, British army intelligence. I loathe them all. You don't have to choose. The enemy of my enemy is not necessarily my friend.

## MAY KEATING AND POLITICAL AWARENESS

Politics began to rear its head when I was six or seven. My mother was the child of a Kildare seventy-acre farmer; a charmer, an innovator, the man to calve a neighbour's cow, but a depressive drunk. She went to school to French nuns in Roscrea. There she developed heart symptoms that were diagnosed, possibly wrongly, as a result of rheumatic fever. The nuns, who had been expelled from France, had a sister house in Spain in or near Seville. The doctors had said the Irish climate would kill her. Her family was clearly non-functional and her mother soon died. And off she was sent, aged twelve, to Spain. She did not come home until she was twenty-one. In the meantime she had finished secondary school and, according to herself, had better Spanish than English. She got a secretarial job where her bilingualism was an advantage. She met and fell in love with a Viscayan mining

---

5. From Shakespeare's *The Merchant of Venice*.

engineer and was getting ready to spend the rest of her days in Spain. Her lover was killed in a mining accident. Then the Easter Rising took place, and on the rebound she came back to Ireland. I have her passport, issued in Seville in May 1916. Her mother was dead, the farm was sold off and her father was in the county home in Kildare. But she met my father and they married.

She later left him and went to Germany to teach in the Berlitz School in Hamburg, where the country was in turmoil due to the hyperinflation.[6] She must have fallen in among socialists because she spoke approvingly of Rosa Luxemburg and disapprovingly of Nietzsche. When she came back to Ireland and to my father (otherwise I and my brother would not exist), she got a job in a prisoners' aid organization called The White Cross, where she encountered a great and neglected lady of the Irish Left, Hanna Sheehy-Skeffington, who influenced her opinions also. She had some miscarriages and stillbirths before the two of us survived, but she never had the daughter she longed for, and she was a housewife. Two small children took up much of her time, but once my brother and I could walk to primary school, she again had time for wider activities.

In the mid 1930s, when Mike and I were at Loreto, what we always (quite correctly) called 'the Franco rebellion' broke out against the democratically elected Spanish government. All of Irish Catholicism, then extremely powerful, rallied the country for the upstart dictator, to the extent that the fascist General Eoin O'Duffy took a Catholic volunteer group of soldiers to Spain to overthrow democracy. Almost all of Ireland followed this shameful lead. A small group of left-wing ex-IRA members and a few Communists went the other way; so did my mother. She was not very political, but she had grown up in Spain and as a result of her school experience she had lost her love for and trust in Catholicism. She got drawn into the small weak movement for the defence of Republican Spain and eventually became one of its leaders. 'I have lived there,' she said, 'I speak Spanish, and I know from personal experience that to describe Franco as an upright, Christian gentleman is three lies in three words.'

In the face of the rising fascism of Europe in which the Catholic Church played such an important role, she remembered the socialism of her Hamburg

---

6. Between June 1921 and January 1924, the Weimar Republic underwent the fifth most severe period of economic hyperinflation in world history. Germany's post-war reparations could only be paid in gold or foreign currency; the mark became devalued with astonishing rapidity. Among the short-term effects were political instability, strikes and civil unrest, widespread misery among citizens and foreign occupation (by France and Belgium) of the industrial Ruhr Valley.

time. She became deeply involved in the Europe-wide struggle of the Left against fascism, and I am extremely proud of it. Later on, I remember a party at home to send off the Irish volunteer contingent of the International Brigade, which was going to fight against Franco in Spain.

Meanwhile, in another part of the forest, I was caught between school and home. The good nuns in Loreto Rathfarnham, deeply ignorant as they were but obedient to disgraceful leadership from the Irish hierarchy, terrified the kids with atrocity stories about the behaviour of 'The-Red-Army-of-Bolshevik-Russia' (one long sound, the symbol of everything wicked) in Spain; especially tales of their murder of priests and nuns. My mother, while recognizing that in a civil war terrible things are done on both sides, was on the side of the government. To add to my confusion, staying in our house in Ballyboden was a Basque priest, complete with an impeccable white dog collar, whose name I can only spell phonetically as Father Laborda. He was on the Republican side, and had come to Ireland to try (unsuccessfully) to counter the propaganda of the Irish Church. Who to believe? Home won. But that put me at odds with all the teachers and all the pupils. It was the first, but certainly not the last, occasion when I was in a tiny minority.

I explained my dilemma to my mother. She was something of a joker. When I ran home from school to be asked, 'What did you learn today?' and when I gave a recital of all the bits (religion included, because it loomed large), she would say about the religious parts, in a totally angelic voice, 'You can believe it if you like. But I don't.' A nod is as good as a wink. I think the conflict of truths troubled my brother Mike a lot. It troubled me not at all. In this I feel extremely lucky, because I never had a battle like the majority of my peers later in life about 'believing or not believing'. In fact, once I reached the age of reason I have always been mystified as to how people could believe any of the narratives of the main religions. It is fair, though, to emphasize that my brother felt free enough to go the other way, to end up making a good Catholic marriage to a Mayo woman who, totally decent and a splendid wife to him, was very conservative, and they reared their children within the odour of sanctity.

Franco was victorious. The First World War loomed, clear to every socialist, invisible to every conservative – who hoped, anyway, that that nice man Hitler would turn east and destroy the USSR. At that tender age, I made my choice. I was against fascism and its conservative, more respectable allies. I was against the Catholic Church and, ultimately, at an age where I could study, became a root-and-branch opponent of all revealed religion, which I still am. I cut my political teeth later on reading the orange-covered publications of the Left Book Club, an important and formative part of my evolving political excitement. I also, in the course of following the war on the Eastern Front in my early teens, became a Communist, which I now recognize as an enormous mistake, for which – until and as the paradigm shattered – I paid in wasted time and pain (though not nearly as much as others did).

The political divisions were evident in our own village of Rathfarnham. One of the local curates, Father Kelly, who was better educated than most of the clergy, had quarrelled bitterly with my mother about Spain, and they used to stalk past each other on the road. (He was the man who said – perceptively, I think – that my father was pre-Christian and my mother was post-Christian.) One day I was walking with her to the village, past the priest's house, when he saw us coming. He cut a rose in his garden and came across the road holding it out and saying, 'Peace.'

She took it and said, 'Peace.'

But he couldn't leave well enough alone. 'I thought', he said, 'that you would respect my cloth.'

'Father Kelly,' she said in her severest voice, 'I do not respect cloth. And just sometimes I respect the person inside it.' It was a temporary truce and not really peace. But they remained wary friends.

For all that she was in a tiny minority in the village, my mother kept on friendly and jokey terms with her neighbours. She was a fine judge of meat and loved a good roast. In the village was an old-fashioned butcher, Mr Lynch. If she had guests, she would go in and say, 'Mr Lynch, I have people coming on Sunday and I want a really nice joint, so give me the parish priest's bit.' They knew she had no religion, and that she was a socialist (in the villagers' eyes she was crazy). But she was a good neighbour and loved a joke, and they accepted her.

There was some socialist and trade union activity in the village, and on the banks of the river there, a timber-frame and corrugated-iron shed was built: the Workers' Hall, or more popularly, 'The Bluebird', where in addition to meetings, dances were held without the supervision of the clergy. One night it burned down and another curate, Father Valentine, was overheard saying, 'I would have sworn it was the hand of God if I hadn't seen the petrol cans with my own eyes.' I didn't know then that the word 'propaganda' was from the same root as 'propagation' (the Society for the Propagation of the Faith), nor that the Church put out a hugely distorted and dishonest version of the history of the world and especially the history of the Church, and that it was permissible to tell lies that good might come of it.

The question of secondary school arose. My mother must have said some-where fairly publicly that when we were finished in the Loreto no priests were going to be involved in her sons' secondary education. In Dublin there was and still is a school that was originally, I think, Unitarian: Sandford Park in Ranelagh, where all the 'quare' people sent their kids; various kinds of Protestants, many Jews and the people of no religion. My mother went to have a look at it. She wore a belted raincoat, had black horn-rimmed spectacles and she rode on an upright Rudge bicycle. She parked her bike against the railings and looked in through the headmaster's study window. She saw him pursuing the parlour maid around his desk. She thereupon decided that this was the place for her sons and made the decision fairly public.

Word must have got around. The family received a communication from Father Stephen Brown SJ, who was the founder and head of the Catholic Central Library. Could he come and visit us? Certainly. Out he came to Rathfarnham. The upshot was that if my parents would relent from their decision to send us to the godless Sandford Park, then the whole of our secondary education would be provided free at the flagship secondary school Clongowes Wood College – in the malicious phrase: 'the cream of the country; rich and thick'. My parents were poor. Nobody much in Ireland bought my father's sort of pictures then. The offer was worth a lot of money. It was declined.

Father Stephen Brown carried a bag of boiled sweets and used to hold them out to me, but not too far out. When I came near, he clamped me between his knees and planted sloppy kisses on my resistant face. I had no sense then that this constituted sexual molestation, but I hated him. I produced the bad pun that he was 'not a Jesu-it but only a Jesu-halfwit'. I must've been an insufferable little puppy, and there are those who would say that in three-quarters of a century I haven't changed much.


## DUNABRATTIN SUMMERS

In the war, holidays abroad were out of the question. Anyway, cheap mass air travel and consequently mass tourism did not exist. Where would Mike and I spend our summers? The answer was wonderful: until 1946, in mid Waterford, where my uncle Joe – my mother's brother – was part of the old IRA network. Joe emigrated after qualifying as a doctor in Dublin; practising first, I believe, in the Caribbean and then in the United States. But the stupid action by the relevant British officers in carrying out the series of executions was the greatest recruiting force that any nationalist could have wished for. From being in 1916 a somewhat marginal viewpoint, physical force nationalism became the core of Irish Catholic political opinion. Joe Walsh came home from America and took up a dispensary position at Bunmahon on the Waterford coast. He then became the medical officer of the West Waterford Flying Column, of which one of the leaders was George Lennon, who subsequently developed strongly left-wing political opinions and was part of the group of Left people to which my parents belonged in the thirties.

In Bunmahon we came into the orbit of a man called Andy Kirwan, who had been the transport officer in the West Waterford Flying Column and owned a pub in Bunmahon. He lived in the next village eastwards on the coast, Dunabrattin, where there is a beautiful small harbour with inshore fishing boats, and indeed, one of the last of the sailing ships that used to bring coal from south Wales. During the war there was no petrol for the public. Cars were off the road. To keep the countryside going, the government issued 'plates' to local lorry owners, who acted as a transport system for every sort of goods. Andy, who in the mid thirties had transferred, like many another, from the IRA to Fianna Fáil, had got a plate. We stayed in his house and travelled all over Co. Waterford in his cheery old lorry. We used to carry fish on Fridays from the local small boats in the harbour all over the county. Our friends the O'Byrnes had two sons, about the same age as Mike and myself. We would go out late on Thursday evening and early on Friday morning, when the local fishermen's catch was being sold around towns like Portlaw and Kilmacthomas. We brisk nippy kids would sell their fish on condition that we could bring what we had caught and sell that too.

This gave rise to one of the most wonderful memories of my life. It was very late July or early August, and the mackerel were in. I arranged with the O'Byrne boys that we would meet at the dock at 4 am on Friday morning to go fishing. I arrived and waited, but there was no sign of them. After a while I took out the rowing boat myself. Pulling two oars, I could just get up to mackerel speed. I took off my shoes and socks and propped my feet on the back seat, fishing two mackerel lines on my big toes. The mackerel were going mad, and by half five or six I had enough, and anyway I was exhausted from rowing, so I headed the punt into the slight swell and very gentle wind and just sat there for an hour or so. I was a mile or so off the coast, alone, with the sun coming up and my fish caught, and feeling pleasantly tired. And I let the surroundings come to me on that perfect summer's morning, and I entered into a state of bliss and awe and delight and wonder at the beauty of the world that surrounded me. It is a feeling that years and increasing knowledge have only deepened. It has never deserted me – even in the worst of times, it never deserted me – and it has brought me endless joy and solace.

I went ashore, took my fish to Andy's lorry and off we went. Portlaw on the River Suir had been a prosperous tannery town, but it was then dramatically poor, in a way that I had never seen before. We were selling our fish, knocking on the doors from house to house. I had five mackerel on my left hand, with four fingers and a thumb through their gills. A woman came out and started bargaining with me. She offered me four pence for the two biggest. And I, pert puppy that I was, was overheard to respond in a retort of which I am deeply ashamed, but which, quite properly, I was never allowed to forget. 'Ma'am,' said I to her, 'take your four pence to the butcher and see what it will get you.'

Andy Kirwan's brother-in-law Paddy Morrissey was, for each of the five summers, almost a second father to me. Paddy was the son of a small farm on the Waterford coast at Dunabrattin, between Bunmahon and Tramore. There was, I think, an aunt who was a local postmistress. He worked as a farm labourer, lorry driver, mechanic and general handyman. He was a wonderful man whom I dearly loved and whose memory I revere. And he possessed extraordinary skills.

He taught me to sail a boat, to drive a lorry (surprisingly, as I was underage and uninsured and it was his brother-in-law's lorry). He taught me to work a farm horse and mow with a mowing machine (no combines, or even reapers and binders) on the small farm that was promised to him, but which in the end he did not inherit. He taught me to calve a cow, and I remember his old father coming along, when the calf was out and before the beastings (first milk) was drawn, making the sign of the cross in drips of candle grease on the cow's back. It was in Waterford that I came to realize the depth of religious belief and practice among country people at that time. In my home my father's practice was minimal – no Confession, Communion, Easter duty or any of that stuff, but Mass – and my mother's was non-existent. Both would have frowned on what they rightly called superstition.

Against that background Paddy played the fiddle, largely self-taught. He played it badly but recognizably, and as the loathsome G.K. Chesterton said, 'If anything is worth doing, it is worth doing badly.' And it didn't stop there. He was orderly and meticulous in what he did and I recall, to my wonder and delight, that he *made* a fiddle. I remember him carving the scroll. It was not a Stradivarius, but heavier and coarser, and the sound that he made as he struggled to learn to play it was sometimes okay and sometimes awful. But how much more admirable than the passive use of an iPod. What struck me, apart from what he taught me, including some nice woodworking, was the breadth of his culture. I worshipped him, and, though he is long dead, he is often in my mind.

## MAY AND SEÁN KEATING'S SOCIAL CIRCLE

The creative community in Dublin in the thirties was so small that everybody came across everybody else. My father's closest friend was Harry Clarke, who I think was a really great stained-glass artist. When Clarke died, for my father it left a gap so great it was never filled. To this day I have a special love for stained glass. Another painter, Patrick Tuohy, who died young in New York, was another un-replaced friend. And Seán O'Sullivan, a pupil of my father's who was a preter-naturally skilful draughtsman, came and went. He was also a brilliant producer of funny one-liners. Viewing a Royal Hibernian Academy varnishing day, he came upon two pictures by George Colley: one a floral still-life, and the other a portrait of a prize-winning greyhound. At the first he snorted and said, 'Colley flower,' and at the second, perhaps inevitably, 'Colley dog.'

O'Sullivan was alcoholic, and while he was institutionalized he was let out one day to go into Dublin on day release in the care of one of the warders. They arrived back late, the warder completely spifflicated and O'Sullivan stone-cold sober. Handing over the unfortunate man to one of his colleagues, O'Sullivan remarked, 'I am not my keeper's brother.'

By some accident, we knew more poets than we did painters. Yeats lived just down the road. F.R. Higgins was, I think, in my parents' house. How else would I have a vivid recollection of what he looked like? Likewise John Lyle Donaghy, one of whose kids was at school with me. Ewart Milne, fresh from Spain, where he had been a non-combatant medical assistant, was a close family friend. And a mile across the fields, at the Bridge House in Templeogue, Austin Clarke lived and held a Sunday night salon. My parents were regular attenders, and I was there a few times. I recall a night when Austin let go a stream of vituperation about the awfulness of 'culchie' Irish society. 'Austin,' said my mother, 'a bard shouldn't foul its own nest.'

I never remember my father inviting a student of his in the College of Art to the house, except one, and that one I recall very clearly. Gerald Gavron, a South African Jew of whom my father was very fond, had fetched up in Ireland because he did not want to be conscripted into the British army. He was a person of great charm and talent, and had become a very proficient ballet dancer, attached, I think, to the famous Ballet Russe de Monte Carlo. When he got to Ireland with his partner, he was able to earn a few bob now and again by putting on a vignette ballet classic in one of Jimmy O'Dea's Christmas pantomimes or summer shows. But by then he had turned to painting, and my father felt that he had great talent.

One dramatic event that I recall was that (not keeping sufficiently in training) his Achilles tendon gave way – on stage.

He was a regular visitor on Saturday or Sunday, and one night my parents got a phone call from the pier in Dun Laoghaire. He and his partner were being deported back to the US. Some loathsome civil servant in the Department of Justice offered in part explanation that he and his partner were not married. And perhaps, with that sort of bigot, being a Jew didn't help either. Gavron had phoned, resignedly, to say goodbye, but his partner took the phone and begged my parents to do anything they could. My battling mother knew the Minister for Justice, Boland,[7] from old times; she got on to him, and the deportation was postponed for a day, and then permanently. Gavron went back to South Africa when the war was over and we lost touch with him.

## SANDFORD PARK

Mike and I started at Sandford Park in September 1938. There was a new head-master, 'Bull' Cordner. My secondary education was extremely patchy. The school was then very small and struggling for survival; in those days not far from collapse, I would think. It had a lovely atmosphere, but the teaching was less excellent, apart from English and science.

We were weekly boarders, and the boy next to me in the dormitory was a Co. Down Presbyterian. We were a small dormitory of about eight boys, but even in that small group there was a mixture of religions. It is impossible to see the animosity towards, or even very much difference from, someone whom you have seen wet the bed. At school assembly each morning, after roll call and announce-ments, the headmaster used to say, 'Those who do not attend Scripture may go.' The substantial group of us who trooped out – Jews as well as atheists, Catholics and sundry others – felt no sense of exclusion.

It was at Sandford Park that I first became aware of Jews and Judaism. Victor Waddington, my father's agent, had an art gallery in Dublin. I remember him from about 1935. His kids Max (or 'Bunny'), Theo and Leslie (who later devel-oped the very distinguished Bond Street gallery)[8] were there, as were John and Martin Prescott and Neville Boland. I had a certain fellow feeling, because they like me were outsiders, because I found them interesting people, and most of all,

---

7. Gerald Boland stood in for Paddy Ruttledge (Minister for Justice from 1933 to 1939) for a period in 1936 when the latter fell ill.

8. The Waddington Custot Gallery, now on Cork St close to the Bond St area.

I think, because my parents had from the mid thirties been members of Victor Gollancz's great Left Book Club, which orange-covered publications I devoured. I recall a publication detailing the Nazi persecution of Jews that was published long before Kristallnacht.[9] The British media (apart from left-wing publications with a tiny circulation), like the British government and ruling class, chose to ignore the rise of fascism; even to support it, as a 'bulwark against Bolshevism' until long after Munich, until Churchill replaced Chamberlain and the 'phoney war' ended. The German and British claim after the war, that 'we didn't know', is a lie. I knew in school in 1939, and I identified with the victims even then.

I went to parties in Jewish boys' houses – and there were girls! I had no sisters, and so later, in full raging puberty, I was short of contact (of any kind) with girls. I was always very small, though I had no sense of it. From my mid teens I was involved in breaking horses, and in 'riding out' for racing stables, in demand because I was so light. I played cricket at school, and rugby – in which, because I was so small, I could only be effective at scrum half, which I was in Sandford's Junior Cup team. I understand the rules in a way that for Gaelic football I do not. And I hate what it has become: brutal, professional, without any of the chivalry or sense of fair play that was genuinely part of it when I was a kid. I realized this when Wales' J.P.R. Williams took out Mike Gibson in a very, very and totally deliberate late tackle. When taxed with this offence he explained, 'It was a professional foul.' Yes, exactly. Half of my love of rugby died that day. I still watch it, internationals and interprovincials, but with that same sense of shame with which I think many people watch pornography.

Sandford Park had some distinguished Left-liberal (in the American sense) former pupils. Among them was a man whom I knew a little when I was on the Trinity staff and admire enormously, Senator Owen Sheehy-Skeffington, a consistent and relentless defender of the liberal ethic, and his cousin Conor Cruise O'Brien, who was subsequently my colleague in government. I shall have more to say about him later. The man who later became the very distinguished writer William Trevor (whom we knew as Trevor Cox) was in my class, and he and I were in friendly competition in our weekly essays.

At Sandford Park I experienced defects that I think mar Irish education to this day. The most serious was that mathematics was not given a central position and was extremely badly taught. The person who did that was James J. Auchmuty,

9. Probably a booklet owned by the author entitled *The Persecution of the Jews in Germany* (1933), which details anti-Semitic behaviour by the Nazis at this early juncture. Kristallnacht took place in November 1938.

an academic who had written a book on the nineteenth-century Irish humanist Lecky. (Another of these remarkable Irish people, men and women, who have been written out of Irish history – most notably Thompson[10] or Toland[11] – because their views did not conform to the consensus.) Auchmuty was well educated and stimulating as a teacher. He ended up as the vice chancellor of an Australian university. But the war was on and he was, I am now satisfied, also a British spy. I say this on the basis of questions that he asked me, in so insistent a way that I remember them to this day. My friend Dominic Campbell, son of my mother's great intimate Nancy Campbell, whom I know since we were tiny children and who also went to Sandford, has written recently in the school magazine that he does not believe this accusation. I think he is wrong.

My secondary school years coincided almost exactly with World War II. My father's brother Claude was in the British Navy (like many another Irish family, we were thoroughly mixed up). One uncle Joe was in the IRA. Son of a 'sceptic' father, code then for agnostic or atheist, Paul became a priest. Apart from the formative experience of the Spanish Civil War, I remember dressing up as an Abyssinian when Mussolini was building his short-lived African empire there. My parents were passionately anti-fascist and therefore pro-Allies, especially after the wartime alliance was formed between the West and the Soviet Union.


## MARY FRANCES

At Sandford Park during the war important things were happening to me, which have influenced my whole life. My grandfather, my father's father, was one of the early Catholics to go to the new Queen's College in Galway where, he said, he found an education but lost his religion. It required a fair amount of courage to be a 'sceptic' (what he called himself) in nineteenth-century Limerick.[12] He had owned what was originally quite a prosperous bakery business in Limerick and

---

10. William Thompson (1775–1883) of Cork was an egalitarian, interested in philosophy (including Benthamite utilitarianism), economics and social reform. He coined the term 'social science' and collaborated with Anna Wheeler (1780–1848); both were pioneers of the Co-Operative Movement.

11. John Toland (1670–1722) of Donegal was a radical scholar, theologian and self-identified pantheist who studied at Glasgow, Edinburgh, Oxford and Leiden – and the first recorded person to whom the epithet 'freethinker' was applied. On the publication of *Christianity not Mysterious*, it was proposed that he be burned at the stake; in 1697 Dublin's public hangman burned copies of the book in his stead.

12. Here the author has a note to self: to read *Angela's Ashes* by McCourt.

an elegant Georgian house in Newenham Terrace, but became more interested in reading books; this first generation without minding the store went bankrupt. This ruined his daughters' chances of marrying the sort of man that their education and talents would have warranted. My father was the eldest, and his nearest surviving sibling was a sister, Mary Frances. She came to Dublin with the rest of the impoverished and now dysfunctional family and had a love affair with an 'unsuitable' man. She came from an offbeat, nominally Catholic family and he was a Belfast Presbyterian. To the Keatings this was of no importance, but it was opposed by his family and the romance ended.

On the rebound, Mary Frances went to Italy, initially (in my understanding) as a kind of senior domestic servant who could teach English to the children of the rich families for whom she worked (though with the Limerick accent that she retained all her life). She ended up as a senior house manager in a Rothschild palace, where she encountered the best food and wine that money could buy. Back in Ireland, her former love married and had three children: two daughters and then a son, Frankie, who was completely incapacitated. And then their mother died. Mary Frances came back to Ireland, took up with the man, married him and devoted some of her great energy to minding Frankie. And then she began to write in *The Irish Times* about food. Writing about food is now almost a major industry. It probably didn't hurt that her husband was Alec Newman, who had become editor of *The Irish Times*. There, over many years, she wrote a respected weekly article under her own name of Mary Frances Keating, and also an anonymous cookery book, which Alan Davidson[13] has praised highly in the sparse arena of Irish cookery books.

Why tell all this about my aunt? The reason is that I went to school in Ranelagh, and Mary Frances lived in Windsor Road, Ranelagh – 500 yards away. As a nine-year-old who was very small, I avoided spats as much as possible, so I used to walk over to my aunt. She had no children of her own, though she loved and cherished Frankie, and I, until I left Sandford, became a kind of surrogate son. By then her basement had become a land of demonstration. And I became her apprentice. At first I was so small I could not reach the table, but she had a wooden box under it that I used to pull out and climb onto, so that I was at a level that I could both watch and then participate in the preparation of what she was trying out. She was a loving teacher and a meticulous technician, so that I fell

13. Derry-born diplomat and author of numerous gastronomy books, including *North Atlantic Seafood* (Macmillan, 1979), in Keating's collection, and *The Oxford Companion to Food* (1999).

in love with cooking before I was fifteen years old. Food and cooking (drink too) became a very important theme in my life. It is still, and, as I will tell later on, it helped me to get through a very bad patch in my life.

## GLENCREE VALLEY

When I was a little boy and we lived in Killakee, probably my mother's closest friend was Nancy Campbell, who lived nearby. And when we moved down to Ballyboden, the Campbells moved to a house on the Rathfarnham Road half a mile away, and Nancy's children, Dominic and Diana, were friends. About 1939 we – Mike and myself – were with Dom and Diana in the cottage owned by Nancy's husband the poet Joseph Campbell at Lackendarragh, a beautiful place at the bottom of Glencree Valley. There were other visitors; an older generation, friends of Nancy's elder son Flann.

Among them was a young man with the reputation of academic brilliance and a characteristic high whinnying laugh. His name was Conor Cruise O'Brien and I was in awe of him. While I was a child he was already a Trinity student and was courting his first wife, Christine Foster. My mother had once been the secretary of Conor's aunt, Hanna Sheehy-Skeffington, in a prisoners' aid organization called The White Cross. Sheehy-Skeffingtons, Cruise O'Briens and Keatings were all of Catholic background, most (though not all) of us vociferously lapsed and all 'liberals'. Conor shone in the group of students and was brilliant company, even for a kid thirteen years his junior and silently vacuuming up the adult conversation. He had gone to the school where I was just about to start, Sandford Park, and he had already acquired a reputation for being a brilliant scholar. So I was hugely impressed and pro-him, though it is very likely that he does not remember this episode at all. Later on, when a few years later I was politicized myself, he was someone spoken of as a socialist. So it was all favourable, though the differences in our ages precluded friendship.

Fuel was scarce in the war and Dublin people resumed cutting turf on bogs in the Dublin Mountains that had long been deserted, on the Featherbed bog near the Killakee cottage where I lived for my first four and a bit years. Further north in Glencree Valley, close to the Glencree Reformatory (which was built as a military barracks after the 1798 rebellion) was the cottage of a great friend of my parents, Edward Sheehy.

From 1941 to 1945 Mike and I spent some very happy times at that cottage. Edward was a brilliant student of Alfred O'Rahilly (the finest mind of the twentieth century) at University College Cork, though he disappointed his mentor by turning leftwards and editing a progressive magazine called *Ireland Today*, now forgotten, which was a precursor to *The Bell*. Edward was delighted with two pairs of extra willing hands to gather and stack his turf; a couple of vigorous teenagers were a godsend for him and his two brothers-in-law Kieran and Eddie Kelly, who were in the IRA. The bog was a wonderful place in summer; it was almost like being at sea. There I first saw a 'dally dooker' or 'dark looker'[14] and a pair of distant rooks.

Among the people who turned out to save the turf was Muriel MacSwiney, the widow of Terence. She had lived in Europe and had become a Communist. She was the victim of a 'kidnap' of her daughter [Maire] by MacSwiney's family, assisted by other nationalists who could not stomach the idea that the only child of the great hero Terence MacSwiney was being reared by an atheist.[15] And she had a second daughter, a beautiful girl called Alix, whom I very much admired from a distance. Muriel had a strange way of working. She was slow, but relentless. Without seeming to, she got a lot done in the end. I don't know where she ended up. She deserved better of Ireland, as the widow of one of our greatest national heroes. But the rule is: conform or we will write you out of history.

There was quite a strong IRA presence in Glencree Valley at that time, and in the cottage of Prof Roger McHugh the kidnapped Wexford IRA man Stephen Hayes[16] was concealed for months, and though all the people around seemed to know, the police did not seem to hear about it or to move to set him free.

The other thing was an exciting piece of technology that we built in Edward's cottage and which influenced me later towards studying biochemistry. Edward's cottage was tucked into a sloping hillside with a tiny stream running down by the gable. It was the classic three-rooms-in-line Irish layout, and in addition to the main open fire in the centre room there was a second fire in the gable next to the stream. We knocked a hole in the gable and brought in a sack of potatoes, some yeast and sugar and a still of coiled copper pipe.

---

14. 'Dark looker' is a folk name for the newt, according to Michael Viney.

15. In 1932, Maire was taken from Germany by her aunts to live with them in Ireland. Muriel saw this as a kidnap; during the ensuing custody battle, however, 'Maire testified that she had arranged the escape on her own initiative because she wanted a stable life.' (R.F. Foster, *Vivid Faces*). Maire grew up happily, by her own account, and married Ruairi Brugha, the son of Cathal Brugha. Her mother rebuffed later attempts at contact and the two never spoke again.

16. Stephen Hayes, Chief of Staff of the IRA, was suspected of betraying the organization. He was subsequently transferred to a house in Castlewood Avenue, Rathmines, from which he escaped to the local Garda station.

The mash was made in a big container that just fitted into the fire, and in it we mixed peeled and chopped potatoes, yeast and sugar. When it had worked sufficiently, we dammed the stream and from the little pond we made, we carried a pipe of very cold water into the hole in the gable, past the fire where it could cool the copper 'worm', and out again to rejoin the rivulet through the front window. And then we ladled the fermented mash into the container, stoked the fire and made poitín. On that occasion we stayed five or six days in the cottage with nothing more than some dripping and a pot oven. We made chips from our remaining potatoes in a pot oven on the big fire, and lived on them and milky tea, the milk coming from the neighbours. It was the first time that I recall being drunk, and one day, going to the nearby well, I saw a little elver swimming round in it. I caught it, brought it back to the cottage and put it in a saucer of poitín, which it lapped at high speed for about ten rounds – and then expired. It was an impressive lesson on the evils of alcohol.

## DALTON TUTORIAL SCHOOL

I sat the Intermediate Certificate just as the war was ending, in the summer of 1945, and did okay. Although Sandford Park was a lovely place in atmosphere, it was not much good at preparing people for exams. The normal routine was that two years after the Inter one sat the Leaving Certificate, and if the results were good enough one gained entrance to one's chosen course in university. But I was impatient. Discovering that I could enter University College Dublin via the National University matriculation examination, which could be taken when one felt ready, I pulled out of Sandford and went to the Dalton Tutorial School in Rathmines. There I met a lifelong friend, and experienced for the first time a really good science teacher in the person of Teller, a Hungarian-Jewish refugee who had a DSc in Botany from the University of London. He was great, and there were a couple of Jewish pupils in my class, one of them his son Joe, and a refugee called Otto Falk. After a hard year, when I was motivated to work, I got a reasonably good matriculation and secured a place in pre-medical in 1946.

Then one awful day, reading the regulations, I discovered that to go to UCD you had to be seventeen when the academic year started in October. Despair. And *then* I read the small print carefully and discovered the magic addendum 'or within three months of that date'. That brought the deadline up to 15 January. I didn't reach seventeen until 7 January, and I thanked my parents for timing me so well.

# On Education

I have been involved in education, as learner and teacher, all my life. I would claim that this experience as a teacher and planner gives me a basis for informed opinions about education. I start with my repeated refrain that one is perfectly entitled to ignore the experts. My reason is that Irish education, especially at primary and secondary level, is full of foolish things. Of course it has been subject to reform, but I give an example from my own primary schooling. The currency was then pre-decimal, and we were taught, as little kids with a tenuous grasp of the basic idea of numbers, how to divide and multiply pounds (240*d.*), shillings (12p) and pence. And in weights: pounds (lb), quarters (4lb), stones (four quarters), hundredweights (112lb) and tons (2240lb or 20cwts). Even for the quite mathematically endowed, these are tricky manoeuvres. Taught in my case by nuns who had the most fragile grasp of what they were at, it produced failure, pain, grief, feelings of inadequacy and hatred of mathematics.

I don't for a moment blame the nuns. But imagine the imbecility of the educational authorities in the Department of Education who, with great pomp and the demand for respect for their high office, forced this into the schools. I decided I would never again respect any opinion just because it came from persons of authority. It was quite a mind-blowing stupidity and incompetence. In later life, whenever I see very large numbers of people doing something incredibly stupid, so serenely that it makes me doubt my own dissent, I think of multiplying pounds, shillings and pence. The fact that within a given society at a given moment there is a consensus that a particular course of action is the correct one does not preclude it from being very foolish.

I'm not in the least surprised that the grandchildren of those who were mathematically debauched by this teaching believe that 'you have to have a special kind of brain' and that mathematics is very difficult. There is no excuse for our present situation. In passing: as I write, the country is troubled by the poor results in maths and science in the Leaving Certificate.

I believe that a raised level of numeracy is central to any successful schooling and that this will become increasingly true in the future. Every few years there are worldwide mathematical competitions to find the best and worst countries, with a bit of variation.[17] Britain is 26th. And to their shame, because they possess the necessary resources, the US comes in at number 29. In general, the US education system is very poor and a model for nobody. Ireland, however, is joint 29th. Denmark, which is of comparable size and wealth, and Iceland, with one-tenth of our population, are ranked 17th and 16th respectively.

In education, we have a separate minister for the Irish language (the first national language, according to nationalist myth), and special subsidies and even marking systems to promote it (mathematics through Irish is apparently easier than through English – another piece of stupidity). But we have no comparable promotion of numeracy. Once the numbers get very big or very small, the vast majority of the population is lost. So, at the beginning of a recession, informed public discussion of the economic situation is impossible. And here comes another indictment of the syllabus-concocting experts: at the time of the French Revolution, more than two hundred years ago, the reformers introduced the metric system. It is obviously better. Better in large ways because calculation is so much easier, and better in the smaller domestic ways. I love to cook. And in cooking with metric recipes, for all practical purposes 1 kg and 1 L (of water, wine, milk, stock) are the same. If you look at a recipe in imperial measure, it is much more complicated. But the educational experts who were working as hard as they could, fortunately unsuccessfully, to root out English were until very recently still happy to retain imperial measure.

Since I have mentioned Irish, when I talk to my grandchildren and their peers (and I hope that I can last long enough to do the same with my great-grand-children), I find that they mostly have a hostile but patiently enduring attitude to Irish. It is just something you have to do. But here is another example of the official stupidity. The people who spend so much time and effort and resources on Irish have produced the opposite of what they wish. They have produced patient resistance in the majority of schoolchildren. Pádraic Óg Ó Conaire, nephew of the great Pádraic Ó Conaire, who spoke Irish as a first language, told me that of all the people who learnt Irish as adults my father spoke the best Irish of anyone he knew. I grew up playing with kids in the Aran Islands, and we must have

---

17. The OECD's PISA (Programme for International Student Assessment) examines literacy and numeracy levels across 65 countries every three years. Shown here are the 2009 rankings for mathematics; in that year, Britain fell within the average range, while Ireland and the US scored below average. Ireland's rankings later recovered to resemble the 2006 results.

been speaking Irish. I can still read simple newspaper articles and understand most of the news. I do not hate Irish. I think it is a beautiful window into a rich past culture (and it was a Keating, Seathrún Céitinn, who gave written Irish its modern form). But I hate the attitude of trying to force it down kids' necks, which is counterproductive, which has done terrible harm to other parts of the educational system and which spreads all the wrong attitudes and feelings to both pupils and teachers.

What I have been enumerating are defects in particular sectors. But I experience a wider problem than that. I believe the situation is getting better, but very slowly. What worries me is that the ferocious curiosity and desire to learn and to know things of the very small child is crushed by our system. They become indifferent, even hostile, to the whole educational system. And in their apathetic or resistant frame of mind, they waste incredible amounts of their young lives. Think of the number of hours per year spent in school or doing homework. Think of the number of years for such a tiny result. With things they want, like text messaging, the kids are brilliant. But over most of the curriculum, there is no such passion or achievement.

Everything has a history. Mass education is recent. Over the Christian period it was considered dangerous. It only gained widespread support when literate people were needed to man the new factories, railways, mines and ships of the Industrial Revolution. But even then it was doled out in a very practical but limited way. The masters of society wanted competent employees, but not troublesome ones. The last quiver of this old concern was during the witch hunts of the 1950s, when a House Un-American Activities Committee (HUAC) interrogatory questionnaire contained the gem 'Do you read books?'

It is only recently, then, that education is seen as a mode of access to the culture of the world, as a source of inspiration and beauty and entertainment, and most fundamentally as a method of reworking one's paradigm. As a source of liberation, in fact. In Ireland, because of British stupidities prior to the national school legislation, the Catholic clergy in hedge-school times earned a special and deserved respect and authority. This was later parleyed into a position of almost unique power after the smashing of the genuinely national element in the national school system. A century and a half later, we are paying a terrible price.

Leaving minority religions aside for a moment, the vast majority of Irish children were educated in schools where the Catholic ethos prevailed, and when one got to secondary level the vast majority of the teachers were Catholic clergy. Irish nationalist history, as I will discuss later, is largely myth; not least in the sphere of education. The British administration of the 1830s made a sincere effort to educate the various children of the country (the poorer ones, at least) together and equally. More than any other single individual, my illustrious East Kildare relative Cardinal Paul Cullen, from Ballitore, was instrumental in wrecking that system and in leading the whole of the Catholic clergy to make sure that the proposed national schools remained national only in name, were divided on religious grounds and became, on each side, centres of sectarian bigotry controlled by the local religious dignitary – the parish priest, in the vast majority of cases. Of course, the Church of Ireland went along. I feel close to and angry about this piece of educational vandalism because my grandmother Martha Cullen taught in the 'national' school in Eadestown, Co. Kildare and was a great-great-niece of the cardinal.

Due to the progress of cognitive science we begin to have an inkling of how a small child vacuums up language, with special hardwiring, which shuts down later. And I think that without pushing current knowledge too hard, we can see the dim outline of the child pursuing the process of socialization, sucking in uncritically and extraordinarily quickly the whole paradigm. There is an old saying quoted by Koestler in *Darkness at Noon*, which he attributed to the Jesuits, but which I have never been able to track down; it states: 'Give me the child and I will answer for the man.' It is certainly a precept that all the Churches use; get the kids when they are little.

The nuns' duty was to indoctrinate us into the 'one true faith'. I remember the catechism: 'As there is but one Lord, one Faith, one Baptism, one God and Father of all, there can be but one true Church, and … no one can be saved out of it.'[18] Small children are not into parsing subtleties of meaning. The interpretation was clear. Life on earth was the route to salvation, for those who did the right things. But the 'no one shall be saved out of it' meant that Protestants would go to hell. This was in the mid 1930s, in a capital city. We were still in the shadow of the War of Independence. The Catholic authorities of the time and their successors must answer to their consciences about the wisdom of teaching small children that Protestants would go to hell.

The practice has been to answer a whole lot of questions that children never ask. They are given a whole certain paradigm as 'the Truth' before they can reason fully. I have argued elsewhere that the paradigm we receive in childhood is an accident of time and place, and that it is the duty of any self-respecting person to

---

18. From *The Turquoise Catechism*.

go on reworking it in the light of experience as long as we live. But if truth is based on revelation and is not subject to any testing, then we cannot want an evolving paradigm. And of course, that is the way that all the Churches want to keep us.

The de Valera constitution is full of pious aspirations about 'the family'. But de Valera's party has been in power for 75 per cent of the time since the constitution became law, and the latest action of a Fianna Fáil finance minister is to increase yet further the size of primary school classes.[19] And as for the pre-school organization, centrally important with more and more women exercising their right to be part of the workforce, pre-school crèches, which are excellent and free in secular France, cost an arm and a leg in Ireland.

Summing up, I think that schools should be completely secular. Religion belongs elsewhere. They should be run by parents and teachers, with oversight from the Department and an input from teachers' unions, and should have a fairly fixed core curriculum and a great deal of local freedom about the rest. The present managerial system should be abolished. Class sizes need to be smaller. Pre-school should be well provided for and free. University staff have other earning methods and so do not need more pay than other levels of teachers. Primary teachers, who in many ways are the most important, need the same pay as secondary teachers. Girls and boys should be educated together. Irish, while being encouraged for those who want it, should not be compulsory. All education, including university, should be free. The regional technical colleges and special skills schools, including apprenticeships in practical skills, need more encouragement and money. And that is enough to be going on with. A country that neglects education shoots itself in the foot, or somewhere even more important.

## ABUSES WITHIN EDUCATION

The churches, and especially the Catholic Church, had persuaded a supine state that they were the right people to take over vast areas of social activity in education, health and the care of the disadvantaged young. And that was the Ireland where I grew up. We know now that they abused their position in an absolutely monumental way, often making a profit from the ill-treatment of their unfortunate and mostly blameless charges, touting around the District Courts to persuade district judges to put more kids in their care. And I'm not just talking

---

19. Bartholomew 'Batt' O'Keeffe, Minister for Education and Science from May 2008 to March 2010, announced this and several other significant cuts to education as part of the budget for 2009.

about sexual abuse, but the striking of pupils by teachers; totally impermissible in any educational situation. The kids were beaten in schools as well as in the cynically named 'reformatories'. It was common. Anything more disastrous to the establishment of a good school atmosphere I find hard to imagine. They were badly fed and badly housed, and in general the atmosphere was such that working-class kids very often hated school, and the reformatories churned out angry, antisocial kids who spent a lifetime in conflict with society. Of course there were the very clever and very strong young who survived undamaged, but alas, too few.

The cruelty, the violence, the sexually inspired beatings have long characterized Irish education. The Department of Education has long betrayed its trust by abdicating its control and responsibilities to the Catholic Church. And they have concealed the documentation of abuse. Alas, the last time I looked (about a decade ago), the teachers' trade unions, at their annual conferences, had oceans to say, very properly – that's their job – about pay and conditions, but nothing about the abusive atmosphere prevailing in the schools where they taught. It took the extraordinarily courageous actions of individuals like Christine Buckley and the TV documentary-makers to bring these things to public attention.

There are huge scandals erupting in the Catholic Church all over the world about widespread paedophilia. While the fact that it is becoming public and that more of the abused are refusing the advice to 'hide their shame' and confirming the abuse *is* new, the problem is not, and the evasion, lies and cynical concealment with which the Church authorities have responded are not new either.[20] When eventually the extent of paedophile abuse in Catholic schools – both so-called reformatories and ordinary primary and secondary schools – came to light in Ireland and also in Australia, Canada, the United States and Britain, the response was revealing.

A nun called Sister Stanislaus, 'Sister Stan', has been built into a figure deserving of affection and respect. The paedophile abuse of children within the Catholic Church came to light in recent decades.[21] Sister Stan denies she had any knowledge at the time of extensive sexual abuse of children in the care of her order, the Sisters of Charity, at St Joseph's orphanage in Kilkenny during the 1970s and 1980s. But in the early 1700s a special Catholic teaching order that had a vast success in establishing schools was shut down in the aftermath of a major

20. An author's note here references *Fallen Order: A History* by Karen Liebreich, which details the scandal within the Piarist Order in the seventeenth century.

21. Article by Mary Raftery, author of *Suffer the Little Children*: "We Were Not Responsible" (13 July 2006) in *Village Magazine* and online.

paedophile scandal. Such minimal documentation as was left in the Department of Education's industrial school files indicates that the problem of sexual abuse of children in the care of religious orders was known – though, shamefully, the records were filleted. The defence of 'I didn't know' is one I find hard to accept.

If John Cooney's biography of Archbishop John Charles McQuaid is right, there is persuasive evidence that McQuaid himself was a paedophile – but we did not then know that in many institutions which were run by the Church, in shameful abdication by the state of its role and moral duty towards disadvantaged children, the most appalling brutalities and humiliations were routinely practised, including sexual abuse. Of course, the obscene abuse of children in institutions controlled and run by Catholic clergy was primarily the fault of those who did it, the nuns and priests who fought very hard to get and keep that control. But we, the citizens of the state, allowed it to happen. And we knew.

My father, who was neither malicious nor foul-tongued, always referred to 'the Christian Buggers'. As for the religious themselves not knowing, that is a self-serving lie. In the 1640s the leading teaching order, the Piarists, was briefly dissolved because of the sexual abuse of children under its care.[22] The Department of Education abdicated its responsibility, which it was supposed to exercise on behalf of all of us.

This is an issue on which I feel an extra sensitivity and an extra shame because it continued, without being exposed and stopped, into the time when I was in government, and indeed much longer. As someone who believes in the collective responsibilities of government, I too bear blame and I am bitterly ashamed to have to say it – even though, with the possible exception of the relevant ministers (Dick Burke in Education and, less likely, Pat Cooney in Justice), the government did not know.

I am not sure even now that it is completely ended. The Church is still in denial. In Ireland, in the dying days of a Fianna Fáil government, a shockingly exploitative deal was done between the Minister for Education, Michael Woods, and the religious authorities in what is to me a terrible piece of State/Church

---

22. The regular sexual abuse of children in the care of a Father Stefano Cherubini came to the attention of the order's founder, Calasanz. Cherubini's family was exceedingly powerful; Calasanz promoted and moved him away from the site of his crimes. Superiors in Rome also knew, but support for Cherubini was such that he was appointed head of the order, supplanting Calasanz, who then published documentation of his rival's long pattern of molestation. This did not block his appointment, but resulted in the temporary suppression of the order. Calasanz was later both beatified and canonized (Karen Liebreich, *Fallen Order: A History*).

collusion. It capped the Church's financial responsibility at an appallingly low level, to be paid in part by the transfer of overvalued Church property to the State. The amount was €128 million in cash, property and counselling services. But the cost of the compensation for the damage done by the abuse topped €1 billion.[23] I know of an instance where a prominent Irish barrister was sent to Canada to study how the Catholic Church there had concealed its assets so that it could evade the financial consequences of its depredation: compensation to the victims. Who is paying the vast majority of the Church's compensation liabilities? You don't need three guesses. You and I: the taxpayer.

So the defence – that 'nobody spoke about these things' and that the Church authorities did not know – is untrue. There is a further evil consequence of paedophilia: homophobes use it to justify their prejudice. But there are plenty of heterosexual paedophiles. It is the derouting of a normal hetero- and homosexuality that causes the violence to children. Because of the persistence of damage and injury through entire lives, the consequences are still harmful and also expensive, both for society and the individual.

I have had experiences, as have I guess most other children, which amounted to paedophilia (literally sexual excitement by children) and which I reckon (I hope) did me no harm whatsoever because there was no violence, exploitation and secrecy attached. There was Father Stephen Brown, with the bag of sweets, who clamped me with his legs and planted sloppy kisses on my face. Since it never progressed I don't reckon it did me any harm, apart from being unpleasant. I have described my romps with the young nun in the playground of Loreto Rathfarnham, but it is interesting to tease out the moral implications. At seven years of age, I had no deep understanding of what was going on. It was just a game. I clearly gave her pleasure, even if I didn't know why. And it is nice to please. But what about the inside of her head? In the long night, did she realize that she was using me as a sex toy? Even if she didn't, how could she reconcile the vows she had taken with her behaviour? How could she enter into a lifetime of duplicity and guilt? And if she continued in an order that taught small children, did her sexual outlets become violent, brutal or exploitative? Though it is a long time ago, and in a sense none of my business, I hope she jumped over the wall.

I have gone on at some length about these childhood experiences and about the worldwide revelation of misbehaviour because I have drawn the conclusion, considered but very firmly held, that no priest or nun should be let near the

---

23. Over €1.36 billion. The *Irish Times*, 9 May 2012.

education of children. I know lots of people who say with truth, 'I went to the Christian Brothers, where I got an excellent education, and nobody ever laid a hand on me.' I accept that. If you live in a 'Catholic country', you will certainly have encountered women and men who have been able to turn this abnormal situation – chastity – to the good. But in my experience these are only a small minority; there are too many who find the vows of chastity impossible and who then begin to express their sexuality in ways that are exploitative of the young in their care. This is why I have made it clear in print that I would not allow the chaste to have control over the lives, or even the classrooms, of children.

Does that mean that there are no reliable teachers from the ranks of religion? Of course not. We all know, and many of us in our own lives have benefited from, the dedicated work of beautiful and noble people who are in holy orders. The problem as I see it is that, as a proportion of the total, they are too few. There are too many of the others. And in the circumstances of teaching institutions, the opportunities for abuse and for cover-up and secrecy are too great. It is a matter of probability. The best suffer because of the villains. But the consequences of child sexual abuse are too great and the damage echoes down the decades. There is even some small evidence that it can produce genetic changes.

If in doubt, don't.

# 2. *The Godless Institution*

## PRE-MED

So three-quarters of the way through my seventeenth year, in 1946, I started pre-med in UCD. The class was huge. The pent-up demand from the war was just getting to university, and there were well over three hundred in the class. Even then, dimly, but now in retrospect with much greater clarity, I recognize that the facilities were overcrowded – but much worse than that, the teaching was pretty terrible. Chemistry was okay. Physics was passable, though in the school tradition of 'submit and memorize', rather than on the real educational basis of 'find out and understand'.

But the biological subjects, my special love, were really pathetic. There was no genetics, then advancing in leaps and bounds. Botany and zoology were still in the nineteenth-century, classification stage of their development, the view being of species as created and immutable – the Christian view, with no hint of the nascent science of ecology, the study of their interaction in ecosystems. Worst of all – and, I am sure, ideologically determined by Christianity – one of the greatest discoveries of all science, evolution, which makes sense of everything, was completely omitted. Propounded ninety years earlier by Darwin and Wallace, it was not even mentioned.

My savage conclusion (that of an arrogant youngster, but alas, I see no reason to change it) was this: if that was the only science that the future doctors of Catholic Ireland ever got, then they were too ignorant to be permitted to practise medicine. Fortunately for all of us, they got to Britain and America at the postgraduate stage, where they could learn something useful. I am eighty now, so all that class have passed on, but when one considers how greedy and arrogant they were in their mature lives, one can only hope that medicine in Trinity was better, and that fundamentalist religious ideology did not stop them from learning about evolution.

My first real academic test was at the end of this pre-med year, when I was seventeen and a half. Out of the huge class, I came second. I was beaten by a man called Philip Awan, who was (I think) overseas Chinese. He was already a BSc, in his mid to late twenties, and had taught science in his home in the Caribbean, but dumb immutable regulations forced him to do pre-med before he could start medicine proper.

## VETERINARY STUDIES

And then my love of horses, a lasting passion all my life, intervened and I switched from medicine to the veterinary course, to the intense chagrin of my doctor uncle Joe. The Veterinary College of Ireland was recognized by the Royal College of Veterinary Surgeons in the UK and was therefore able to confer membership of the latter, a qualification recognized all over the world. But for reasons of past history its funding and management, including its administrative staff, were based in the Department of Agriculture. Bluntly, they were not up to the job, and they had no understanding of how to improve an institution in a subject that was rapidly being transformed by science and taken, all over the British Isles, into the university system. Some of the teachers had great experience from practice and possessed a great deal of mother wit and common sense. When I qualified fifty-five years ago, the training was practical (and made, I think, reasonably good veterinary practitioners) but it had a long way to go in science.

I had the good fortune that all through my veterinary studies I was up against a competitor: Sidney Davies, an ex-serviceman who was married and had a child. He was deadly serious and his dedication and excellence pulled a performance out of me that left to myself I probably would not have achieved. Later on I was elected Dean of the Veterinary Faculty in UCD, to my great delight as I was not exactly a typical vet.

The part of the veterinary course from which I derived a great deal of benefit was 'seeing practice'. Before qualification, the student had to spend six months during the summer vacations with practitioners, keeping a detailed notebook and travelling with the vet on his rounds. My practical teachers were quite diverse people. One was an Irishman, Leo O'Higgins, who had served as an officer in the First World War, practising very close to Heathrow, and ran a quarantine service for people bringing in pets. His was primarily a small animal practice, and while I retain a love of dogs and cats, I found that in many instances the owners were neurotic and were grossly overfeeding their pets to the point of provoking various illnesses. That was an experience that caused me to think hard about the relationship between humans and domesticated animals. I have no doubt that lonely people derive enormous benefit from a pet, both psychological and physical. But equally I have no doubt that the relationship between our species and those creatures that we have domesticated is often exploitative and abusive. There is little about this in the veterinary course. And the intensification and enlargement of scale of enterprise I have seen in my lifetime has made the problem worse. This is a topic for later.

When I qualified there were no postgraduate scholarships open to Irish veterinary graduates. What saved my intellectual life was a British organization that in my time was called the Animal Health Trust. I am forever indebted to them. Since I had a good record in my studies, the man running it, Dr Reggie Woodridge, took an interest in me and gave me a research scholarship. He had fixed up for me to go to Cambridge, where Doctors Hammond and Marshall had an important centre for the study of mammalian reproduction. I convinced him, rightly I think, that I was a bloody fool. Anyone who, at the age of twenty-one, is offered a chance to do a doctorate in Cambridge and turns it down *must* be a bloody fool.

What I said to him was that my education in the science subjects in pre-med had been pathetically inadequate, and that I wanted to spend a year in a good place studying physics and chemistry, with a bit of biology, of a modern kind. Very generously, instead of throwing me out, he arranged for this at University College London, the utilitarian Benthamite 'godless institution' in Gower Street. And during that year I discovered a love for, and tiny aptitude in, mathematics. It is perhaps the greatest regret of my life that my mathematics teachers up to then had been less than satisfactory, and things that I now find easy, even obvious, I had up to then thought very difficult.

After that year the blessed Animal Health Trust signed me up to do the special BSc in Physiology/Biochemistry. It was the last year in which you could do them together, and in every way these glorious years in London were the most intellectually exciting of my life. I was influenced by some great scientists. It was the extraordinary personality of Prof. J.B.S. Haldane, in the special Chair of Biometry (created for him), who showed me the full scope of mathematics in biology. By happenstance, and God knows where he even heard of it, my father had the very great pioneering work of D'Arcy Wentworth Thompson, *On Growth and Form*, and I was familiar with this from childhood, so to a degree my mind was prepared. Haldane was not just a great and inspiring scientist, but also a Communist. He was part of a remarkable group of Communist community intellectuals (Leslie Morton, Eric Hobsbawm, Desmond Greaves), some of whom were Irish.

My professor was Sir Lindor Brown.[1] He and his staff gave no lectures. They provided a list of the lectures in the London medical schools and told us to pick what we wanted. They fitted us into research projects in subjects that interested us, so we got to the research coalface right away. The class consisted of eight people, all graduates already and three of them PhDs. One of the latter, Prof. Heinz Wolff, later became a famous popularizer of science on UK TV. It was immensely exciting. And when it was finished Prof. Brown, who apparently liked me though he had not shown much sign of it, said one day, 'I have got the chair in Oxford. I cannot offer a post, but if you come there with me we will always find you something to keep you going.' So within a few years I had been offered postgraduate places first in Cambridge and then Oxford. Again I declined, thereby convincing him, like Woodridge, of my basic instability. This offer was all the more remarkable because he must have been asked about me by some bit of British intelligence (Cold War, remember?) and used to call me 'that revolting Irishman' (an old joke). I told him that I was going back to Ireland, without a job. That convinced him. He dropped me.

## COMMUNISM: THE EARLY YEARS

I am here concerned to pursue the evolution of my ideas. As a kid of the 1930s, the first major event in my awareness of the world was the Spanish Civil War, and without at all knowing what it meant, it was the first time I heard the word 'Communism'. When I was six and the Franco rebellion broke out, and triumphed partly through British non-intervention and active fascist intervention for the generals, my mother was passionately in the camp of the Republic. Though it

---

1. Physiologist and Fellow of the Royal Society (1903–1971).

was initially a broad social democratic government, in the end the Communists came to play a leading role. Even in Ireland we knew Communists, and while my parents were not Communists themselves, they respected them. I gradually came to Marxism in my middle teens, when the standing of Communism was high, when the Soviet Union had played the greatest role in defeating Hitler and the local Communists had been the bravest, most resolute and most effective of all European resistance movements. For organization and determination and courage, the Communists were spoken of with respect, even in Ireland. And there were then great Communist intellectuals that we knew about in France, as well as great artists.

In the Popular Front-inspired organizations that preceded World War II, there were Communists and others. I knew some of the Communists. Nice ordinary decent people. That was my experience; that was where I was coming from. By the age of eleven or so, I accepted the analysis that the West's strategy was to build up Hitler to destroy Communism. He spoiled the plot by turning west. The result was that the British ruling class, who had been appeasers and indeed collaborators of fascism, threw out Chamberlain and found the patriotic outcast, Winston Churchill. The Cold War, which had started at the moment of the victory of the Russian Revolution in November 1917, was temporarily adjourned. Uncle Joe with his pipe and moustache became almost cuddly. That was my world.

The British newspaper *The Daily Telegraph* published excellent war maps. I pinned one of the Eastern Front to the wall and followed the front with coloured pins. Voroshilov, Timoshenko and Budyonny were heroes. The long, drawn-out battle of Stalingrad and the even longer siege of Leningrad were followed with attention. And while the Red Army, hitherto despised by Western 'experts' and with much of its general staff destroyed in the great purges, started to turn back and defeat the invincible Wehrmacht, my delight grew. By some trick of memory, I recall in particular detail the great tank battle at a place intriguingly called Kursk.[2] And after that, the Soviet army triumphed.

One of those milestone Left Book Club books was by an American left-wing writer, Leo Huberman, and was called *Man's Worldly Goods*. It was an easily accessible account of Marxist ideas, and I took it on board there and then on first reading.

---

2. An author's note reads: 'Magnetic anomaly'. Kursk is the largest magnetic anomaly on Earth, first discovered in 1773. Further investigations attributed the anomaly to the remarkable richness of iron ores in the region, spread over an estimated 120,000 km².

At the age of fourteen, fifteen and sixteen I will never forget the excitement of reading Marx, Engels and Lenin, very carefully and repeatedly. I revered them and accepted what they said uncritically. And so for the next nineteen or twenty years Marxism was the core of my beliefs. My first experience was of *The Communist Manifesto*. Jack White was a friend of my parents and used to visit them in Killakee, where he left behind his copy of the *Manifesto* (printed in Dun Laoghaire), which I pounced on whenever I came across it – I cannot exactly remember when. But I do recall the excitement. Shortly afterwards I got my hands on *Das Kapital*, Volume I, and I have been reading Marx, with a shifting viewpoint and reaction, ever since. He is not easy. In my view he has suffered desperately from simplistic interpretations by half-educated people. But even allowing for this I now think that he was wonderful; in certain aspects he showed a stunning insight and prescience, but he contains very large and debilitating errors.

In 1946, under the encouragement of George Gilmore, I joined the Labour Party in Rathfarnham.[3] By 1948 or 1949 I had moved left and become a completely committed Communist. Indeed, in all my teenage brashness I taught Marxism in the small (and sometimes competing) proto-Communist groups in Dublin. I was never a member of an Irish Communist Party – because there wasn't one – but had there been I would have been, and I was a member of its precursor organization, the Irish Workers' League. I recalled Spain and World War II, when the most resolute opponents of fascism were the Communists, in the Resistance as well as in the Soviet Army.

It was still possible for me to dismiss reports of the gulag, and the message of Koestler's wonderful novel, *Darkness at Noon*, as capitalist propaganda. That is what I did. I swallowed it hook, line and sinker and with great passion, and I began to build a circle of friends among British and Irish Marxist intellectuals who in retrospect were wonderful people, straight, decent and very brilliant.


## SAGE AND HIS SALON

Accident, chance, happenstance – call it what you will – have played an enormous part in my life. So I am about to describe the chain of accidents that brought me into the company of the most extraordinary group of people I have ever met.

---

3. The author was in fact the founder of the Rathfarnham branch, which was named for him after his death.

In 1951, when I went to study as a postgraduate student at University College London, my first landlady was Stella Jackson, whom my family had known as the partner of the Irish poet Ewart Milne in the period between the victory of Franco and the outbreak of the war in Europe. In the large flat where Stella Jackson and her partner lived was a man called David Barton, who had gone to A.S. Neill's Summerhill School, and his Swedish wife Kirsten, who had gone there as a teacher. Among their friends was a physicist called Mike Bernal (I think he stayed in the flat for a while) and he was interested to meet a young Irish Marxist who was also a vet.

The reason, I discovered, was that his father – the famous J.D. Bernal, 'Sage' to everyone, the most remarkable man and the most brilliant mind I have ever encountered – was born on a dairy farm in Co. Tipperary. I believe the nick-name 'Sage' was given to him by Julian Huxley, himself no mean scientist and the first head of UNESCO. Sent from Tipperary to the English Catholic school at Ampleforth, the Jesuits taught Bernal too well and he became a Marxist. As an extremely brilliant young researcher in physics at Cambridge, he was elected a fellow of the Royal Society at twenty-seven. The future of militant Marxists in Oxbridge just as the Cold War was warming up was not bright, and Bernal became Professor of Physics at Birkbeck College, the successor to the old Working Men's Institution founded by Michael Faraday just down the road from UCL, and lived a few hundred yards away on the Russell Square side.

At Bernal's Sunday night salons in his house on Torrington Place, I occasionally – being as invisible as I could and soaking up the conversation with great delight – got an insight into a most extraordinary group of people. The result of the invasion of Cold War attitudes into academe, this last great flowering of Communist intellectuals in Britain has been swept under the carpet and neglected. (There is a great piece of scholarship awaiting someone unearthing it …) So I was excited by ideas and new knowledge as I had never been before and – in a group – have never been since.

At the centre was Bernal. Among the others who were Irish and had Irish connections was the great Marxist classicist Benjamin Farrington, a Dubliner and Professor of Classics at Swansea University, who developed a completely new take on classical studies. His brother Tony lived in Dublin and was a brilliant geologist, married to Doreen Synge, a relative of the playwright J.M. Synge. They were friends of my parents and had a cottage in Ticknock, where my brother Mike and I spent a lot of happy times. Their sons Brian and Conor were of an age with us. I have clear memories of George Thomson, a classics professor in Birmingham, who though he was not Irish, learned the Gaelic language, visited the Blaskets and wrote about Peig Sayers, and contributed much to Gaelic scholarship.

Aged sixteen, I had spent a long and wonderful summer on a farm on the River Stour in Constable country on the Suffolk–Essex border. This was owned by Max Morton, related to Stella Jackson by marriage, whose brother Leslie Morton wrote what I found to be an immensely revealing book, *A People's History of England.* Leslie was a member of the historians' group of the British Communist Party – as also, I believe, was the remarkable historian Eric Hobsbawm, author of what is to me the greatest synthesis of history (mainly European) from the French Revolution to the end of the twentieth century, running to four volumes. I believe too, though I can't be certain, that Hobsbawm was there. Certainly we never spoke.

I remember the strange, complex Cambridge biochemist Joseph Needham, who during the war had been in what was then called Chungking.[4] It was the seat of Chiang Kai-shek's government, and Needham was some kind of scientific attaché.[5] Good scholar that he was, he learned Mandarin Chinese, apparently not just well enough to write it but also to speak it, and was given access to government archives. With a brilliant research career behind him, while still a young man, he wrote on China in all its multifarious and wonderful aspects. He fell in love with a Chinese scientist who came to Cambridge to further her career in science; a passionate love that lasted the rest of his life.

I remember, about 1953 or 1954, Needham telling us that he was writing a book about the history of science in China.[6] This history of Chinese science and technology in its social context, over literally thousands of years, must be one of the very great works of scholarship of the twentieth century and has changed the Western view of China. For someone reared in the chauvinism of Western science, it makes chastening reading. But it is exciting and wonderful, and if your mind is open to change, then it is mind-altering.

I think that the 1950s was the time of the last great flowering, in various fields, of Communist intellectuals in Britain and France. About other countries I don't know enough to say. I was never again in my life privileged to know genuine intellectuals of such quality. Not all of these were Communists. Some were; about others I don't know, but they were all politically strongly on the left. The

---

4. Now Chongqing.

5. Needham held the position of 'scientific counsellor' at the British Embassy in Chongqing.

6. *Science and Civilisation in China* remains an ongoing project today, under the guidance of the Needham Research Institute; currently it numbers twenty-seven books.

wonderfully inconsistent and manic Needham never was, but they all respected Bernal immensely, and they thought that Communism was a perfectly honourable and decent belief system. Sitting at their feet, quiet as a church mouse lest I miss a sentence, I thought the same.

But the tide of contrary evidence was rising. The volume of shocking information coming out of the Soviet Union was so great and authentic that it could no longer be dismissed as 'capitalist propaganda'. Communist intellectuals of impeccable honesty and the noblest of motivation became, quite rapidly, an extinct species.

## THE CONNOLLY ASSOCIATION

Before talking about that, there are two separate important things in my life in London. I was extremely active in the Connolly Association, an organization for the Irish in Britain, which in its broadest aim sought to persuade immigrant Irish in the UK that they should take an active part in the British Labour Movement, both political and trade union, and should support the Left in Ireland. It was led and guided by Communists like Desmond Greaves and myself, though that was not clearly said, and it had espoused the nationalist cause, which I supported then but now consider wrong. If there was an IRA physical force grouping in existence at all in the UK during those years, I had absolutely no contact with them, nor did I know of any such contact by any of the Connolly Association leadership. Had there been such, I feel I would have known, since I was very close to Greaves, who ran things. It is a thing that Hobsbawm would know and I would dearly love to know. Tony Coughlan has written that he was never a Communist, and of course I believe him, but he certainly worked with us and was trusted by us.

I learned that the clerical leadership of the Irish community in Britain and the Irish government became concerned at the amount of headway that the Connolly Association was making in Britain. So it was decided that any money would be given to a more conservative organization for Irish emigrants in the UK. This was the Anti-Partition League. In our organization work among the Irish, we kept on coming into contact/conflict with them. Their message was a brilliantly articulated version of the nationalist story with a touch of 'Celtic' feeling and of chauvinism. I had close contacts among the junior diplomats: Florrie O'Riordan, my cousin Paul Keating and a few others. One summer in the early fifties, I was home on holiday when I met up with Paul. He was very explicitly not Communist, but he had been a Fabian in Trinity. I stuck into him about the political line of the Anti-Partition League, which was reputedly intellectually backed by the Department of External Affairs in Dublin. Their policy line was the standard stuff of the Fianna Fáil government that succeeded the coalition of 1948–51. In other words, it was old-fashioned green nationalist rhetoric, but well written. To my amazement, Paul told me (perhaps he should not have) that the APL publicity materials were written by Conor Cruise O'Brien, my friend of Glencree fourteen or so years before. By then he was a brilliant junior diplomat in the Department of External Affairs; a star, running quite a brilliant staff. I was surprised, and noticed it as a change from the opinions that I knew he had held as a TCD student. Years passed and we went our separate ways, mine leading back to Ireland. By then, under the *nom de plume* of Donal O'Donnell, Conor had already gained a considerable reputation as an essayist and literary critic – on the liberal side.

The Connolly Association got me into places that a nice middle-class kid like myself would never have seen, like the old grey gloomy Gorbals in Glasgow before it was redeveloped and the camps on the Isle of Grain where a large Irish contingent of workers had a special dormitory, church and priest; the Poles the same. For a week some of the hardy ones would work two shifts, sleep one shift, and with money in their pockets go into Chatham on a Saturday night and tear the town apart. Sunday was for recovery and then it began again. It was in Chatham that I first saw 'No Irish' signs in the windows of boarding houses.


## HONEYMOON IN PARIS

In early May 1953, I got married in Caxton Hall registry office, to Loretta (Laura) Wine from Dublin,[7] the only child of Alec and Claire Wine of the Grafton Street antique dealership Louis Wine. I always understood how awful for the family her 'marrying out' was, especially as we did not ask permission. They were thoroughly decent and nice people and we later became friends. (Conundrum: 'What do you call your mother-in-law?' Answer: 'Nothing for the first few years, and then "Granny".' It was like that.) But there was also the question of food. I loved her Ashkenazi food, which her husband did not really appreciate, and harking back to my aunt Mary Frances I got mother-in-law Claire to teach me. It wasn't a trick. But it showed her I could not be *all* bad. As a foodie, I still cook a mean Ashkenazi dinner around a boiling fowl. Since I had exams, and Laura, after a spell at the

---

7. Customarily called 'Laura' by the author and others close to her.

Conservatoire in Paris, was studying too, we were married on Saturday and went back to work on Monday. But we went to Paris for the celebration of the revolution on 14 July. We hitchhiked to Dover and took the boat.

Claire Wine said that we were motoring in Europe. We were, but in kind people's cars. We were thumbing. On the great day we joined the procession and were on one of the great boulevards, walking totally peacefully towards the Bastille, when our section of the procession was cut off in front and behind by armed helmeted police out of side streets. The next thing, without warning, there was the clatter of machine guns. Unbeknownst to us, we had happened on the Algerian contingent. Six were killed on the spot in front of us and many more injured. I recall a café chair upturned over a large pool of fresh blood, and wedged between the legs was a piece of cardboard on which was scribbled, *'Içi un camarade était tué par les flics'.*[8] And at the entrance to the Metro station nearby, when parts of the crowd were smashing cast-iron café tables to use the legs as weapons and were levering up cobblestones, wiser heads were saying, 'Go home, comrades! You can't win and they want to kill you.' For the previous dozen years I had been troubled by the murder of Dinny O'Brien and now here it was again – violence, death in pursuit of political aims. I have detested physical force ever since.

Had it ever come to 'the revolution', which we discussed and which in the atmosphere of the Cold War was thinkable, I would not have fought; not then, not ever.

---

8. Translated: 'Here, a comrade has been killed by the cops.'

# On Marxism

So, I slipped into Marxism easily, and I had wonderful teachers. From about nineteen I read Marx continuously and carefully. Sometimes I still do, and having at first only encountered his obvious published classics, as well as the two volumes of *Das Kapital*, I later received a further injection of insight with the English-language publication of the *Grundrisse*.[9] Even by 1950, the Marx I knew from his own writing was different from the Marx who appeared in Soviet periodicals. I found him very complex. Subtle, difficult, deep, flexible. And using – revelation! – the dialectical method. For Lenin I had respect, though his work produced less excitement. For Stalin, even then: none. I still have the pretentious brown-bound volumes of his collected works. Lots of volumes. Lots of words. But I could not find fresh original exciting thought.

In some ways, the early Marxists were very typical of a mid-nineteenth century philosophical mode of expression: use big words where little ones would do and establish a system. In a way, it reminds me of the post-war French philosophical development after the breakup of traditional Marxism. Often they had something interesting to say, but you had to excavate it from the debris of a self-consciously 'clever' mode of expression.

I already knew that Marxism was not easy and that, in pursuance of the traditions of German scholarship, he did not strive to make his meaning clear. I knew that he was a bully, that he got drunk and knocked off policemen's helmets and that he had seduced and made pregnant his wife's maid. Already in my early twenties I was annoying Desmond Greaves by my propensity to make jokes, even about Marxism. And I knew that there were many in our movement who were utterly simplistic in their understanding, and who had switched the certainty of revealed religion for the certainty of the triumph of the proletariat. All this I knew, and yet my Marxist conviction survived Hungary, if not Czechoslovakia.[10]

---

9. First published in English in 1973.

10. The Hungarian Revolution of 1956 and the 'Prague Spring' of 1968 respectively.

My mind, in the face of the widespread hostility of the Ireland of the Cold War, to which I had returned in 1955, was clenched. It took a long time to unclench.

Who am I – a vet, a farmer, a politician, a journalist – who am I to think that I can spot the error at the very core of Marxism, which I admire so much? But, un-humbly, I do think that I know. It is this: Marx, the dialectician, was not dialectical enough. And he knew no science, even though he had the genius to recognize the extraordinary step forward of Charles Darwin in proposing evolution as central to understanding the way the world is.

If I am to explain its major error, then I must begin with a very brief exposition of my understanding. At the core is dialectical materialism. Dialectics as a technique is as old as the ancient Greeks. How it connects with Marx is that it was he – impatient, bullying, arrogant – who made the incredible juxtaposition of materialism (which goes back to the early Greeks, before the brilliant imbecilities of Plato) with the dialectical method (again going back to the wonderful early Greeks, codified and polished by the German philosopher Hegel, but on an idealist[11] basis. Hegel, like Sophocles, was a dualist: existence was compounded of both spirit and material reality, of which the former was more important.) What Marx did – a stroke, I think, of extraordinary brilliance – was to take dialectics and add, 'But there is no dualism. There is only material nature.' Thus, his philosophy was dialectical materialism. Marx inverted the dialectics of Hegel to base it on the real existence of reality out there, regardless of human consciousness or human observation of that reality. Materialism and dialectics: what an ideas system! I still believe that, incorporating new things that Marx and Engels could not have known, it is the best shot humankind has made at a sound and true philosophy, and is now in the process of being made even more profound.

In the twenties, Stella Jackson's father Tommy (Thomas Alfred, or T.A., Jackson) had been a prominent British Communist. A largely self-taught working-class intellectual (he was a printer by trade), he wrote a well-respected book on Dickens and, more important to me, a history of Ireland called *Ireland Her Own*.[12] Tommy was such a wonderful person that I will allow myself to digress. One remarkable and dangerous characteristic is that he was funny. 'How can I be taken seriously', he used to say, 'when I am named after an apostle who couldn't believe and a king who couldn't bake?'

He lectured wonderfully on dialectics. One bit I often repeat. What was dialectics? Tommy Jackson's exposition of its essential components revolved

---

11. In philosophy, idealism is the group of philosophies which assert that reality, or reality as we can know it, is fundamentally mental, mentally constructed, or otherwise immaterial.

12. Published in 1947.

around what he said was a well-known Bethnal Green saying: 'There is a difference between scratching your arse and tearing the skin off.' Tommy might not have invented this, but I think it is one of the best, and certainly the funniest, exposition around.

1. Nature consists not of static things, but of evolving processes (the itch).
2. The application to the itch (thesis) of the scratching hand (antithesis), resulting in pleasant relief, constructs temporarily the synthesis of the scratching process; a unity of opposites.
3. Small itch – gentle scratch; more intense itch – more vigorous scratch. This is an example of quantitative change. It answers the question 'How much?'
4. Very intense itch – very powerful frantic scratch, so that the skin reaches the limit of what it can endure and tears. So quantitative change (harder and harder scratches) changes suddenly into qualitative change – a tear.
5. The scratch negates the itch, but ultimately causes a tear, which results in an even bigger itch. As a result of the unity of opposites (itch and scratch) we find the negation of the negation – not relief, but a bigger itch.

But here, to me to this day, is the paradox: Marxism in dialectical materialism offered the best shot so far of a systematic philosophy that deals with the way the world really is. It inspired the noblest and best all over the world for nearly seventy years (ending, in my eyes, with Plekhanov and Rosa Luxemburg) in a consistent fight against imperialism and oppression. The movement, on lots of major issues, was consistently on the right side. And yet, over and over, when in power it was unable to guarantee liberty and freedom of thought and of artistic creation. Where did it go wrong, and how did its simplistic application by ignorant people open the door to the murderous violence of Stalinism – and a terrifying and paralyzing overgrowth of the state in place of the withering away that Marx had predicted? It is not then simply a question of wicked people like Stalin. It is deeper than that. There must be something in Marxism itself. I am going to be immodest enough to suggest what I think that something is.

There were important things that Marx did not know, and could not have known because they simply were not known. Since, almost simultaneously, Marx wrote *Das Kapital* and Darwin developed his Theory of Evolution, huge advances have been made. Engels had written a splendid essay on what science might become, 'Dialectics of Nature', but in the last quarter of the nineteenth century, in all sorts of important ways, crucial bits of science did not yet exist. Physics of a mechanistic kind, yes.

Up to Marx's time, biology had been descriptive and analytical. The great work of Cuvier is an example. But botany and zoology were still classifying and collecting things. Though Darwin had published in 1858 and Marx read and recognized the magnificence of his work, evolutionary ideas were slow to penetrate biology. This was partly because of the laziness and poor quality of the teachers and partly because of the influence of Roman Catholic pietism. When enough data were accumulated, biology passed from the cataloguing stage to the answering of some of the big 'how' questions. Darwin and Wallace began the process not just of explaining how living things got that way (evolution), but of how they fitted together (what is now ecology) – analysing dynamic, evolving, interacting biological systems (culminating for now in Gaia), which reveal themselves to a dialectical analysis.

Before leaving dialectics, I have one more recollection. In 1957 the British Association for the Advancement of Science[13] visited Dublin. The greatest Irish biochemist, E.J. Conway, was lecturing on, I think, cell membranes and the sodium pump. There were few listeners; he was a poor speaker and in his choice of subject he was before his time. The elegance and simplicity of the equipment he invented, I found extraordinarily beautiful. He had some kind of speech defect and spoke very softly. But, mumbling to himself, he gave a beautiful and brilliant discourse. I recall him saying one day, *sotto voce* in an almost empty lecture theatre, 'I'm sorry if this seems like dialectical materialism. The problem is that nature is dialectical.' Yes, indeed.

In Marx's time, there were no electron microscopes; there was no cybernetics; there was no biochemistry. There was no genetics – apart from the work of the monk Gregor Mendel, a contemporary of Marx, who in a monastery in Czechoslovakia was laying the first analytical basis of what became the science of genetics. The discovery of DNA lay in the wall of time, and the great debate about the relative influences of nature and nurture had not been joined, much less resolved. But Marx was a child of his time. It would be un-Marxist to think that he could be other. He didn't know everything, even of the knowledge then existing.

The great weakness – indeed, error – stems from the mathematics of the time, which was linear. Nature had immutable laws, which physics could uncover. Marx was ideological, harking back to the cosmology of Johannes Kepler and the mathematics of Newton and Leibniz, which provided a magnificent, beautiful and inspiring new model of the universe and a new way of calculation. These swept all before them, posing and answering a host of extremely important questions.

---

13. Now the British Science Association.

But not all questions. And like every new triumphant paradigm, it claimed too much for itself and was accorded too much intellectual respect.

The assumptions of the Newtonian synthesis were linear and mechanistic, and Marx, for all his love and brilliant use of dialectics, was not dialectical enough. His mistake was to be too Newtonian, and although he would have hated anyone saying so, he was not totally dialectical; he had not time to completely rework the paradigm of his youthful education and he remained a bit of a mechanist. Marx claimed that he could see and articulate certain, inexorable laws of social revolution relating to the defeat of a mature bourgeois society by the risen forces of the proletariat. The 'iron laws of history' said that Communism would overthrow capitalism. Well it didn't, did it?

Until the second half of the twentieth century, one hundred years too late for Marx, Einstein and the new physics had not yet destroyed the certainty of Newtonian physics. Newton believed that his laws of motion were absolutely and unalterably true; Einstein proved him wrong.

> Nature and Nature's Laws lay hid in night:
> God said 'Let Newton be!' and all was light.[14]
> It did not last: the devil howling 'Ho!
> Let Einstein be!' restored the status quo.[15]

But Marx came before Einstein. He thought that there was a rigid causality, which we now know to be nonsense, but which fed his general certainty that he was not just partially (which he was) but totally and permanently right. Had he been less mechanistic and more dialectical, he might have seen the danger of this line of thought. There was no mathematics of chaos and complexity, in my view the most important advance of the second half of the twentieth century. The public discourse contained no metaphors about the effects of falling leaves and butterflies in the Brazilian jungle on the weather in Europe. Marx was just too early. The new post-linear mathematics of people like Mandelbrot and Prigogine gives us a very powerful tool to deal with complexity and chaos at a level above linear processes. And most of the important things in nature (blood flow and the climate, for example) belong in that domain.

In passing, the fractal pictures of Mandelbrot are some of the most beautiful and exciting shapes I have ever seen. The inspiration of this digression is

---

14. Alexander Pope, 'Epitaph for Sir Isaac Newton'.
15. J.C. Squire (1884–1958), 'Answer to Pope's Epitaph for Sir Isaac Newton'.

to make clear that I totally respect C.P. Snow's 'two cultures' theory.[16] Someone who inheres totally in either cannot, in my view, claim to be educated. And the act of scientific discovery is often a highly intuitive and beautifully creative act. I learned a little mathematics later in life, having failed to appreciate in my youth not just how powerful mathematics was, but how beautiful. Art and science are a continuum. There are different emphases, but no boundaries.

Finally, on a personal judgement, comes at last the emergence of a science of mind. The works of Freud, Jung, Adler and their contemporaries are interesting, sometimes beautiful – and sometimes, especially in Jung, really frightful. They are exciting works of creative imagination. And they have the huge merit of asking some important new questions. But they do not provide the answers. Apart from a few shafts of brilliant insight in Freud, they are not science. They are not knowledge. Freud is beautiful, intuitive makey-uppy. Jung is, on my reading, a racist mystic. Adler was the best of them for common sense. However, cognitive science, primitive as it is, begins to offer us – if not yet magnificent results – at least magnificent vistas and hope. Only now, when scientists can watch the responses of a living conscious brain under controlled tests and challenges, do the outlines not just of the science of the brain, but of a science of mind, begin to emerge. In all these areas the recently available computers can handle the numbers. Cognitive science is real and developing very rapidly and is providing the kind of useful knowledge that Freud never could.

To me as an onlooker, the two most important conclusions are that human behaviour and chaotic behaviour are at the core of all the most important processes, physical or chemical, and that there are beginning to be ways to deal with this chaos intellectually.

All of this knowledge – new, beautiful, exciting, powerful – was not available to Marx. In fact, looking back on him I am struck by how much he was a creature of his time, both in economics and in philosophy. Unless you believe that truth is given, on top of a mountain, by God to a specially chosen man, graven in stone, then we can only work with the knowledge we have got. This kind of culture (writing, counting, storing and recovering recorded knowledge) is extraordinarily recent in human history. It could not have existed without the rise of urban civilization. In evolutionary time, that is a moment. The blink of an eye. So it is

16. 'The Two Cultures' is the title of part of an influential 1959 Rede lecture given by British scientist and novelist C.P. Snow. It argued that 'the intellectual life of the whole of Western society' was split into the titular two cultures – namely the sciences and the humanities – and that this was a major hindrance to solving the world's problems.

not surprising that we have not got around to everything yet. Indeed, the most powerful tool, the experimental method of modern science, is widely understood and vigorously in application only for a few hundred years. Marx was subtle and flexible, and only idiot followers, who were very little acquainted with his writing anyway, set his thoughts in stone.

Though he was fiercely combative, he did not stop learning new things at twenty. I believe (not 'I know' – there is no evidence) that he would have welcomed and adapted to the new knowledge of the last century and a half. He was very human, a very great human, profoundly worth studying, traduced by simplistic followers – at least in the European incarnation. Perhaps the wise old Chinese will do it better. Nothing stands still. *Panta rhei.*[17]

I was never very happy with the sense in the Communist movement that things, including very large and important things like the victory of the working class, were unrolling in an inevitable and almost fore-destined way. It reminded me at certain moments of the kind of 'predestination' mocked so brilliantly by Robert Burns in 'Holy Willie's Prayer':

> O Thou that in the Heavens does dwell,
> Wha', as it pleases best Thysel',
> Sends ane to Heaven an' ten to Hell
> A' for Thy glory,
> And no for onie guid or ill
> They've done before Thee![18]

There are no 'iron laws'. Anywhere. Ever. One of the problems of Stalinism was that half-educated people swallowed Marx, who is subtle and difficult, as if it were the catechism. Consider the terrible effects of thinking there are. If the revolution was inevitable, then anything was permitted to make it safe: if I am right, history will justify me; if I am wrong, I will pay. The Gletkins[19] of the world, often (mostly, I would guess) committed the most terrible crimes in defence of the revolution.

But the problem goes deeper than that. Let us assume a totally sincere and intelligent revolutionary in the 1880s (and I think that those people were extremely

---

17. 'Everything flows.' Encapsulation of Heraclitean thought found in Simplicitus and Plato's *Cratylus*: 'Everything changes and nothing remains still … you cannot step twice into the same stream.'

18. From *The Poetry of Robert Burns – Vol. II* Centenary Edition.

19. Character in Arthur Koestler's *Darkness at Noon* (1940): one of Rubashov's interrogators.

moral in their private lives, extremely honourable and extremely intelligent – the salt of the earth, in fact). But they didn't doubt enough or laugh enough, or hold their beliefs lightly enough.

Marx predicted and called for the proletarian revolution. Lenin, in the extraordinary circumstances of Russia in the First World War, achieved what looked very like it. The great masses of Left opinion in the immediate aftermath believed this *was* the revolution. There was a problem. Having rather surprisingly taken power without a great deal of policy as to what you did with it, the new Soviet Union built its economy on the pattern of the German war economy. This is fine in war, but it is bad at supplying the consumer goods that the public wants. And the Soviet Union inherited a civil war on top of the destruction of the world war. The public did not get what the utopians had promised them. As always, people listen to their bellies first. And there was famine. The initial euphoria of the revolution evaporated. They came to oppose the Communist State in significant numbers. But Marx had promised the proletariat victory. This was 'the Revolution', and in defending the inevitable revolution one had the justification of history to do – in the short term, of course, and for the sake of the revolution – the most terrible things.

The crucial thing for me is that by the late 1940s or early 1950s there began to be so much evidence that, far from being the socialist utopia, the Soviet Union was a pretty terrible place and that it was no longer possible to dismiss this evidence as capitalist propaganda. I was rather late in realizing this. The 1956 Hungarian Rising and its brutal suppression should have shaken me, but I kept on; worried, cautious, with doubts, but certainly not rushing to the outstretched arms of the anti-Communist bandwagon.

The Cold War was in full swing and I was able to sustain my belief, in the knowledge of the extent of US provocation and financing. Of course, it was true about what the CIA and others were up to. But they were only taking advantage of an exploitable situation. I regret that I did not keep a diary of the evolution of my thought, and I did not have any Irish intimates that I felt I could talk to. And I was desperately busy: three children arrived in this period between 1956 and 1965. There was a house built, agricultural journalism, the building-up of the subsequently abandoned TCD veterinary school, as well as wonderfully enlightening periods of research in France, Denmark and Sweden.

But Czechoslovakia 1968 was too much, even for an old [Bolshevik][20] like me. In a marvellous 1970 film about the Czechoslovakian rebellion made by the great

---

20. Word missing from the notebooks. This is the most likely intended word, according to family.

Greek filmmaker Costa-Gavras, *The Confession*, when the tanks appear at the end of the boulevard a student with a bucket of whitewash is writing, 'Lenin, wake up, they have gone mad.' I agreed, but I went beyond blaming Lenin for the error, and went right back to Marx. I think that left-wing people have been pondering what went wrong ever since.

I have been reading him on and off for more than sixty years, and though I am not now a Marxist in the traditional sense (I've added some bits and rejected others), I remain in awe of his mind and in agreement with very large parts of what he said. If I can have a dialectical approach *and* use the new knowledge of a century and a half to modernize it, then I am still a Marxist.

# 3. Snakes and Ladders

My life, as will emerge, has been an exhausting series of ladders and snakes, and in the decision to return to Dublin I slipped on an enormous snake. I came of age and qualified as a vet in 1951 and, like so many of my fellow young, set off for England. Looking back over those London academic years – studies, wider reading stimulated by Bernal and company, travelling Britain with the Connolly Association to wherever there were Irish, finding time to enjoy my new home with my new wife and some of the wonderful range of theatre and cinema London had to offer – I don't know what Laura and I did for sleep. But they were great times.

And then came Dublin. Out of some kind of perversity that at this remove I don't quite understand, I joined the staff of the veterinary college in Ballsbridge, Dublin at the beginning of 1955. Poorly equipped after the war as University College London had been, the transition from people of great scholarship and competence to the atmosphere I found in Ballsbridge in the mid fifties was the greatest shock of my life. It is a long time ago and I'm not going to throw stones into the past at people who are nearly all dead. It is enough to say that out of the whole of the staff there was one person I admired and liked. To make things, if possible, even worse, the college's administration was by civil servants from the Department of Agriculture, who though individually decent and honest were given no long-term plan, no serious budget and fundamentally no direction. There were no properly trained technicians and no properly equipped labs. The classes were about fifty students; the courses took four years after pre-vet. For the four years of the course proper, there were thirteen teachers, professors and lecturers for about two hundred students. Truly, I stood on a snake. It was awful.

Finally, in 1960, an almost unbelievable judgement of Solomon was put in place – except that neither parent loved the baby enough not to cut it in half. In the end (to tend the Catholic and Protestant domestic animals of Ireland, presumably) the school was divided unequally, with the larger and subsequently viable part going to UCD and a small, neglected and ultimately unviable part going to Trinity. I am happy to say that an excellent, properly funded school with good research has arisen and is turning out good students. I have to add, rather sadly, a phrase from a priest friend of mine, Father Pat Collins, who when we were teasing him about the ending of priestly celibacy with terrible sadness said, 'Too late for me, I'm afraid.' Notwithstanding its hopeful beginning inspired by Sir Horace Plunkett, the department turned into the upas[1] tree of Irish administration, in whose shade everything withers. And I think that half a century later, they are still pretty awful.

## DOMESTIC MATTERS

At this time, the late 1950s, life was getting a bit hectic and I was a bit taken up with domestic things. My children were born in 1956, 1958 and 1960. And I had (I should be saying 'we' all the time, because during that period my marriage was close and good) a thoroughly pleasant and rewarding experience.

In 1958 I bought two acres on the Dublin side of Tallaght and engaged an architect to build us a small house. In the early thirties my father had designed and caused to be built by a contractor, with whom he dealt directly, the house in Ballyboden where my sister-in-law Kitty, Mike's widow, still lives. So the idea of building rather than buying 'off the peg' was quite familiar to me. In 1956 I bought my first car, a Volkswagen Beetle, and Laura and I drove around the surroundings of Dublin. Every time we saw a modern house that caught our eye, we rang the doorbell and said, 'Please, we admired your house. Would you tell us who designed it?'

One day in Howth, looking down the slope towards Dublin Bay, we saw the roof of a modern house that looked as if it grew there. In response to our

---

1. *Antiaris toxicaria*, the upas or poison arrow tree, is found in tropical regions of Africa, Asia and Australia. Its sap is highly poisonous and was used to coat arrows and darts. Alexander Pushkin's poem 'The Upas Tree' (1828) first drew the West's attention to its properties.

bell-ringing, a very tall man came out (we are both small). In response to the query, he replied, 'I did.' We had happened on Andy Devane, who in retrospect (with Seán Kenny) was the greatest architect in Ireland at that time. Devane had gone to America to work for Frank Lloyd Wright, who was then at the summit of his career. The two hit it off. And when the vacancy came up, I understand that Wright wanted Devane to head up his design studio. But our Andy chose to come back to Ireland. He was working in the firm of Robinson, Keeffe and Devane, who mostly built churches. There wasn't much other work in the Ireland of the mid fifties, though Devane carried out very large commissions, such as the much-admired Allied Irish Banks building in Ballsbridge. He was used to big jobs, and here was a mid-twenties couple with a tiny amount of money wanting a small house in an unfashionable place. We must have amused him, because he took us on.

One of the features of the main room, a music room with a wonderful view across the Dodder Valley to the Dublin Mountains, was a panelled gable in a beautiful wood. But when the estimates from the builder came in, we were way over budget. We stripped out everything that could be described as non-essential, including the panelling. One day at lunchtime I drove out from the veterinary college to see how the house was going and there, installed, was the panelling. In horror, I said to Mr Murphy the builder, another excellent person, that it had been stripped out. 'I know,' he said, 'but Mr Devane is giving it to you.' Building that house was a thoroughly happy experience. Later, wishing to farm, I bought a further twenty-eight adjoining acres that came available for £6000. There are always wiseacres who say, 'Oh, you paid too much,' or, 'If only I had known, I could have got it for you for half the price.' And such there were.

I have described all this at some length because Andy Devane was one of the noblest, kindest and generally most decent men I ever met. I have very hard things to say about religion in general and Catholicism in particular, but I cite Andy as a really noble person, and one of the most devout Catholics I ever met. After the traumatic death of his wife, he gave up architecture in Dublin and went to work with Mother Teresa in Calcutta. I think she is a phoney, more concerned with snatching souls than with saving bodies. I agree with what Christopher Hitchens says about her in his book,[2] but clearly that was not Andy's experience, and he derived inspiration from it that moved him to do good in a completely disinterested way.

---

2. *The Missionary Position: Mother Teresa in Theory and Practice* (Verso, 1995).

## RESEARCH

I recall one bright spot from the late fifties. A man with whom I disagree about many things – and enormously admire and like – is Paddy O'Keeffe, who with a group of likeminded agriculturalists and in a very philanthropic frame of mind established and promoted the *Irish Farmers Journal* into a very powerful force for change in the countryside. Around him were very interesting people, like the late Michael Dillon and John Mooney, and all of these became friends from whom I learnt a great deal. Inspired by their experiences in New Zealand, they had established the Irish Grassland Association, of which I became a member and in stimulating company visited many progressive farmers in Northern Ireland as well as the South. It was before physical force Republicans destroyed the goodwill and neighbourliness that was beginning, admittedly very slowly, to blossom between the two communities. The unionist farmers we visited at that time – provided we respected the constitutional arrangements under which the vast majority of the Northern Ireland population chose to live (there are Roman Catholic unionists too) – were friendly, curious, excellent farmers and happy to share information and experience.

In the late fifties, the Kellogg Foundation (the cornflakes people) offered scholarships for postgraduate work in United States universities to Irish vets and agricultural graduates. I was chosen along with others to submit a research scheme, but was turned down. I believe that this was because of my politics. I probably would not have got a visa. But fair play to the Department of Agriculture, whose greatest admirer I am not: they realized that people less qualified and with poorer academic records than me would end up with US graduate degrees, which would put them in front of me in the career race. As compensation, and it was a move from which I derived great stimulation and delight, in 1959 they sent me to do small pieces of research in France, Denmark and Sweden. But my experiences in France and Denmark only made me more acutely aware of how inadequate my situation was in Ireland.

The first good impression of my 'honeymoon' in France turned into a full-blown love affair with that country, which still enthrals me, notwithstanding the police murders on Bastille Day 1953 and indeed others as they retreated from empire. It was there that I started a piece of research for which I could later get no funding, but which I still think was (and is) a good idea: a natural follow-on into animal nutrition of the enormous work of the visionary Dr Tom Walsh, who produced a detailed survey of the mineral composition of Ireland's soil. I wanted a mechanizable and easily managed method to see how this translated itself into the mineral nutrition of domesticated animals, which is subject to great variation and among which many mineral deficiency diseases are known.

How to find out? Blood was out. Laborious to take samples, hard to transport and keep, and not so easy to analyse. The answer was hair, even better than blood because it gave a history of the beast's nutrition during the whole life of the hair: a profile. Easy to take (with a scissors); easy to store (in an envelope); easy to transport (through the post); and easy to analyse in a very mechanized, labour-sparing way (with a spectrophotometer).[3] The research I did in Paris, I think was fairly important and original. I can never understand why it is not used where there is overgrazing and erosion to find the deficiencies and 'top dress' from the air.[4] Many underdeveloped countries clearly need this. A great bonus was that, to the limit of my meagre purse, I systematically ate my way around Paris in all its wondrous culinary splendour. It is a city I still find magical.

While I was in Stockholm, I got a letter asking me to choose which university I wanted to work for, as we were to have two veterinary faculties in Dublin. The permanent pensionable post, the statutory lectureship for which everyone then yearned. Alone, with no one to discuss it with and knowing nothing of the small print, I opted for Trinity. This was a mistake. I did not know until later that there was a powerful group within the Trinity College management who did not want a veterinary faculty at all, and that the college's commitment to its veterinary school was marginal at best.

In Denmark I had not enough time to get a piece of research underway, so I spent the time studying the farming, the agricultural co-operative system and the relations between the vets and agriculture. One vet I travelled with gave me an impressive lesson that changed my life. When we went and did a case, not alone did he treat the animal, but he conducted a health seminar with the farmer. Not just what was the illness, but why.

When I got home, I told my friend Paddy O'Keeffe what I had seen. He said that that was a bit different from Ireland. Irish vets were competent and vigorous but they didn't communicate very well with their clients. Would I like, he said, to write a weekly column in *The Irish Farmers Journal* explaining disease and its

---

3. Spectrophotometry is the quantitative measurement of the reflection or transmission properties of a material as a function of wavelength. A spectrophotometer is able to determine, depending on the calibration, what substances are present in a target and their exact quantities through calculations of observed wavelengths.

4. The practice of addressing soil deficiencies by spraying the missing nutrients from the air.

causes directly to the farmers? 'Yes, I would,' I said, 'yes.' I was meticulous in not telling farmers how to treat animals or to go beyond their level of knowledge and judgement, and this saved me from the wrath of my own profession, though they did not like it then, and Paddy kept me strictly anonymous. For many years I was its veterinary correspondent: my first step into the media world, to be followed by many more.

Soon after I started my column, Irish TV was launched and it was strongly supported by the best boss I ever worked for, the Swede Gunnar Rugheimer. The usual suspects were discreetly asked to suggest a vet for agricultural broadcasting and I think that it was Paddy O'Keeffe who suggested that they give me a try. My response to this offer changed my life.


## CHILDREN AND CHILDBIRTH

One older brother, no sisters. That was my family. Femaleness was largely a mystery. But I had no difficulty in loving women and children, and wanting a wife and family. I remember a solemn debate among 'professional revolutionaries' (which is how I, at twenty, would have described myself) about whether we had the right to inflict our insecurities on a wife and family. (A bit like the Catholic priesthood, though we made no pretence of chastity.) I'm very glad biology prevailed. I married at twenty-three and we started our family three years later.

An atheist, I felt that the Abrahamic religions (Judaism, Christianity and Islam) hated women, that it was because of the 'sin of Eve' that women were condemned to bring forth children in pain and danger, and that modern science could improve things. My wife and I believed that the male domination of reproduction in the Jewish and Christian religions (with the exclusion of women from the making of doctrine and culminating in the murder of the witches) had dehumanized and encumbered with guilt what ought to be the most human and beautiful of experiences.

When Laura and I decided to have children, perhaps before the beginning of her first pregnancy, we began investigating what was called 'painless childbirth' in a book[5] by the obstetrician Grantly Dick-Read. It was very decent, indeed a noble endeavour, but a bit woolly. As someone with a degree in physiology and a vet's experience, it did not satisfy me in regard to precisely what the woman should

---

5. A British obstetrician and leading advocate of natural childbirth methods, Dick-Read wrote *Childbirth Without Fear*, first published in 1942 under the title *Revelation of Childbirth*.

do, what role (if any) there was for her partner, and for others. We looked further and found better, but alas it was in French: *L'Accouchement Sans Douleur* by a Dr Fernand Lamaze, who worked in the French Mineworkers clinic.[6] Laura had more French than me, but a bonus was that after a tiny (and pathetic) experience of being taught French at school, I started to learn it seriously to read Lamaze. It told Laura exactly what to do and what I could do to help, and we found a doctor who did not actively object, though he was not enthusiastic. There were no classes or websites in the mid 1950s. We set about the exercises at home, and were booked into a Dublin nursing home. Laura, though she was subjected to the traditional anti-woman complexes of traditional Judaism in her rearing, was great. In due course we went to the nursing home.

We were both ready for me to be present and help, but at the crucial moment our relatively liberal doctor failed to insist on my presence, and I was put out of the room. The whole system depends on the pregnant woman and her partner, or whoever she worked with, co-operating. I was only let in to see my newborn daughter, Carla. So our first try [at the Lamaze method] was a failure.

With child number two, Eilis, we were cuter. We changed gynaecologist and made it a condition of employing him that he would accept that we would do our utmost to do a Lamaze. We did, and it was very successful. I got into the birthing room in the nursing home and played my subordinate part in what was a very happy experience. And this time the nurse was impressed and started to be curious. Labour is well named. It is hard work, and there can be manageable pain, which does not in most cases call for anaesthesia. I think that the total consciousness of the mother and the presence of her partner are joyous and life-enhancing experiences. I think this helps the mother's bonding, which if things are normally happy and supportive is switched on easily. But I think that men have a right to be present, and to bond to the newborn from the beginning.

When it came to our last, our son David, I think we can say it was a triumph. Third time around, we were wiser. We lived in Tallaght then, and by good fortune we had a wonderful local midwife, the first person we met in the whole business of having our children who was not stuck in the past or hostile, but curious. She was anxious to experience and participate in 'Lamazerie', and indeed was ultimately converted. The doctor agreed that we would do a home birth. With phones, ambulances and nearby hospitals, we did not think this either irresponsible or

---

6. Dr Fernand Lamaze (1891–1957) was a French obstetrician most famous as a popularizer of psychoprophylaxis, a method of pain management in childbirth commonly known as the Lamaze technique or 'Lamazerie'.

dangerous. As it turned out, the doctor was detained, sailing in Dublin Bay. My wonderful wife kept her calm and her courage and carried it off with aplomb. We had done the exercises together for months, and the bond between her and those assisting her, the midwife and me, was never broken. We were able to keep control of the birth process. While it was desperately hard work, and not comfortable, there was no anaesthetic, even if the presentation was an OP.[7] There was no tearing or need for surgical repair. It went like a dream, a happy dream, with no doctor present. It was all quick, with incredibly little trauma to the baby.

Much the best bit was to come. The birth was in the late evening. The older children, Carla (four) and Eilis (two), went to their own beds with their mother there. When they got up in the morning their mother was still there, but so was their little brother. No drama. Mother had not disappeared to a nursing home, to reappear after varying periods with a new jealousy-provoking sibling. David just slid in, without fuss, to join his sisters. I have told this story at some length to indicate that it is possible at home. And it is every woman's, and every family's, right.

Of course there are some times when the best of modern medicine is absolutely necessary. But when it works, it is wonderful for everyone involved, mother, baby and partner, and if things go wrong there are wonderful drugs, well worked-out surgery and splendid hospitals all quickly available as a fallback. The fathers who are excluded or exclude themselves are missing something very precious. I know that there are plenty of men who would run a mile from the birthing room, or who would faint or otherwise be a nuisance. And there should be no pressure. Those who want to stay away should, I think, do so. But they are missing a great experience.

The reasons I have described this set of experiences at some length are:

- We ran smack into the same ignorance and prejudices that had existed in Victorian times.
- These were coming to an end.
- The second and third births were extraordinarily happy experiences for me – and, I am persuaded, increased my bonding to my children.
- I am convinced that home births are as safe as hospital ones, and often safer.
- They are less stressful for everyone involved and I would urge that anyone contemplating childbirth at home, with a partner or close friend participating, and making the best shot at breastfeeding, should do so.

---

7. In an occipito-posterior presentation, the baby enters the birth canal facing upwards, rather than towards its mother's spine.

Carla's birth was the beginning of an enlightening, if sad and mostly tawdry, experience of the peculiar Irish mixture of religion and sex. I had wanted to be present at the birth of my first child. In 1956, this proved impossible. A few days later, I entered the room in the nursing home where my wife was learning to suckle the child. She had not much clothing on, and the nurse who was there made a big deal of rearranging her clothing so that I could see as little as possible of her leg or breast. I was more amused than angry. I told her that she was a bit late, since having been there at the start of the baby, there was not much of my wife that I had not seen. But that sort of smart alecry only made relations worse. I should have shut up. All in all, not a happy experience, though Carla was strong and healthy. It seems to me that then, at the cost of great pain and repression, the Irish medical services (including nurses, who ought to have more sense than male chauvinist doctors) were extraordinarily dirty-minded about sex. I am glad to say that I think it is much better now.

I had an illuminating experience when I went to register Carla's birth. Since there was no religious ceremony I had to go to the local registry, in my case in Ballsbridge, to register her birth and have a birth certificate made out. The registrar was also a medical doctor. And when the paperwork was done he said, gratuitously, that there had been a long time since our marriage before the first child. Though it was none of his business, I said that when we married we were both students and not in a position to have children. I considered then, as I do now, that access to contraceptives was a basic human right and I told him so. Then, again gratuitously, he offered me advice. People who use contraceptives, he said, often find that when they want children they are unable to have them.

Whether this was a lie, motivated by the desire to bolster his religious beliefs (contraception was then against the laws of the State and the Catholic Church), or just ignorance and stupidity, I have no way of knowing. I had a shorter fuse then than I have now, and I blew up. I told him that I knew more about the physiology of reproduction than he did; that what he said was not true; that he was the registrar when he was in that office, not a doctor of medicine to whom I had come for advice. That as well as being factually wrong, he was using his official position to promote a Catholic anti-contraception campaign, churning out religious advice based on false science. So he was not just using it, but abusing it, and he was disgracing an honourable profession.

I tell this trivial little story to illustrate that Ireland was not then, and is not now, though it has improved, a pluralist society. We have a long way to go.

# On Women, Religion and Sexuality

## CATHOLIC IRELAND

Here, based in part on personal experience, I want to draw together my thoughts about woman–man relationships in my lifetime in Ireland. I think we have an illustration of how superficial, wrong and harmful Christian, especially Roman Catholic, teaching and particularly practices and attitudes are in regard to sex. They are a source of great pain and damage to a society trying to observe them. A country like Italy knows perfectly well, and has done for a millennium, that these teachings are what you ought to say, but are not expected to do. Catholic Ireland, in its incarnation as a new state in 1922, was possessed of the zeal of all new-founded institutions. Upper-class Irish Catholics caught the whiff of late-Victorian puritanism from within the UK. (In addition to this was the Catholic counteroffensive of the turn of the century against the left-wing, secular, humanist and liberal forces emanating from the French Revolution.)

On top of this was the attempt, finding its culmination in the alliance of de Valera and Archbishop John Charles McQuaid, to make the Free State into a Catholic state, ignoring the rights of Protestants and of people without religion. The new state was bigoted and Church-dominated. And the entirely Catholic populace could and did try to force its will on society; some ass could say in all seriousness that there were no prostitutes in Ireland, and the Church expected and encouraged the parents of an unmarried pregnant daughter to drive her from her home to hide her shame in a city or abroad.

## SEXUALITY IN IRELAND

When I was in my teens there was very little – and distorted – knowledge about sex for myself and my peers. I was particularly disadvantaged because I had no sisters. When I was young, people did not discuss sex within their families. And though I revere my parents, whom I think were both quite extraordinary people in many ways, I very much regret that about sex they were no good at all. Even the matter of pregnancy was euphemized into being 'in an interesting condition'. For men, women's monthly cycle was unmentionable. The myth was that women were without sexual desire. Women who knew about and expected to have orgasmic sex were labelled nymphomaniacs. And in regard to homosexuality we knew almost nothing. We thought it was a men-only phenomenon and that it merited some of the most powerful words of condemnation in the language. Even though then, as now, it was ubiquitous, it was never discussed in any informed and serious way. But beating up 'nancy boys' was quite okay. In fact it was, if mentioned, gently encouraged; certainly not a mortal or even a venial sin.

Since the propagated and prevailing view was that sex was dirty, the way we discussed it and exchanged information about it was both ignorant and disgusting. 'Marry or burn': only the sacrament of matrimony could sanitize it. Sex outside marriage was a sin. Homosexual sex was a greater sin. The word 'masturbation' was simply unsayable, except in circumstances where adolescents were lied to in the most damaging ways by the suggestion that the masturbator would go blind, go mad or grow hairs on the palms of their hands. I recall in my teens teasing believers by saying, 'If God had intended us not to masturbate he would have made our arms a good deal shorter.' But there is no evading the charge that the churches invented and promulgated guilt-building lies.

That 'making love' (a phrase I like because it implies that there is more love at the end than at the beginning) or having sex was a very important, very pleasurable and positively health-giving activity was an utterly foreign thought. Church and State propagated the opposite and, as a consequence, the idea that good sex was a skill to be learned, and that it was important that both partners learned to be good at it, would have been looked on as very sinful.

There is a story told that when a missionary in a Cork slum told his audience that sex was only permitted within marriage for the purpose of making children, a reformed drunk went home, got a box of whitewash and wrote in huge letters on a vacant wall: 'In this building we only fuck for the greater glory of God.' But more widely, in Islam, in Christianity and among Orthodox Jews, there is a drive to breed for victory. The more souls you can control, the stronger your religion. It seems a sad commentary on humankind that the largest numbers belong to the most disciplined, centralized, fundamentalist and brutal religions, while the nicest of all in my book, the Quakers, are very few.

## ABRAHAMIC RELIGIONS AND SEX

I suppose, though I cannot be certain, that my serious thinking about women's sexuality and about childbirth arose from reading somewhere that the Catholic Church hated women. The extent of the repression of young female contemporaries was extraordinary. Not even the most ferocious repressive brainwashing could eliminate normal sexual curiosity and desire and exploration among young women. But these were accompanied by terrible guilt and unhappiness. Femaleness has been broadened out into a wider, more all-embracing source of wickedness and sin. Male randiness is fine ('Any good man would do the same') but female randiness, until very recently, was not allowed. There was allegedly no such thing as female orgasm. Conjugal rights meant that any man could have intercourse with his wife at any time, regardless of what she wanted. (I could not call it 'making love', because when the man was finished there was less love around, not more.)

And then, by some accident, I read a history of the development of male gynaecology, after the murder of the 'witches' and the male takeover. And I began to believe that the accusation contained a great deal of truth. As a vet, I had seen lots of mammalian births and, from mares to lambs, had assisted with many. And I didn't experience the Book of Genesis description of childbirth. What I did know was the power of suggestion. If a woman was warned not just of 'labour', which it certainly is, but also of 'pain', it was the punishment of Eve for the sin of curiosity. There was no corresponding pain for her partner at the beginning of her pregnancy. From the time when men took control of birthing and drove out (often burning) the wise women they called witches, this history has been shocking and terrifying. I ask anybody who is sick of my wittering on about Western religion and women to please read a history of society's approach to childbirth since the middle ages, written by a serious scholar (preferably a woman).

The biggest minority in the world is actually a majority. (I suppose that sentence is an Irish bull like that cow over there.) I use the word 'minority' because in power, in social roles, in average pay, they are disadvantaged. I refer, of course, to women. There is a school of history which claims that the Judeo–Christian–Islamic model of what is in many cases only to be called a woman-hating patriarchy, where the vast majority of the power rests with men, was preceded by a period of women's rule – *Mutterrecht*, matriarchy.[8] I am not convinced. Not that I wish it to be a

---

8. *Das Mutterrecht* (or *Mother Right: An Investigation of the Religious and Juridical Character of Matriarchy in the Ancient World*) by the Swiss anthropologist J.J. Bachofen was published in 1861 and posited a theory of gynaeocracy in prehistoric societies – the precursor to many other such theories.

fiction, but I don't think that research has yet settled the question. The Scottish verdict 'not proven' seems appropriate for the moment. Male and female bodies are different each from the other. (Hard to think of a more obvious statement.) But male and female minds are, I believe, different too. And the social roles of the sexes are obviously different.

One hundred thousand years ago, most women were either pre-pubertal, pregnant and/or nursing, or dead. The average age of death was earlier than the average onset of menopause. So obviously in a hunter/gatherer economy, roles were different. But even the term 'hunter/gatherer' betrays the inbuilt male bias. It seems that notwithstanding the special demands of reproduction, the gatherers (women) contributed more to overall diet than the hunters (men). Perhaps we should begin to talk about 'gatherer/hunter societies'. Maybe in these times the head of the hunting band was the boss. Maybe it was the wisest woman. Maybe they got by without a boss, and had a society where the sexes were equal. Equal but different. It looks as if the rise of a surplus-producing agriculture in Mesopotamia, Egypt, India and China led to the establishment of civilization, religions which became in the West monotheistic, and led to enormous differences between the power and respect allowed to women and men.

I recall an argument with the wife of one of my political heroes. She was well educated, extraordinarily decent and kind and, in her own eyes, a feminist and a liberal. But when I said that the Judeo–Christian–Islamic group of monotheists hated women, she blew up at me. Let me very briefly say why I hold to my belief.

The basic narrative of the three religions is the Book of Genesis, the myth of origin of pre-Iron Age city civilizations. I have said elsewhere that I find it loathsome and very harmful because of its attitude to our own now gravely overpopulated earth. But it is just as bad about women. Look at the basic metaphor. Humankind enjoyed Paradise (the Garden of Eden) and would be there still but for the sin, not of humans, but of woman – specifically Eve. She plucked the fruit (what else would you expect the gatherer to do?). She tempted her partner, who seems to have been an easily led duffer. But for the 'sin of Eve', we would be in Paradise still.

Why does Christianity blame women for so much? We are all, the whole of humankind, forever excluded from Paradise because of the sin of one woman. And that 'sin' – curiosity – is, in my book, a virtue. Why do some of the worst parts of Islam carry out the sexual mutilation of women? Why is a menstruating woman so dirty in the eyes of good Jews? Menstruation is an ordinary bit of female physiology. Of the myths built up to make women feel dirty, and hence inferior, none was more potent than the taboos and dreads that surrounded menstrual blood.

The Latin poet Lucretius said (wonderfully, from my point of view), 'Nothing in nature is alien to me.' The reproductive cycle in women is the very core of human existence. If after an absence of a fertilized egg settling down in the previous cycle, the womb tidies itself up and gets rid of the half-formed nest preparatory to the next egg release, what is taboo or terrifying about that? But in Judaism, sex during menstruation is taboo. And for a time after the period ends it is still taboo, until the ritual cleansing in the communal bath. And genuinely Orthodox women must shave off their 'crowning glory', their hair, and wear a wig.

Lest the other western monotheisms start feeling superior, at least Jews don't go in for women's sexual mutilation. What could be a clearer example of a male wish to dominate all aspects of women's lives? And before Christians preen – who burned the witches? Catholics and Protestants. In my reading of it, a witch was simply a wise woman who knew the herbs, was the healer and, most dangerously for her, the midwife at a time when many Christians wanted to take over the management of birthing – often with obscenely anti-woman results like symphysiotomy, which lasted up to quite recently.[9]

Sexual mutilation is common in modern human societies. Castration is a common punishment. As a way to holiness the Russian Skoptsi sect[10] did this routinely. The Vatican thinks it so unimportant a mutilation that it only officially gave up castrating boy sopranos in their choirs in 1870.[11] And a great deal of vocal music is written for castrati. I have seen the statistics recently, in a serious newspaper, that a majority of Egyptian women are subjected to the abomination of female circumcision.[12] Male circumcision is widespread, and not just among

---

9. Symphysiotomy is a surgical procedure in which the pubic cartilage is severed and the pelvis prised further apart to faciliate vaginal birth in cases of mechanical difficulties during labour. It has been claimed that Ireland was the only country to choose this over the Caesarean section solution. According to Prof. Oonagh Walsh's draft report, the last Irish symphysiotomy was performed in 1984.

10. The Skoptsi ('the castrated ones') were a secret breakaway sect from the Russian Orthodox Church, first recorded in the late 1700s. They believed that on expulsion from Paradise halves of the forbidden fruit were grafted onto Adam's and Eve's bodies, forming testicles and breasts respectively, and so their amputation would return members to a pre-lapsarian purity. There may have been up to 100,000 Skoptsi in the early twentieth century. Repressive measures were stepped up under the Soviet Union and by the late 1970s the sect had almost vanished.

11. Castrato Allessandro Moreschi performed in the Sistine Chapel until 1913. Some historians believe that Domenico Mancini, a private pontifical singer between 1939 and 1959, was also a castrato, despite the ban of 1870.

12. Now more commonly referred to as 'female genital mutilation' or FGM. Estimates from 2014

believing Jews. To me, all these practices, from chastity to sexual mutilation, are aberrations marking the youth of humankind. I expect us to grow out of them as I expect us to grow out of murdering women 'taken in adultery' and gay men – and, of course, of the death penalty in general.

The ultimate craziness was the belief that there was a special virtue in the denial of any expression of sexual love. Celibacy would have you believe it was holy, notwithstanding the evidence that it drove a proportion of those who tried to practise it into often brutal modes of diverted expression. To me, the belief that there is a superior bonus to be earned in God's eyes by what is inaccurately called celibacy – which means refraining from marriage, when what is meant is 'chastity' (refraining from sex) – is preposterous. But call it what you will, the rest of the Christian churches don't go in for it. Nor do Muslims or Jews. Even Orthodox Catholic clergy don't all attempt to be celibate. The Roman Catholics do. Of course, it avoids a tug of war between the Church on the one hand and the family on the other about the disposal of the often very considerable wealth accumulated by those who have sworn to 'poverty, chastity and obedience'. And of course, there was often a little bit over for the relatives. A priest's niece was often a good mark for a dowry in the Irish countryside.

We are living at the end of 3000 years of dominance by the Abrahamic religions in the Western world. But the grip is still so powerful on our culture and our morals that the ability to do terrible harm to individual humans is still enormous. And in revolutions, be they political, economic or moral, the winning side has a tendency to go too far before a decent balance is reached. I am still looking out for an answer why from some evolutionary psychologist or sociologist.

Sexual activity, the physiology, the psychology are hard-wired into all creatures that reproduce sexually (not all creatures do). In the early evolution of life it was a minor pathway of reproduction, which became dominant, it seems, to juggle the genes more and allow a more rapid evolution, and thus one more precisely and delicately suited to numerous evolving ecosystems. Humans possess a uniquely evolved culture, one which allows us to add a complex social context to the broadly similar anatomical, physiological and psychological sexual capabilities.

Sexual drive is, in my view, still inbuilt and so powerful that you thwart it at your peril. Many people are chaste through no fault of their own. But those exempted, I am inclined to prefer people who take the risk of committing to a partner. I think life is much better in the context of commitment, and sex is too.

---

are that up to 133 million girls and women worldwide have been affected by FGM. Prevalence rates for Egyptian women aged 15–49 are estimated at 91 per cent. [Source: WHO.]

That is not to condemn promiscuity outright. I think there is a sexual learning curve in the young, which involves a promiscuous phase, and the thought of requiring a woman to enter marriage as a virgin fills me with horror, but I would affirm that really fully human and joyful sex is impossible without commitment. However, I believe that the vows of much Christian marriage are nonsense.

We live much longer than people in the time of Christ (if he ever existed, but you know what I mean). And both partners have the right to evolve and change. Since nobody has the right to regulate *how* they evolve and change, they may, perfectly honorably and decently, evolve away from each other (and if we look around we can see that they often do). They cease to love each other in the physical sense and cease to wish to live together. And again, if we simply observe our own society we can see that, perfectly honorably and decently, they can fall in love with somebody else. So statements like 'Marriage is for life' or 'What God hath put together let no man put asunder' are simply wrong (note also that woman is passive in this formulation). And being wrong, they are harmful, because they imply guilt when marriages don't work. Alimony, the 'high cost of leaving', is built on this presumption of guilt, not to say sin. But in my experience there is much more misery engendered by forcing married people, and especially married women who have nowhere to go, to remain in bad marriages, where mutual hatred comes to predominate over the memory of good and happy times. Christian marriage, in a time of equality and individual sovereignty for women as well as men, is harmful and quite inappropriate. In fact, I never cease to wonder why women continue to be so loyal to a religion that fears and hates them. And why much of humankind continues to be loyal to religions that harm them.

## SEXUAL ORIENTATION AND EXPRESSION

Extreme sexual repression demanded of women by Western monotheistic religion produces its opposite. When the controlling power of religion began to fade, the kids of the world slipped into a period of promiscuity, enabling the moral censor to say, 'Ya, I told you so.' But I think two things about this swing of the pendulum. Firstly, it seems to me utterly natural that just after puberty there should be sexual experimentation: 'Am I straight, bi or gay?' I think it is okay for the kids to be experimental. But this experimentation, if the individual's development is proceeding as it should, is a prelude to something much more rewarding and wonderful, which is a stable long-term relationship. What the kids don't know is that sex gets better in the context of a loving relationship.

As a farmer, I know that the expression of sexuality in my dairy herd is quite complex. Why should it be more simple in the much more complicated human species? The preachers who can call homosexuality 'unnatural' have never looked at a farmyard. Because there has been so much murder and physical assault and discrimination against gay people, a culture has grown up of concealment and of blackmail that adds to the load of misery. From my point of view, I see absolutely nothing wrong with homosexuality. Giving and receiving love and intimacy is a physical need. The attempt to deny or thwart this human need seems to me a crime against our species, as it is indeed of those species close to us on the evolutionary tree.

Of course I see excessive and self-harming sexual behaviour by both sexes in circumstances where millennia-long prohibitions are suddenly lifted. But it should be no surprise. Action and reaction are equal and opposite. And the call to return to the old repressive ways is not just immoral, but impossible. We just have to give people a while to get used to a new freedom.

There is one aspect of human sexuality that even in our new era of glasnost is hardly discussed at all. I refer to bisexuality. This failure comes partly from the general prurient silence of those who proclaim themselves our moral teachers. But I think there is a deeper cause, stemming from the baleful influence of Plato and the perpetuation of his nonsense by the scholastic philosophers. Things (not processes) were all of a piece, without nuance or shading or partial truth. In between two totally separate things in themselves there could be no legitimate halfway positions. The ancient Greeks, pre-Plato, knew better. There is a dialectical relationship between the sexes.

I loved the story where the judge says, 'Are you guilty or not guilty?' and the defendant's lovely dialectical answer is 'Yes – my lord'. Similarly with sexuality: the generality of simplistic thinking in the Christian world affirms 'you are male' or 'you are female', as if these were completely separate, watertight states. But again if we looked at life around us, or even looked in the farmyard, we would see that the two compartments are not watertight. Any truthful examination of ourselves and those close to us would find feminine traits in men and vice versa. This is in my view perfectly normal.

I think every human must be a little bit bisexual. However macho boys may be, is there anyone who has not had a pleasant experience of a bisexual kind in the course of growing up? And, if you look at team games, as played by both sexes, they have to my mean nose a distinctly homoerotic whiff. I object to this not in the least. What I do dislike, and what I find in society's response to so many aspects of human sexuality, is evasion, denial, ignorance and the inability to see the elephant in the drawing room. I understand, with the depth of prejudice that exists, why some people would resort to evasion. And I would never force anybody to come out against their will. But I would prefer a world where they would be free to be absolutely open and upfront about their sexuality, and I believe they would too.

Over the last thirty years I have tried to cherish and nurture the feminine traits in myself. So I have no disapproval of people who are not sure and do not definitely fall into either camp. I believe that the state of being bisexual is much, much more common than is presently recognized – and as far as I am concerned it is okay, and far, far better than concealment and disingenuous role-playing. I hope in the next few decades we see the same acknowledgment and acceptance of bisexuality as the last few have shown towards homosexuality.

## EQUAL RIGHTS FOR WOMEN

I know a large number of straight men who love sex with women, but who don't love women. I had better be clear about my use of the word 'love'. I'm not talking about the wonderful one-to-one relationship. I'm talking about a general attitude. And my experience is that the female/male differences complement each other. That being half of a couple is very rewarding, but even more widely, women's attitudes and behaviours complement men's. Our species consists of two different sexes and an important bit around co-operating and forming a completeness and wisdom that neither commands alone. And now I have finally come around to the real point: I think our species' survival is in peril. That is not alarmism. It will certainly last my time. And we are a clever adaptable little species. We are the masters of our fate. We can avert it. But what do we need to do? We, the old men who mostly ran things (not of course as old as me, but still well on), what do we have to do? Lots of things, but one of the most important that I can think of is to admit women as equals to our decision-making processes, to call on their nurturing, cherishing, caring, peacemaking qualities.

I hear people (even formerly militant women) saying, 'But that is old hat.' The battle was joined a couple of hundred years ago, a fringe movement in the French Revolution, and since then there have been Mary Wollstonecraft, Ireland's Anna Wheeler (a close friend of William Thompson of Cork), the suffragists who won the vote, and then in the late twentieth century the Gloria Steinems and Germaine Greers and Marilyn Frenches. Let me shock you. The battle for women's equality has hardly started: women's pay; the percentage of women in top management in the great corporations; the percentage of women in governments and parliaments; and the percentage of heads of universities.

When I was young I swallowed Communism whole; there were quite a lot of good things as well as utopian foolishness. One was the emancipation of women – in Marxist terms, 'the slaves of slaves'. That is what we believed. But it is not what we did. It is one of the proofs of betrayal. Maybe the old Bolsheviks tried. But the next generation, the Stalinist chieftains, were male chauvinist. And a depressingly high proportion remains the same.

Women have gained some freedoms, but at the cost of taking on multiple burdens, which exclude them from time for further study, from creative activities in the arts, from athletics, and from mere time for joyful play. The evolution of the economy and of technology in the developed world has meant that middle-class women can have 'labour-saving' devices beyond the dreams of their grandmothers, but they cannot have servants. Yes, a woman can have it all. A career, kids, a lovely home. But it is often at the cost of exhaustion. She may be earning half the household income. She is bearing the children, and giving them more than half the care, and she is cooking the meals (or arranging for them to be 'sent in'). She has gained freedom at the cost of exhaustion, because not a large proportion of men are cooking, or using the dishwasher or the washing machine. One of my granddaughters, while still in her twenties, has a law degree, is a qualified accountant, and has a husband and two children (my great-grandchildren). But in our society, which claims hypocritically to be 'family-centred', a crèche is horrendously expensive. And the only way to get her children there is if they are driven by herself or her husband.

If we are serious about equality, we must recognize that to be fully developed persons, using all their talents but bearing kids too, women must be provided with support systems that far exceed what men need. They must have shared domestic responsibilities, they must have enough support to have time off to read books, to expand their knowledge, to write policy documents, to participate in local community organizations and the wider world of politics. We need their wisdom, their ways of problem resolution, their caring and cherishing skills. But how can they contribute these things if we require them to be career women, child-bearers and homebuilders, all at the same time and without the support of community and society?

Freud, in a piece of male chauvinist nonsense, said that women experienced penis envy. Perhaps they do. But surely, and I think more significantly, I experience 'baby envy'. Except for a very small and very pleasant contribution at the very beginning, I cannot make a baby (an entity that seems to me a little more important than a penis), though I recognize that you cannot have one without the other (except for IVF).

Our society is rich. Our society, in its imbecilic male chauvinist way, spends really quite incredible amounts on armies and armaments. A fraction of this would build a society where the support structures are such that women could have it all, over time, gently, as they age, and as is appropriate to their age.

It is not just that I love women, which I do. It is, much more importantly, that at this particular moment in our precarious career, humankind needs women's attitudes in peacemaking, cherishing and in non-male-led wisdom. But to think that women's equality has been attained is patent nonsense. For women to deliver what the world so needs, we must re-route our expenditures away from armies, and towards the world's largest minority so that it really can become a majority. Please. Quickly.

# 4. *Genesis v. Gaia*

MAY KEATING

Medical knowledge about the heart was not as developed in the early 1900s as it is now. But when my mother was about ten years old, the local doctor in the country town of Roscrea (where she was at school) diagnosed her as having serious heart valve lesions, which he said were due to rheumatic fever. She knew this threat hung over her for the whole of her lifetime, and she chose to ignore it. And then in March of 1965, she went to bed one night, a night of snowfall, and woke early complaining that her limbs were cold. Because of the snow it was decided to postpone going to the doctor for a few hours. And then she died. Quickly, painlessly and in her own bed. Not a bad death, but at 69 it was much too soon.

Let me make it clear that in what I have to say next, I am not judging or apportioning blame. I did not live in the same place and I had not seen her for some time. When I did get to see her, after she was dead, she was in the midst of a full Catholic burial – shroud embroidered with the cross, a cross in her clasped hands, a mass with unctuous condolences from the priest. I know that the people who decided on this course of action believed it was for the best. Had I been consulted, I would have protested vigorously, but I wasn't. I do not believe that in the few weeks since I had seen her that she gave up the vigorous humanism of all of her adult life for the religion of her childhood. I therefore believe that all of the actions taken after her death were in violation of her wishes.

All this had a very curious effect on me, which I could not control and which I much regret. The person they buried was not the mother I loved so much. Instead of experiencing grief, mourning and purgative resolution of my sense of loss, I was filled with anger, which froze my emotions. I am ashamed to say that it remained so for years. The knot was slow to unravel and dissolve. Of course, it eventually did. I have passed through the grief to now feel extraordinarily proud and extraordinarily lucky to be the child of a woman who from her early twenties was an active and vigorous feminist, socialist and humanist.

## TELEVISION

In the mid sixties I was completely blocked in my scientific career. Trinity College, which I had opted to work for when the old veterinary college was divided (the judgement of Solomon), in this particular instance had behaved in a way that I consider disreputable. While it is not written in the contract of individual scientists who join the staff of universities that they are offered laboratory space, the support of technicians, some equipment funding, and the means to attend a significant number of conferences where they can meet others in the same specialisms, none of these things was available to me. No lab space. No technicians. I was never, ever able to attend a scientific conference, unless I paid for it myself, and this I declined to do. So I got restless. I was absolutely determined to stay in Ireland, and indeed in Dublin. Though I thought hard about going elsewhere, I moved away briefly from my chosen field.

In 1965 Irish television (Raidió Teilifís Éireann, or RTÉ) was new. I had made a few programmes freelance. I got an RTÉ carpenter to make me an outline of a ewe in plywood and to paint her up. He cut the relevant shape out of her flank and put in a cardboard womb, into which I inserted a lamb. Not a real one, of course, but a leggy foam plastic one, with wire inside so that it could be bent in all directions. I bent my lamb into the various positions that occur in lambing. Normal first, then one leg backwards, then two, then the head and neck, and from behind I 'delivered' the lamb each time after correcting the malpositions. Prudes could not object: it was plywood and a doll. But it made sensational TV, and in the new, single-channel state of Ireland, it caused a stir. This was something really new for Ireland.

A little later the controller of programmes at that time, Gunnar Rugheimer, a Swede who had worked in America, threw all his weight behind using TV to loosen up and modernize Irish farming. He was not entirely satisfied with the man who was doing the agricultural stuff on an ad hoc basis. The expanded farming service in the new TV station was to shake up Irish farming and to introduce new knowledge, such as the making of silage and the grassland management techniques that Paddy O'Keeffe had brought back from New Zealand. I was invited to take on the job of Head of Agricultural Broadcasting in Raidió Teilifís Éireann. The bait was that I was also appointed as Head of Adult Education, but various forces were to block my doing much under that latter heading. I had no expectation of a career in front of the camera. The university grudgingly gave me two years' leave of absence, at the end of which I had the choice of which career to follow. We advertised unsuccessfully for a presenter, and Gunnar said, 'Would you have a go yourself?' I did, and one thing led to another. My TV career began; brief in a full-time sense, but a wonderful exciting breakneck gallop.

Before any announcement had been made, Gunnar indicated in discussion with me a change in the conditions of employment from what I had already been offered. I immediately said that no announcement had been made, I would cause no row, but I was going back to university. He grinned at me and said, 'I was just trying you out.' He was an unusual thing, a politically conservative Swede. We did not see eye to eye politically and he was a hard player, but subsequently the best boss I ever worked for. He delivered exactly what he promised, quickly, and he never passed the buck. When the attacks came concerning my appointment, he along with the Director-General Kevin McCourt showed admirable – and for the time, unusual – courage in resisting the witch-hunters.

When my appointment was announced there was consternation, both among some members of the television authority and the leadership of the Department of Agriculture. For the latter I was a loose cannon, and I was a vet, a farmer and a journalist, not an agricultural graduate; God knows *what* I would say. I had no association with the farm advisory services, which the Department then ran (though it was subsequently taken away from them). So they had no control over me, and that worried the hell out of them, and the senior civil servant who liaised with me played a dirty game. Such is the small community nature of Irish society that, through a few intermediaries, a member of the television authority sent me a message that he knew what I was up to and would 'get me'. They need not have worried. I accepted (which I do not now) the prevailing consensus about how to farm, and passed it on to the viewers.

I have always found the Department of Agriculture to be highly politicized, opaque in their policy-making, and shall I say … habitually less than frank. The person in the department that I dealt with was Dr Harry Spain. At some point I had to go to a conference in Europe and I said to my excellent number two, Joe Murray, 'While I am away, make no agreement with Harry Spain.' On the first morning back at work, Harry Spain phoned me. 'While you were away I had a meeting with Joe Murray and we agreed … such and such' (I don't even remember what the issue was). I normally try to be correct and courteous with people working with or for me. On this occasion, I let out a roar that shook the building. Joe was in the next room. 'Come in, please,' I said. When he was with me, holding the phone in front of my mouth so that Spain could hear me, I said, 'Joe, Harry is on the line and he said you agreed such and such.' Joe instantly denied that that was so, and I believed him. 'Harry,' I said into the phone, 'Joe is with me and he flatly denies your version of your meeting, or that there was any agreement.' I didn't get a retraction or apology, just a grunt. But the matter was never raised again. This is how it was, I'm afraid.

## TELEFÍS FEIRME

Rugheimer had given me a wonderful brief. We were to put a farm school, *Telefís Feirme*, onto TV at prime time for two years over 48 episodes. We were to organize viewing groups all over the country. Good old Paddy O'Keeffe (again) carried the group notes for all the participants in each week's *Irish Farmers Journal*, which had a very large circulation. A benefactor provided a hard cover so that participants could cut out the programme notes and put them in the binder, making at the end a complete record of the subject matter of the series. Group leaders (who were in the majority of instances completely inexperienced) got more expanded weekly notes, so that they could be a step ahead of their class. These were posted directly to them 'under plain cover', as they used to say about importing contraceptives in good old McQuaid's golden days. In village halls of one kind or another all over the country, viewing groups were organized to meet once a week and watch a subsidized TV set (very rare in rural private homes in the sixties). The viewing schedule was arranged so that at peak viewing time the group could stay together and watch a very popular entertainment programme after *Telefís Feirme*, and then settle down with their group notes and their group leader to discuss our programme.

Let me outline the full complexity of a very ambitious plan. Firstly, co-operation was required from a whole host of rural groupings. If memory serves me rightly, the Department of Agriculture's farm advisors had been newly freed from the restrictive hierarchy. They were now employed by the Institute of Agriculture, An Foras Talúntais, and they came on board. This was a huge relief to me, and it had been by no means guaranteed. Without them we were sunk. The Irish Farmers' Association helped a lot, as did Macra na Feirme,[1] their youth branch (there were daughters too, plenty of them, but in 1960s Ireland women were a bit invisible). I was really delighted that a Catholic rural grouping called Muintir na Tíre, 'the people of the countryside', established a viewing group.

Modern readers must realize that there were no video recorders. The only ones were the enormous Ampex machines in RTÉ, which required a minder all to themselves, and you got into the queue to get to use them. So there was no tape editing. The programme comprised my talking to the camera with the aid of wonderful animated graphics made by the genius Gerrit Van Gelderen, who was behind the set making things move. On one occasion, he persuaded viewers that a graphic tractor engine was running by blowing, through a drinking straw, puffs of the smoke of his cigarette through a hole in the set where the tractor exhaust was. In addition, there were drop-ins of specially filmed sequences, and the studio floor was littered with actual living or inanimate agricultural objects with which I interacted. Without video editing, this presented horrendous problems. Each film sequence needed an exact lead-in to get the projector going. If we made a mistake, there was no editing it out or tidying it up. We went back to the beginning of the programme and went again. The effort of memory, to come in on time for the total duration, to give the necessary cues on time and in the right sequence, to memorize the whole programme and to be able to get it into the can in one go from start to finish – these were tasks so enormous that had we not been such total newcomers and so ignorant about TV, we would not have undertaken it. Lack of knowledge saved us. In retrospect, I think the doing of it was almost impossible – but we didn't know, so we did it.

I have had a few thumps, a few bits of ill luck in my life, but at other moments I have enjoyed extraordinary luck. Television was new. The people working in it with whom I came into contact, from whom I learnt anything I did learn, and who taught me openheartedly and without condescension, were an absolutely extraordinary and wonderful bunch. Making TV or film is a team activity – unlike writing, which is lonely. If it is not a happy team in TV, I suppose good work is possible, but not easy. I was curious about everything, since I was so new

---

1. Translated: 'Sons of the Farm'.

and ignorant. I now know in retrospect what a wonderful group of cameramen (alas, no women) I got to know and to work with. Stuart Hetherington, Godfrey Graham, Seamus Deasy: wonderful, hard-working and above all very artistic people, as they all proved in areas far removed from agriculture. We even had the inimitable Charlie Roberts as a floor manager.

And finally, and to me most important of all, Sheamus Smith, my beloved 'silver fox' – though his hair was not silver then, and I may have caused some of the grey hairs. Originally from Mayo, Sheamus had gone to America and learned his trade with, I think, the Disney organization. The promise of the new TV station brought him home and originally he did not settle in. But when we started working together, I found all the qualities that I lacked. Firstly, he knew TV and taught me everything I learned. Secondly, he is a brilliant people person. I'm a bit of a cow at a gate, and if I like or dislike people, it shows. Sheamus is much more subtle, and smoothed over some of the 'china shop' situations I created. He is a brilliant organizer of detail: he is infantry, while I am cavalry. Sheamus is very good at the media, of which I knew nothing. He secured us a good press. And he is a very gentle and kindly man. (There is a bit of steel, but mostly out of sight.) Sheamus became a lifelong friend, though ultimately he did a job I disapprove of, namely: he became film censor. I can say wholeheartedly that without him *Telefís Feirme* would not have been the success it was. As I write in France, I hear that he has a book coming out about his life.[2] I have no knowledge of what is in it, so if he talks about me and blasts me, then damn you, silver fox, but I love you just the same. I have forgotten people, of course, and am no doubt committing injustices by omission, but they were a wonderful and – I hope – a happy team, though I know that in the excitement of what we were doing, which we believed in, I drove them to work too hard.

Looking back, it seems impossible. All sorts of people who were not best friends co-operated without rancour. Not one TV set was stolen or vandalized. The group members, many of whom had only experienced an unsympathetic and authoritarian primary education, discovered real talents for study and self-expression.

There was one little further complication, the tensions of which I tried to keep away from my people. When we dreamed up this scheme, Rugheimer said to me bluntly, 'We will give you a prime-time viewing slot.' He continued ominously: 'If you lose the audience, you lose the slot. We will continue to broadcast the programmes

---

2. *Off Screen: A Memoir,* Gill & Macmillan (2007).

at some other non-prime time. But then you will lose the viewing groups. We will complete the series, but the wider scheme will collapse.' So there it was. The new urban TV set owners were just that: urban. Could we hold our audience?

What I think saved us, and we used it quite consciously, was Hamlet's other meaning. He says to Ophelia, 'Did you think I meant country matters?' What he means is: sex. I had originally got myself into this impossible position by, as an invitee, delivering a foam, rubber and wire lamb from a plywood cut-out ewe. But if we did no more than teach the euphemistically called 'facts of life' (are they still, I wonder?) to a generation of Irish kids, it would have been worthwhile.

I never really wake up until I am frightened of failure; Rugheimer had frightened the hell out of me. I remember the dread of opening the audience research man Fred Litman's weekly reports: would the audience hold? Miraculously, it did. We kept the audience over the two years and we kept our slot. We got through and wound it up. We had done the business. Approximately 1000 groups stayed together for forty-eight sessions, over two periods of autumn to spring. At the end we were able to hold exams, properly supervised by the agricultural advisory services, mark the papers and issue [over ten thousand] certificates to those who completed the forty-eight programme course.[3] So there it was. We had done something genuinely new. Our diploma sat between pictures of President Kennedy and Pope John XXIII on the mantelpieces of thousands of Irish homes.

In addition, we made a documentary every week in *On the Land* and a ten-minute news and feedback programme from all over the country. We made so much documentary so fast that I made all the mistakes, but it was a wonderful training for later work. I recall from that time that when a group of staff was having a few drinks we played a game of composing spontaneous limericks. My executive producer Barry Baker, a wise old bird from British TV, came up with one I think is fair and apropos:

> Whenever I find myself meeting
> The man that they call Justin Keating
> I carefully wait,
> Then examine the bait
> To discover which Keating I'm meeting.

Our work began to be recognized. The Swedes got interested. In the middle of things I was invited to present a paper at the Second World Conference on

---

3. The author's estimate was that between 11,000 and 17,000 certificates were issued.

Educational TV in Paris in, I think, 1967, on the subject of the presenter in educational TV, while a Swede presented the matching paper on the director. Television is quite different from the classroom, of which I had some experience, having taught a class of fifty veterinary students for ten years. My effort at encapsulation was 'one half of a conversation between equals'. You had no power to hold your viewer and you must not permit the common classroom offence of patronizing or talking down. The Indians got interested in what we were doing and one of their people came to have a look at us. And when it was over, the recognition came. I was given a Jacobs Award, the major prize in Irish broadcasting at the time, but I think I was more pleased to have my ideas and techniques and work used by Swedish, Indian and Japanese people who were examining the use of TV in teaching. At the Berlin Film Festival, I was given an Ear of Corn Award for work in agricultural film-making.

I started to be given the opportunity to branch out a bit. I made a series about Ireland and the sea, based on the thought that, though an island, we behaved and thought as if we were landlocked. We called it *Surrounded by Water*. And a little later RTÉ started looking towards the looming question of our relations with the EEC, as it then was. The brass decided to make a major series of thirteen programmes on the question *Into Europe?* (it lost the question mark along the way), and to do it on location, a first for the station, with a big lorry fitted out for film and sound and technicians who rotated from Dublin. They asked three of us to submit for the whole series. The late Brian Cleeve was one, John O'Donoghue another, and I was the third. But perhaps they felt that none of us was balanced. They took four of mine, in France, Belgium, Denmark and Sweden. This experience again changed my life. In making a documentary about state/private enterprise as part of the French system of '*planification*',[4] we went to the Languedoc to see what they were doing. Forty years on, we can see that the system was a vast success, but it was not popular then. In Genk, Belgium, we looked at Turkish immigrants in the Ford factory, an issue that has become a huge problem with the rise of fascist xenophobia, and north of Copenhagen I made a documentary called *The Retailing Revolution* for which I chose a young, unknown Swedish firm called (wait for it) IKEA.

---

4. The management of resources according to a plan of economic or political development. The term was coined in France in the 1950s.

## DEPARTURE FROM RTÉ

When I said that a member of the television authority sent me a message on my appointment that he would 'get me', he had, in fact, a point. Up to the suppression of the revolution in Hungary I had considered myself a Communist. I did not have a sudden conversion experience about Hungary, but it started the rot. I began a root-and-branch examination of my belief system. It took me a quarter of a century to work out fully my present idea, but by the 1960s I was no longer a Communist. My disillusionment was slow (late 1950s to the beginning of the 1960s) and painful – like a vocation or a marriage that comes to an end.

I did not denounce my old comrades at the top of my lungs. They had been some of the most passionate, honourable and hard-working people I ever knew, as well as some of the best educated and intellectually exciting (Bernal, Thomson, Dutt, Hobsbawm, etc.). I felt a real sense of loss in breaking with them. And I did not go about with a banner around my neck saying 'I am no longer a Communist'. So this particular TV authority member had a point. If I were still a Communist, and for all he knew I was, then he was right to fear my digging myself in at the centre of the national television channel. After the success of *Telefís Feirme*, my position was even stronger.

And then, like Icarus, we flew a bit too high. In discussion with Gunnar Rugheimer – and like lots of ideas, it is now impossible to say who thought of it first, or if anyone did – we had an idea. 'Why not', we said, 'expand the methods and techniques to put a total third level, or upper secondary level, syllabus on air?' This was before Jennie Lee in Britain with her Open University,[5] long before the great growth of similar efforts worldwide. Extra channels were coming over the horizon, and video recorders, and their importation would loosen up a bit of the existing rather stiff and old-fashioned university system. When the idea of a television university got abroad, people were roused. *Telefís Feirme*, success or no, was ended, and there was no consideration of my wider idea. I had learned at first hand in the Trinity Veterinary School how hard and how slow was any change.

There was a funny way thought up of dealing with me: I was to be promoted into impotence. Rugheimer said he could make me assistant controller of programmes, in tandem with Jack White, but by then I saw that TV was in a process of gradually being emasculated by the need to compete for the mass audience out there, with multiple channels and a zapper in your hand where you

---

5. Founded in 1969.

could change programmes. I believe it was H.L. Mencken who said, apropos newspapers, 'No one in this world … has ever lost money underestimating the intelligence of the great masses of the plain people.'

TV stations fought for advertising revenue. The price of the advertising depended on the number of people who saw it. So the dumbing-down began to be visible on the horizon, though it had not yet come to Ireland. Even to this day, idealists in TV make some splendid and courageous programmes. But they are rare. The idealism of public service broadcasting was beginning to be eroded by the requirements of the marketplace. In my time none of this had happened. But I began to feel uncomfortable about the direction of development; I had an inkling of the way TV was going. When I tried, however ineffectually, to look into the future, I did not see a lifelong career in it for me. I did not want promotion or authority. I wanted to be able to make programmes that I was proud of and that said something important. But I didn't see it happening.

I am profoundly glad I made the decision. My leave of absence from Trinity was coming to an end. To the surprise (and relief) of a lot of people in RTÉ, I went back to teaching veterinary students. But Trinity was no better; the opportunities for research were still hopeless. No trained technicians and no serious research funds were available to me, and the teaching load was too heavy, but I needed to draw breath and get over the exhaustion I felt. Other ideas and hopes were beginning to stir in my mind.

## HORSES

The particular focus of my love was horses.[6] As a tiny child, say three and a bit years, one of my very earliest recollections is sitting on top of Mr Doyle's horse, going up the field above my parents' house in Killakee. The Doyle family would come along behind us on a Sunday morning, going to Mass in a trap pulled by the same horse.

Small farmers then, and big ones too, used to have a wonderful multipurpose beast, not very big – 15 hands or so. Wide and strong and docile, but not too much of any of those virtues. Put to a thoroughbred stallion, they bred the famous 'Irish hunter'. They can plough. They have enough speed and spirit to put a saddle on them and ride to hounds. My uncle, around the time I was

---

6. In 1992 Justin Keating was appointed Adjunct Professor at the University of Limerick, where he helped to develop courses for the BSc Honours in Equine Science and the Certificate in Equine Studies for Horse Carers. He retired in 1997.

born, practised medicine in Waterford from the back of one of them, before the boreens were improved enough to get a car up them. And all over the country they would pull Doyle's and tens of thousands of other traps into town to buy groceries or go to Mass. I grew up surrounded by them, those little horses; and with the unshakeable certainty of feelings that emerge from one's earliest years, I love them still, though they are hard to find now.

Before I was into my teens I went as a pupil to one of the heroines of equestrianism in the mid twentieth century, Iris Kellett, who had a riding school in the centre of Dublin at Mespil Road – land of almost unimaginable value nowadays. She now lives in Co. Kildare, not many miles from my home place, and I wish her health and long life, and send my thanks for all that she taught me.

Then in my sixteenth summer I encountered my first real witch. (I hope her children don't mind the term; for me, it is one of the strongest words of praise I know.) Witches are women. They have an extraordinary contact with the earth. They have green thumbs and can think like a vegetable or fruit tree. So they know what plants need in order to thrive. And they can think like a farm animal. That means that, accepting the awful relentless discipline of the farmer who must live, they can still give the beasts love, and the beasts recognize it and love them back. They love horses, and are mostly very good with them. They use the terrible phrase 'to break a horse' because everyone does (and to my shame, I did it in my late teens for money), but they don't like it. They know that if you really 'break a horse', it will never be any good. They know the same sorts of things about relating to horses that the North American Indians know, and that the aggressive male-dominated society of the 'developed world' is only just beginning to learn.[7]

The real witch (no conical hats or cauldrons or grimalkins) was a woman called Pearl McCarthy, *née* White. She lived just outside Clonmel (in Irish: Cluain Meala, the 'vale of honey') in the Suir Valley, with the lush land of South Tipperary to the north and the high poor land of Waterford beyond the river. Even the name of her house was beautiful: Gort na Flúir, the 'field (or meadow) of flowers'. Pearl managed a stud farm belonging to the Hely-Hutchinsons, which produced the best thoroughbred yearlings for the sales. She was a genius with hens too. As a teacher she did not say much, but just watching her was an education of the best sort. That magic summer in Pearl McCarthy's house had a lot to do with my switching from studying medicine to becoming a vet and subsequently a farmer. Sixty years later, I don't regret the switch.

---

7. An author's note refers to *The Man Who Listens to Horses* by Monty Roberts.

When my second daughter Eilis reached the age where she wanted a pony, the whole horse thing began again. What we got was a tinker's pony and when I saw him getting down on his knees to enlarge a hole in the hedge I knew we were getting near time for something better. Eilis and myself got on the road to find one. I was losing all hope of finding what I wanted, and Eilis thought I was the cruellest father alive, when we walked into the yard of Roger and Geraldine Harvey and there stood a pony like a miniature thoroughbred. The sire was a successful National Hunt stallion called Highland Flight. The dam was a pony called Minuet that had belonged to Iris Kellett. There was only one possible name: Highland Fling. I didn't hurry to express my enthusiasm, but we did the deal there and then and brought him home. Eilis, then aged twelve, set about training him and it was soon clear that in the pony world he was a genius, ending up as a champion of Europe in honourable retirement in Sweden.

Years later that same daughter married a Tipperary man, Paddy Quinlan, a beautiful horseman who has been on national equestrian teams, who is gentle and patient in a way that delights me and is consequently able to get a tune out of a difficult horse. At that time, the subjects I was responsible for in the veterinary faculty were at the beginning of the course – anatomy, embryology and histology – but there was one exception. I taught the final year students how to examine a horse so that they could write the all-important certificate of soundness. The principle is this: any fool can fail a horse. You can always find some little fault if you look hard enough. It takes judgement and confidence to pass a horse. The certificate indicates that the horse is sound for the purpose for which it is intended to be used. A horse that could not stand up to eventing can be perfectly sound for the show ring.

One day, Paddy said that he had found a potential show jumper that he liked, and asked would I come along and have a look. That particular horse had warts on a light coat (potential melanoma) and a really twisted foot. But put him at a fence and you got that whoosh, that push, that makes a potential champion. By the time I was finished pulling long faces and saying, 'Tsk, tsk', the owners were ready to *give* us the horse. I was there, I must emphasize, not in any professional capacity for any fee, but as one of the family. We brought the horse home, Paddy developed him beautifully and he ended up being exported to the United States, where he gained a place on the Olympic team that won a gold medal in the 1986 World Championship in Aachen (ridden by Katie Monaghan).

A well-made, fit thoroughbred really striding out seems to me one of the most beautiful things on earth, on a par with an orchid or a porpoise. If I did not understand how evolution occurs, the argument from design would be much the most convincing in regard to the existence of a supreme being. Equally beautiful and deeply calming is the site of a brood mare in a good pasture with a foal, the little creature all hocks and knees struggling on to its feet and knowing how to look for suck. People who live close to animals and look hard at them have no difficulty in believing that some important behaviour is hard-wired, not learned.

# On The Care of the Earth

One of my last actions before leaving television was to offer the programme planners a series called *The Care of the Earth*. Even though I think it was a good title, I did not know then what I know now. And in the text I begin to express, however ill-informed, the beginnings of an environmentalist's conscience. 'We hold the earth', I wrote, 'in trust for future generations, and we will be judged by the state it is in when we pass it on.' Things are much more serious than I thought. But in my life things seem often to converge.

Why did I, the child of a painter, became obsessed with plants and animals to the extent that I became a vet and a farmer, and also a farm journalist and broadcaster? The basic feeling for the earth, in my case a lifelong love and interest, came, I think, from the wonderful good fortune of growing up on the top of Killakee Mountain and being free to explore the then ruined Massey estate. When we moved down to be close to our primary school, my mother set about making a garden, and my father planted an acre of woodland. My parents were lucky in that their bit of land shared a boundary with a great gardener, Sir Frederick Moore, then in charge of the Botanic Gardens. In passing, he was an example of the very best of the former British public servants who stayed on in the new republic and contributed so much to its upbuilding. Although, in the times when the nationalist distortion of history was the dominant dogma, this was deliberately forgotten. He passed over the fence some interesting plants as presents to my mother to forward her enterprise.

There is a sad story about the thirty acres in Tallaght,[8] but immediately upon selling it I went further south to Ballymore Eustace, guided by the sentimental wish to get as close as possible to the home of my farmer grandfather Joe

---

8. An author's note on this episode was one of those not expanded into a full piece. He had been approached by private property speculators, but chose to sell the land to the county council for housing at a far lower, agricultural-level price. However, it was publicly alleged that he had made a huge profit on the sale. He was able to produce evidence of the figures, which refuted the charges entirely, although erroneous references are still in circulation.

Walsh, who was dead before I was born. The townland is Walshestown, though we pronounce it 'Welsh'. Dairying was the tune. I built a big herd of pedigree Friesians, got a big quota when the quota system came in, and built a state-of-the-art herringbone parlour. I loved my farm, a few miles from where my mother was born and lived until she was eleven years old. I had paddocks and was grazing intensively. But over the years, I came to notice that there was quite a lot of mastitis and also infertility, so that cows went off to the factory long before their natural life was completed. I loved my fields, and the soil. As I studied the soil, I came to feel what an altogether delightful and entrancing thing it is. And then, looking closely, horror. I fertilized heavily, but the soil was deteriorating – getting shallower. However much it got in inputs, it seemed to need more.

What I had learned at university and by membership of the pioneering Grassland Association was a 'high input, high output' model. In my time at Raidió Teilifís Éireann, I had put on a farming school telling the official tale. High inputs, high outputs, plenty of man-made fertilizers and chemicals. The then-current mantra was what I preached: intensify production. More and more. Up and up. Not alone did I preach it, but on my own farm I practised the post-war model, putting my acres where my mouth was. Forty-odd years later, though there are still old people kind enough to compliment me for my TV, I am ashamed of it. I think I was saying the wrong thing. For the sort of person I am, a great many lessons were learned by doing and not by studying. My own actions, when analysed, forced me to change. In the beginning, as Goethe said, was the deed.

On a thumbnail: the only route for farmers to make money was to use very large inputs to get very large outputs. With my then almost non-existent knowledge of economics, I swallowed the agricultural economists' arguments that purported to prove how much more profitable this model was. I say 'purported' because they did so by totally ignoring the real costs to the rural community, and to the state as a whole, of what modern radical economists were calling 'externalities'.

What, you may say, are externalities? These are all the subsidiary effects that cost society money, and must be paid for. They are paid for, of course, by guess who? Not the causers of (for example) the pollution of water quality from overuse of fertilizers. They are paid for by the distant unknowing taxpayer, who ought also to be unwilling, but is never asked. Later I came across the work of Jules Pretty,[9] who applied these ideas to agriculture. The discovery of these results was a major step in

---

9. Prof. Jules Pretty OBE is an author and academic whose work focuses on sustainable agriculture and the relationship between people and the land. He is Chief Editor of the *International Journal of Agricultural Sustainability* and won his OBE for services to sustainable agriculture.

my ideological revolution; it fired me and made complete nonsense of what passed for analyses of farm productivity and farm efficiency by orthodox economists.

## CHEMICAL CONCERNS

Where was the seed of doubt planted? In Copenhagen, I think, where I was doing a small piece of research. That long ago, the professor of pharmacology, looking at the outpouring of drugs and chemicals being pushed at farmers, said to me, 'It is not farming any more; it is chemical warfare.' I did not believe it then, but the phrase 'chemical warfare' stuck, and much later I came to recognize its wisdom.

I was never very interested in the diagnosis or treatment of individual animal diseases. But with an initial input from J.B.S. Haldane at UCL, I became very interested in the mathematical modelling of diseases. It soon became clear to me that the prodigious expenditure by the Irish state on the eradication of tuberculosis in cows was largely wasted. But the next discovery was much more disturbing. I came to believe that the serious new diseases of humans and animals were man-made (AIDS; avian flu; the spongiform encephalitis disease of cows and many other animals, and human beings also). There is a wonderful book about this: *The Coming Plague: Newly Emerging Diseases in a World Out of Balance* by Laurie Garrett. I was then acting as a consultant to one of the largest food companies in the world, and I predicted BSE. It was years before the balloon went up, but when it did their efficient computerized system of records spewed out my warning note, which at the time of writing had made no sense at all to the recipients and so had simply been filed away.

Many years ago I was veterinary consultant to a pharmaceutical company that was strong in animal drugs. I also served on the ethics committee of the company, which ran trials of new human medicines for the pharmaceutical companies. Individually, the people I encountered were perfectly decent and honourable, but collectively I began to have my doubts. These are some of the reasons.

After the war the huge chemical industry, which had grown up to provide all the combatants with everything from high explosives to poison gas and napalm, found itself without the safe custom of the armed services. What to do? Partly, of course, there were the products first mass-produced in the war – antibiotics, sulfa drugs, etc.[10] One response was to turn over to agricultural chemicals. The factories

---

10. Sulfa drugs (or antibacterial sulfonamides) are synthetic antimicrobial drugs derived from a sulphur-containing compound. They were an early 'wonder drug', used to kill bacteria and fungi through metabolic interference.

were there with their skilled workforces. The chemists were there, willing, able and indeed anxious to develop new chemicals that had never been experienced over billions of years by existing life forms. Extremely energy-costly nitrogen fertilizers, killers of fungi, killers of arthropods, killers of weeds – a range of new products the like of which the world had never seen. In my biochemical studies I was further struck by the fact that life on this planet, billions of years in evolution, uses extraordinarily similar methods of encoding the developmental rules for each creature, and in managing energy.

Promising drugs are now synthesized by scattergun techniques, and tested for action in a mechanized large-scale way. The ones selected are the ones that interfere with the biochemistry of living things. Testing for toxicity to humans is based on small, short-lived laboratory animals, usually rats and mice. But mice live for weeks. Humans live for decades. The core of our metabolism is our liver. I hope that my liver, which I have not always treated very well, and which has been going for nearly eight decades, will survive a little longer. The tests to which some of the drugs I have been given as medication during my life were subject before their commercial release tell me very, very little about their long-term toxicity.

It boils down to this: without profit there would be no pharmaceutical investment in new products. Some of the new products are the result of prodigious research efforts, and the companies cannot wait forever for financial return. And as I know from being a member of the government and of the European Parliament, the scale and budget of the pharmaceutical lobby is a wonder to behold. The same applies to the whole of the chemical industry, which manufactures products for agricultural use. Their bottom line is to sell more and make more money.

The difficulty is that in the course of this process doubt and morality get eroded. What is done is often not what is most needed (a vaccine for malaria, for example), but what is most profitable. And the same imperative applies to farmers; the largest volume of product at the lowest price. But that is short-term thinking. When the bank manager is shouting at you, as most bank managers are at most farmers nowadays, you just cannot afford to think long- or even medium-term. As for engineers and scientists, in this environment there is a terrible tendency to believe that just because you can do a thing, you ought to do it. We have a moral crisis, or at least a moral deficit, because the old religions have nothing to say about these issues, and a humanist morality is slow to develop in the climate of an unbridled market economy.

Daily the 'experts' turned up to tell even the most cash-strapped small farmers that the way to proceed was not to go up the market with the maximum development of niche special products with maximum added value. I've told the tale too, I regret to acknowledge. But the economic experts who buttressed these practices did their simplistic calculations on the basis of a single enterprise. Let me give a particularly stark example.

As a student I worked on a farm in Suffolk, and then, as my veterinary studies developed, in Middlesex and Staffordshire. I had passed through Norfolk, which I recall. Many years later, I passed through the same countryside. Production was immense. Peas and other high-tech vegetables were sown, sprayed and harvested over huge acreages by huge machines. So what am I griping about? Just this: there were very, very few people. They had moved to town. Their homes were derelict or bulldozed. The villages were dead, and with them the local post offices, the local schools, the local pubs and small grocers. The whole village community had disappeared. The economic point is that all the infrastructure became worthless. Villages bulldozed. Hedges bulldozed to make huge fields. And as the hedges went, the vast majority of the birds disappeared.

Economically trivial, but none of us is just an economic being. I missed those birds. Most serious was that if you cease to use a village school, you must build a new one somewhere else. Which costs money. If you abandon houses, you must build new accommodation, which costs money. If you use farm chemicals in a way that damages the water quality (and this is very common), you must clean it up before it is fit to drink. That costs money. All these costs are externalities, because the damage is done by individual enterprises (farms or factories), while the cost is borne by the taxpayer (you and me). The principle of 'let the polluter pay' is neatly sidestepped. Farmers are partly to blame, but they are not well organized, not well educated economically, not prone to take a long or wide view and are thus easy victims of sophisticated advertising. The real villains are the industrialists who are faithful to their bottom line and oblivious of or indifferent to the consequences.[11]

## THE 'ROAD TO DAMASCUS' MOMENT

What were the influences that turned me? The seeds of disenchantment, but not yet a full-grown tree, had been planted early. Like many another change of opinion in my life, I cannot remember exactly when the rot started. In some

---

11. Here the author had jotted notes: 'Bhopal' and 'Monsanto'. The 1984 Bhopal disaster in India was the world's worst industrial disaster, in which over 500,000 people were exposed to toxic gases. The Monsanto Company was responsible for Agent Orange, the chemical defoliant used in the Vietnam War that resulted in 400,000 deaths and 500,000 children born with birth defects.

vague way my doubts were developing, but what I did remained unchanged.

Then a number of things came together. Along came one of the great friends of my life, whom I still think of every day, Hans-Henrik Krause; a Danish theatre director and actor and a real intellectual. He introduced me to Brecht and to the Frankfurt School of social theoreticians,[12] but most important of all, he gave me a book that I treasure to this day, *Small is Beautiful* by E.F. Schumacher. If I like a book, I write on it (in pencil, so that it can be erased) and when I reach the last page, realizing that I cannot master an important book with one reading, I go back to page one and start again. I devoured Schumacher. Cogently reasoned, it really rang bells. I did not altogether accept it then, but the seed was sown. Years earlier, in 1962, Rachel Carson's epoch-making *Silent Spring* had come out in America. Again, I had noted it but did not fully take it in. Slow and cautious by nature, I am not subject to falling off my horse with dramatic effect on the road to Damascus or anywhere else.

I needed some clear-cut trigger. Emotionally, the most important moment – the particular event that provoked my crisis – may seem trivial: the nearest I came to a dramatic conversion was with my cows. My state-of-the-art herringbone milking parlour was designed for the cows, but they had not had long enough to evolve for it. I employed a very hard-working, decent and efficient farm manager to look after them, as I was away quite a bit. I was very busy, and in poor health. One day I arrived back from somewhere or other and went to the milking parlour to have a look at the herd. My man, in his up-to-date diligence, and in the pursuit of cleaner milk in a regime of intensive milking, had not just clipped the long hairs off the end of the cows' tails, he had amputated the end of the tails them-selves. It was current practice, so they could not splash cow dung over the shed by flicking their tails, and when you are trying to produce reasonably clean milk from almost two hundred cows going through a parlour, it is perhaps justifiable. But when I saw the truncated tails of my lovely cows (even with those freeze-branded numbers on their backsides, you get fond of them) a thunderbolt struck me. It *was* the done thing. I had not told him not to. I did not reproach him; he was a good man, doing his best. But for me, it was a special moment: I realized that this was not a permissible way to relate to beautiful creatures like cows, or indeed to relate to nature in general, or to farming the earth. This was what in my own mind I now call 'the Genesis way', where Earth and all therein were made for man and for his use: 'Be fruitful, and multiply; fill the earth and subdue it;

---

12. The central members of the Frankfurt School were: Theodor Adorno, Herbert Marcuse, Jürgen Habermas, Max Horkheimer, Leo Lowenthal, Friedrich Pollock and Walter Benjamin.

have dominion over the fish of the sea, over the birds of the air, and over every living thing that moves on the Earth' (*Genesis* 1:28). And I did not believe in the Judeo-Christian dawn myth. No way.

A host of books about global warming applied the clincher. There are too many people on the earth. Trying to outlaw contraceptives seems to me as near to wickedness as it is possible to get. While I am not suggesting for a moment that farming is the sole cause of rising carbon dioxide in the atmosphere, it is an important one. The way that I advised people to farm nearly half a century ago contributed in its own small proportionate way to making the earth uninhabitable. So I am now utterly green. I have put an enormous amount of insulation into the house where I live. I consider every aspect of life from the point of view of reducing my carbon footprint and that of those around me. If you have a huge carbon footprint, you release extra quantities of greenhouse gases into the atmosphere. The halting of the growth in greenhouse gases – and better, its reversal – costs almost incalculable money, and perhaps if we fail it will cost us our survival. We are a clever, busy species. Our doom is not certain. But we had better wake up.

For my own part, in my late seventies and ill as I am, I am just beginning to develop an organic smallholding that is on its way to organic accreditation, near my roots in Co. Kildare. A cynic might observe that that is just play, that I can afford to, and that for the ordinary small farmer, trapped in debts and with inflexible fixed investment in his present farm enterprise, such a choice does not exist. All this is perfectly true. I think that shortsighted policies by Irish agricultural leadership since World War II have produced a situation which cannot continue and from which there is no easy way out.

Huge amounts of public funds have been diverted in all the developed countries to research on more intensive and efficient agricultural production. If anything like comparable amounts of time and effort went into organic research, I believe the levels of production would not be much less than in our present chemical way. The New Zealanders, no mean agricultural researchers, have some evidence of converging costs. And when real costs are worked out – which must include externalities – then I believe that the equation 'organic = expensive' will not stand up.

So over the years I got greener and greener. While I am not exclusively organic, I eat as much organic food and drink as much organic wine as I can conveniently lay my hands on. And one of the bonuses is that I am beginning to form the opinion, though as yet without a firm underpinning of science, that organic wine gives one less of a hangover than normal wine. I'm not sure – but I am continuing my research!

## HEALING NATURE

I will outline my idyll and my dreams for Ireland and the world, of the healing power of contact with nature, and of the role that I would wish human beings to play in the care and protection of the Earth. Readers will know how much I have been influenced by James Lovelock's *Gaia* and his later writings.

I think that urban humans, and urban children in particular, are bereft because they do not experience the sense of awe and beauty and wonder and delight that comes from intimate contact with nature, and I think that this is the reason that so many crackpot beliefs about the supernatural, from the mainline religions to some of the bizarre cults, find currency. Furthermore, I believe that we have windows in the formation of our paradigm during our growing up, not just for the acquisition of language and musical skills and other bits of socialization, but that we have special skills and needs in relation to animals and plants. The beneficial effect of pets on lonely people is well attested; but I think, because of its extraordinary importance, indeed its importance for the survival of older societies, that we have some hardwiring in our brains relating to plants and animals. I have come to believe that we must relate to our earth in a more living and symbiotic way, and that the wellbeing of both the earth and humankind requires that we co-operate with, and cease to try to dominate, the environment.

In my old age I feel that my own profession of veterinarian has neglected its responsibilities to the creatures we care for. We are much more than the 'efficiency engineers of the livestock industry'. Indeed, if this is our approach, we permit the atrocities of the great cattle-feeding lots or huge milking parlours or pig houses or poultry farms to continue and grow, and permit the plagues that will inevitably be engendered to thrive. I think on balance, using evidence and arguments, that we as a species are permitted to kill and eat animals, though I have wrestling matches with myself about this, and I have a great deal of sympathy for the vegetarian argument.

What I think is *not* permissible is to approach nature with the Old Testament teaching that we should increase and multiply and fill the Earth, and that the animals were put there by a benevolent god for our exploitation. I think the whole morality of how we relate to nature needs revision. It is not 'for us'. We are part of a whole balanced long-evolved dynamic ecological system, and we can use our intelligence to have a symbiotic relationship with the rest of it – or we can become parasitic, as I believe we have done. I cannot work out where this parasitism may end.

Ultimately, the green movement, Gaia, the campaign to protect the environment, is the most important issue of all, because if we fail our species has no future.[13] One of the twentieth century's greatest biologists has pointed out that most species lasted about 100,000 years, and we have had our span. Seeing humankind so wilfully profligate in breeding and in consuming the resources of the only earth we have, I am inclined to pessimism. But that is no reason to stop trying. As George Bernard Shaw said, 'At least you can give the hangman a kick on the shins.'

---

13. See the author's article 'The Greening of Humanism: On the need for a greater ecological awareness' in full in Appendix A.

# 5. Entering Irish Politics

I had almost from childhood been intensely interested in politics. The first party I joined was Labour, in the village where I grew up, Rathfarnham. I remember an extraordinary mixture of people: Joe Charlton, who subsequently became a very successful accountant; Joe Good, who had been part of Michael Collins' execution squad; Jack Cooney,[1] who lived high in the Dublin Mountains, above Ticknock; and Joe Collier. I was at sixteen much the youngest, and I learned a lot about the real world from them. But they weren't 'Left' enough for me. After a while I fell in with the Johnny Nolan review group and left Labour. It took more than a decade before I grew through the Communist paradigm and came to hate political violence more and more vehemently. By the time I was back in Trinity after TV, I had come to believe, as they now do, that dramatic superficial gains are no good.

While I was in charge of over one hour of television time each week, I felt it inappropriate to belong to any party. But I rejoined the Labour Party in late 1967 or early 1968. When I did I had no thought, at least at a conscious level, of a life in politics; but I was restless, perhaps even in retrospect a little bored, though I don't know why I should have been. Deep inside, I guess I was looking around for a new challenge. It came in a quite dramatic way.

---

1. Author's handwriting is unclear; this could be 'Conroy'.

One night in 1969 my wife and I were at a party. When we came out and got into the car, I decided from the tone of her voice not to start the engine but to hear what she had to say. Laura has a wonderfully terse, pithy way with words. What she said was, 'I heard you giving out all night. One of two things: you should either shut up or do something.' When she put up this valid ultimatum, I decided to have a go. That was February.

By June I had been elected a deputy and was in the process of realizing that I was making a big mistake. It started in a new housing estate in Palmerstown. As was frequently the case with new building estates, the developer had suddenly discovered other pressing commitments when it came to finishing up properly. I knocked on a door and a lady came out and walked me to the pavement. She showed me an area of compacted mud at the side of the road: a rectangle six foot by four foot, which should have been grass. 'You get the local authority to take that in charge,' she told me, 'and I'll give you my vote.' No party or policy considerations; a simple transaction. Tip O'Neill memorably said that all politics is local but this, I thought, was going too far. How naive I was.

Anyone who contemplates a life in politics should spend a while working at local level to see what it is really like. There is a myth that deputies and senators make policy, and that we live in a democracy. We don't. Real power is elsewhere; certainly not in the hands of the people, which is what the word 'democracy' means. Parliamentary politics, except for a tiny elite few, is a simple transaction. The deal is this: the deputy or senator agrees to function as lobby fodder and as a social welfare officer for the constituency. It is not even necessary to do much, but one should be free with promises ('No problem') and simply be there, pressing the flesh at every funeral and dogfight. In return there is 'respect', better than average food and drink, and more of both at very keen prices – or free. There are also increased sexual opportunities, and for those who seek it there is money, in the form of bribes from lobbyists. A nice life, and harmless. Both sides of the transaction get something. The real powers in society use the charade of parliamentary democracy 'to ensure that the "great beast" [Alexander Hamilton's name for the people] does not stray from its proper confines'.[2] I will come back to all this. In the meantime I must emphasize that this condemnation of our political myths is not because I hate democracy, but because I love it. I just wish we had it.

When I became a deputy, life got hectic. I was farming and Trinity College refused to reduce my teaching load, which was enormous – but they reduced

---

2. Chomsky, *Hegemony or Survival* (Hamish Hamilton, 2003).

my salary by three-quarters on the grounds that I had a deputy's salary. I do not blame the university as a whole for this, but I had succeeded in getting under the skin of Provost McConnell (something I'm quite good at) and I think he would have been happy to be rid of me. Anyone who gets rich as a deputy does it in other ways. At that time, supports and allowances were minimal and there were endless sports cups, football jerseys, rounds of drinks and favours for people who told a sorry tale, so that I was much worse off as a deputy than as a senior lecturer in university; but later, as the Minister for Industry and Commerce, when the issue came up of money from my department to support an industrial officer for the university, I enthusiastically agreed. I think it was the first such in Ireland.

## EUROPEAN REFERENDUM

The big item during my first Dáil was the matter of Europe. In 1972 my own outlook (prejudices) coincided with the policy of the Labour Party, so when I was appointed spokesperson on Europe I campaigned hard all through the first half of that year for a 'No' vote. Jack White, assistant controller of programmes in RTÉ and a friend, said to me one day, 'I can't understand why you are urging a "No" vote in the referendum. You are the most European person I know.' We had worked together on the major RTÉ series *Into Europe?* a few years before, and he was in a position to judge. I took his words as a compliment, but responded that being European in outlook and being for the Economic Community were not the same thing. It was longstanding Labour Party policy to oppose entry. I was trying to change the party policy in regard to coalition. I thought that that was enough.

For my part of the *Into Europe?* series I had studied the whole enterprise fairly carefully, and presented the different aspects of my chosen themes in as objective a way as possible, as a matter of professional honour. Anyone who pretends to total objectivity is either a humbug or a bit foolish. Facts are infinite. The very act of selection, which is based on one's whole paradigm, is an act of bias. But one can – and, I think, should – examine the facts rigorously and face what one finds. Calling for a 'No' vote in the upcoming referendum was something that I could, in good conscience, do. There were two reasons for this. Most important was that I was perfectly certain that the 'Yes' side would win by a large majority – and also that the 'Yes' campaign was not quite truthful; we needed a real debate and to see the European Community as it was.

The principal untruths as I saw (and see) it were two. Firstly, that it was just a trading enterprise (the Common Market), and neither our sovereignty nor our neutrality was at any risk. Anyone who has read the founding fathers, Monnet and Schuman, knew that this was not true. Entering the Common Market was just the first step in a long, long journey. The second untruth was that if we did not take our chance then, in 1972, we would not get the chance again. At any moment between then and now an application to join would have been accepted. I overestimated the dangers and thought it well that the Irish electorate saw the EEC, warts and all.

On the other hand, the Labour campaign had a certain freedom (or at least I had) because I knew we would be heavily defeated. In the circumstances, the party waged a vigorous campaign against joining. Conor Cruise O'Brien took no part. He said that he felt like a dog being washed. In that campaign I had difficulty in fighting off the nationalists, the political wing of the IRA and the remains of the Communists, who I thought were preaching chauvinism with a defence of the nation state that was a hundred years out of date and irrelevant. There was a possibly apocryphal Italian diplomatic telegram, when meetings were going on to decide about the disposal of the defeated Italy's erstwhile African Empire: 'Fight to the bitter end', it said, 'and lose.' Quite so. The man who was later President Paddy Hillery (one of the few people in Fianna Fáil for whom I had some respect) later confided that at one moment the 'Yes' side was worried. They had no need to be. Referendum voting day in May 1972 rolled around and the vote was somewhere near 5 to 1 in favour of joining. I was able to go on TV that night and say, 'That is a totally clear answer. The voters have spoken. I am a democrat and I respect the answer. Henceforth, I will work wholeheartedly to maximize the benefits and to help us avoid the drawbacks I have referred to.'

In truth, in the event there were very few drawbacks. The Department of Foreign Affairs was full of brilliant dedicated staff who carried out a great negotiation and secured for us more than we really deserved, or than the present crop of new entrants will get. They got everything right except for fish (our own fault, in a way. We won't eat the stuff and we don't know how to cook it, so we have no thriving home industry on which to base large-scale exports – a resource wasted). The rest I think was done brilliantly. We did extremely well from membership and from the welcoming and accommodating attitude of the original six (France, Italy, Germany and the Benelux countries). And from the Europe-wide perception of Ireland as a poor disadvantaged place, which was perhaps a decade or so behind the reality. However we resist, the CAP is doomed, but we did very well in the good years. To paraphrase Mandy Rice-Davies, 'I would say that, wouldn't I?'[3]

I have one enduring benefit from that campaign culminating in the May 1972 referendum. By the end (and I drove 30,000 miles by voting day, as well as going by train) I had formed a firm friendship with Garret FitzGerald. By then, most people had dropped out and we found ourselves pitted one against the other at meetings all over the country. Sometimes we travelled together, and he was a joy to debate with because he was very well informed and very fair. Also endlessly good-humoured and courteous. That referendum was one-third of a century ago, and we have remained fast friends ever since. Mabel FitzGerald (northern Presbyterian), Nancy Campbell (Church of England) and my mother were close friends before I was born, and I remember going to a field day in the Bray house of which Garret writes so lovingly, but I don't remember him. My only memory is of a donkey, which kids were allowed to ride.

In January 1973 we joined formally and that same month I was one of the first Irish group (not directly elected but nominated by the Oireachtas), with Conor Cruise O'Brien, to go to the European Parliament. Later in that same year, as a minister, I was a continual attender at the foreign ministers' council meetings, which after the summit meeting were the most powerful of the council meetings. I was there because I was Minister for Foreign Trade, and in part because I was very close to Garret FitzGerald and was happy to stay quietly in the background. In fact, I believe (but this would be subject to verification) that I was the first Irish person to take the chair in the Council of Ministers. Chairmanship circulated in alphabetical order. We came after the French. And late one night, all the French had gone home. The chair passed to Ireland. To Garret, by rights, but he was in the loo or somewhere, so quite unprepared I had to move into the chair. Fortunately, I had excellent civil servants at my elbow. I am now a federalist in my approach to Europe, for reasons that I will talk about later on.

---

3. Mandy Rice-Davies (1944–2014) was a British model/showgirl best known for her association with Christine Keeler and her role in the Profumo Affair, which in 1963 discredited the Conservative government of Prime Minister Harold Macmillan. Her riposte, when it was put to her that Lord Astor denied ever having met her, became so famous that by 1979 it had entered the third edition of the *Oxford Dictionary of Quotations* and is now abbreviated in Internet slang as 'MRDA' ('Mandy Rice-Davies applies'), to indicate scepticism towards a claim due to its very obvious bias.

## THE COALITION GOVERNMENT

Another debate had been going on inside the Labour Party. The power elite in every market economy country has immense resources with which to seduce left-wing working-class leaders. It is a spectacle that many radicals have watched in all the social democratic and socialist parties with the growing desire to puke. As a current example, Tony Blair chose to spend a holiday in the palatial villa of Silvio Berlusconi. Fuelled by this sort of disgust, the Irish Labour Party had long had a policy of non-cooperation with other parties: 'No coalition'. If you have no power, nobody would bother to bribe you and you can remain true to your principles.

I see the point of this. When I was young, and with the experience of two coalitions in which Labour participated to no benefit (1948–51 and 1955–7), I supported that policy. But I saw the force of the contrary argument: that by refusing the risks and seductions of even limited power, one kept the political voices of the working class out of the scale pans of government. It was just that I did not trust the leadership.

When I became a deputy, the party leader was Brendan Corish, who in my judgement (validated by time) was an utterly incorruptible and wonderful man, rightly both loved and trusted by the party membership. In my experience of him, he was living proof that it is possible to spend a life in politics and retain one's honour and decency. I never knew him to behave in a selfish or partisan way. He was the very best kind of socialist politician of a now almost forgotten kind, and he won me completely when he said, under a rather rough challenge from me about his failure to intervene in the Fethard-on-Sea boycott of Protestants in 1957, that he had been wrong and that it was one of the mistakes of his political life which he most regretted. Moral stature of a rare kind.

I thought that the rest of the leadership and potential leadership was fairly dependable to stand by Labour policy (and in this I turned out to be not entirely correct). In some cases it was the hope of enormous wealth, and for others, like Conor Cruise O'Brien, it was a genuine decent evolution of political ideas, which – even when I disagree, as I often do – I can entirely accept. I admired Conor Cruise O'Brien very much then. The news of him was good. He did a magnificent demolition job on the CIA intervention in the matter of European literary studies via the US-supported magazine *Encounter*.[4] And he was involved in the Congo

---

4. Cruise O'Brien wrote an article in the *New Statesman* in 1963 on how the literary magazine *Encounter* (founded by poet Stephen Spender and journalist Irving Kristol in 1953) was accepting funding from the CIA.

after a posting to the United Nations. There he showed magnificent courage, though in the end Belgian imperialism, through its puppet Tshombe and the murder of Premier Patrice Lumumba, succeeded in destroying the independence movement and re-establishing the hegemony of the Union Minière Company and the Belgian State (with a bit of CIA help). All good. The next step in the story was that in the general election of 1969 both of us were elected to the Dáil. From the beginning, our relationship was not easy. And since our differences are material to the cause of Irish politics in our time, they are worth discussing. At a Labour Party conference, Conor spoke in favour of Castro's Cuba. I agreed, though I could hear the votes dripping away and I was close enough to rank and file Labour deputies to know of their dismay. And then, four years later and rather to my surprise, we entered government together. By then we had visited each other's homes and were fairly close friends. Conor is one of a handful of people who were really good company. He was charming and entertaining and endlessly funny. And he has enormous self-belief and is an expressive expounder, so he had a major policy influence on Fine Gael as well as Labour. But we started to diverge early.

The problem, as it existed on the ground, was that Fianna Fáil had been in power alone for the previous dozen years. I had early on decided that there should be no coalition with Fianna Fáil, even if they would have us (no coalition was at that time a core value of theirs, though it became utterly peripheral when they lost an overall majority of Dáil seats). I felt that the obscene moral decay and corruption perceptible since the point at which Charlie Haughey succeeded Jack Lynch as Taoiseach was beginning. I know that in January 1993 Labour, fresh from a very successful general election, entered the government led by Albert Reynolds. Members of the Labour quota of ministers were and are my friends. But if Labour ever enters a government again under a Fianna Fáil Taoiseach, I will leave the Labour Party. An empty threat; an old sick man who has no constituency within the party carries no weight whatsoever.

In 1970 I thought we should change our policy. Such was the love for and trust in Brendan Corish that if he remained opposed, he would carry the party. Any fool can refuse to change their mind and call it 'adherence to principle'. It takes courage and greatness of character to change. I think that Brendan's decision to move to favour coalition was one of enormous importance and released the development of the modern Ireland, which in my view is very much better than the old one. Noël Browne, an extremely charismatic figure, led a walkout not only at the 1970 conference, before the vote enabling the party leader to participate in a coalition government, but again in 1973.[5] But just because they walked out and the vote was carried, it did not mean that opposition ceased. Having played what I believe was a significant part in changing party policy, I made the serious mistake of thinking that I was indispensable.

Things were moving with extraordinary rapidity. Fianna Fáil had been convulsed by the Arms Crisis, the dismissal of senior Fianna Fáil ministers and the Arms Trial. In the election of February 1973 they lost a majority after twelve years in office. Negotiations with Fine Gael were successfully concluded, and a simple two-party Fine Gael/Labour coalition was formed. I ran for the Dáil in a four-seat constituency and won. Brendan Corish, who was Tánaiste designate as well as leader of the Labour Party, had the job of allocating portfolios (with some advice). When we came to form a government, I was part of no grouping. I knew that Conor Cruise O'Brien, Tully and O'Leary were opponents and I was part of no discussions whatsoever about who got what job. I was absolutely at ease with the idea that if I did not like what I got I would decline the black car. I did not drive to Wexford to lobby, and insofar as memory is clear, I awaited the outcome with very little anticipation and not much caring.

Corish afterwards told a story about breaking the news, which I have no reason to doubt. I had made no representations to anyone, ever, about being in government at all. Corish phoned each of the ministers designate in turn to ask them to serve. About his contact with Jimmy Tully I know nothing at all. When he phoned Michael O'Leary (who got the Department of Labour) with the formula 'Are you willing to serve in the government?' O'Leary immediately said 'Yes' and rang off without enquiring as to what department he was being offered. Then he phoned Conor Cruise O'Brien, who was put into Posts and Telegraphs – which did not interest him, though he was immediately christened 'Con the Post', in a genuflection towards Dion Boucicault's *The Colleen Bawn*. He asked what department he was getting, and accepted, although he wanted Foreign Affairs and behaved throughout our years in government as if he were Minister for Northern Ireland. But he did not succeed in doing much harm. When Corish rang me, I am told that I immediately asked, 'As what?' That accords exactly with my recollection of my mood. He told me, 'Industry and Commerce', which was also responsible for natural resources and science. I was completely gobsmacked. Apart from his own job as Tánaiste, I had the most senior department; in terms of the size, power and importance of my department, it far outranked the others.

5. Both conferences referenced took place in Cork; however, in 1970 the issue was coalition, while in 1973 the debate was on natural resources, an account of which is given later.

Seán Lemass had effectively run the country from the office I came to occupy. As it turned out, the department was a poisoned chalice.

So that was the stakeout in the Labour third of government (five ministers of fifteen) in the period 1973–77. We were all, I think, mindful that previous coalitions had collapsed quickly, cementing Fianna Fáil in almost continuous power, and all determined that we would go the distance. Liam Cosgrave as Taoiseach was perfectly correct and fair, but distant. Everything in regard to Labour he did through Brendan Corish. Brendan was as deaf then as I am now.

There is an old joke that ministers are chosen to know nothing about the day-to-day subject matter of their departments, the more easily to be managed (dominated?) by their civil servants. Certainly I am a vet, a farmer, a broadcaster and journalist, in my aspiration a scientist, who knew very little about industry and commerce, although I was able to clearly attach 'science policy' (sensible enough) and 'natural resources' to my portfolio.

There has been comment by some of my colleagues about how correctly the old and blind President Éamon de Valera behaved at the change of government from Fianna Fáil to our coalition. Not with me, he didn't. My father had painted him; they spoke Irish together; they had been members of the Gaelic League from 1912, the year my father came to Dublin; and due to the influence of Seán Moylan, whom my father had also painted and who was a Fianna Fáil Minister in the 1930s, he voted Fianna Fáil for a time. The President took me aside and said, 'I know your father well. How is he?' I replied that he was fine (he was then eighty-four years old). Then he said something admiring of him and after a moment, he added, 'I was surprised to see his son in a group like this.'

My period in government, however, contained actions more worthwhile, interesting and useful than those I have been writing about just now. In particular there were the twin themes under the heading of natural resources: mining on land, and oil and gas on the continental shelf.


## THE OIL SHOCK

There is a story that Napoleon, when asked what quality he most wished his generals to possess, responded, 'Luck'. From the war's end, for a quarter of a century (well, from 1945 to 1973) the world economy had gone on and on and on and up and up and up. And then, when I was a beginner – both as a politician who had never served his time or learned his trade on the lower rungs and as a minister in the major economic department – the world economy walked over the edge of a cliff with the first oil shock, when the price multiplied in a few months, many raw materials disappeared off world markets at any price and a raging inflation set in.

In a sense it was a triumph of crisis management, because the country never realized how desperately serious it was. This was easier to maintain as an attitude because a lot of the government had themselves no grasp of how serious it was. My own Labour people had neither grasp nor interest. Garret understood, of course, but then he understands everything. Neither Taoiseach Cosgrave nor the Minister for Finance rushed to my political aid. Prudently, they stayed as far away from the whole thing as possible. But the Taoiseach never struck me as being overwhelmingly numerate. Richie Ryan (FG) knew, and worked extraordinarily well and quietly. In my estimation of ministerial quality he is one of my goodies, along with Peter Barry. Fianna Fáil made hay and I became known as the Minister for Prices.

About the quality of the oil shock, which has only now after one-third of a century been exceeded in the league table of the severity of depressions, a small open economy like Ireland's suffered some special disadvantages. The five-fold increase in the price of oil caused a worldwide recession, but that applied equally to everyone, both in diminishing world trade and balance of payments problems. But we had another, even more dangerous, problem. Oil is the source of many downstream products essential for the functioning of modern industry. If they became dearer, we would somehow pay, but if they disappeared off markets, due to preferred customers getting first call, then large sections of our industry would grind to a halt. And when that happens, you get a domino effect spreading to other sectors of the economy. If the panic in Ireland were severe enough, hoarding here could cause the very shortages that we most feared.

When I went into the matter of our oil supplies, what I discovered shocked me. National governments – not just of our little country, but bigger ones – had ceded control over energy supplies to the great companies. Provided the oil kept coming, the companies were left totally dominant. They had better global communications than Ireland had. They had a whole series of inputs into their tanker fleets, and when the ships were on the sea or the oil in tank farms, they could play what tunes they liked on supply and demand. The advice I got from my senior people, entirely correct in the circumstances, was to sit quietly and do nothing to annoy them. In the event, they kept us supplied. No panic or hoarding took place.

The possibility arose that there might be oil and gas in serious economic quantities on the Irish continental shelf, and I was faced with the previously neglected matter of setting out the conditions for their exploitation. Britain had a long tradition of making legal claims on the ocean floor anywhere they could: witness the huge area around the Falklands/Malvinas. The big possibilities were in the open ocean west of Ireland, as distinct from the Marathon gas field in the south Irish Sea. We set about making a formal claim on everything that we considered was ours west of Ireland, though there were already British claims out to Rockall. The technology of deep drilling in the open ocean was much less developed then than it is now. At the pre-1973 world oil prices our continental shelf was of no interest, but it became so, and the big oil companies started looking around and doing some seismic measurements in the best areas.

I carried my old distrust of the great oil companies from previous times, but when I had a hard look, that feeling proved completely justified. Some of the books I studied about the future of oil convinced me that it was a rapidly wasting asset, that maximum production would be reached somewhere around the end of the century, and that consequently the price would rise. I knew too that the companies, mostly US and British, had set up puppet regimes in the Near East, aided by British and then US arms, and that they bribed and killed (which was only necessary very occasionally) as their quasi-imperial needs required. Anyone who doubts this might do well to have a look at the recent history of oil in Nigeria. (The Internet exists now, so there is much less justification for the excuse 'I didn't know'.) I knew, too, that apart from bribes and intimidation in some instances, it took very little to persuade a locality to lobby vociferously for free access for the companies. Indeed, sometimes the promise of a few temporary low-skilled jobs and a set of football jerseys (with cup) is enough.

I knew that my time in office was brief. And I was convinced that nobody in either of the coalition parties, and still less in Fianna Fáil, was bloodyminded enough to stand up to the power of big capital. The recent worst of the Irish political elite would not just sell their mother, but thank God that they had a mother to sell. So I formed a very private strategy. I wish I could have trusted my fellow Labour ministers enough to have shared it with them. I didn't. Perhaps impermissibly, I decided to go it alone. On examination of the legal situation, my people told me that I did not need new legislation to draw up the rules for the licensing of the continental shelf. It was possible, in conjunction with some splendid civil servants, for me to draw up the rules for the licensing of blocks on the Irish continental shelf without recourse to government. And this I did. Absolutely deliberately, I made the bluntly and consciously rudely called 'state take' very large. And we had not one, but three ways of scraping off more profit for Ireland if a particular field proved to be as profitable (highly unlikely) as some of the best Saudi wells.[6]

I have a wonderful recollection of a meeting in Holland with senior brass in Royal Dutch Shell. I exuded dislike, distrust and disapproval. In those days I fought an intermittent battle to stop smoking. I had been off for a few months prior to the meeting, but the stress of my private policy broke me down. At the meeting I was smoking again. I cadged cigarettes off Joe Holloway when my own ran out. But ostentatiously, I would not even accept a cigarette from the people across the table.

What saved Irish oil and gas for a while was not my unpleasantries, but the fact that in real terms the price of oil fell back dramatically over succeeding years, and the companies, while they would have been happy to put away rights on our continental shelf for a future date, had much cheaper oil for current needs.

## THE TARA MINES CONTROVERSY

Of the various issues facing me in my new department, the matter of Tara Mines, the extremely rich and valuable zinc ore body that had been discovered near Navan in Co. Meath, was the most pressing. The discovery of the ore body was, I believe, initially due to the soil survey work of my friend (and later on, my predecessor as Chairman of the National Council for Educational Awards) Tom Walsh – or 'Doc', as he was affectionately known. The remarkable figures for the zinc levels were noticed by some Irishmen who had been active in mineral development in Canada: Pat Hughes and a number of others. The ownership situation for Irish ores I inherited was a mess. Ore bodies, if they are big enough, are like a plum pudding. The main part might belong to the state. But dotted through it, the plums were in private hands. That was the situation in Tara. The land on which the largest part of the ore body lay had been purchased for a derisory price from the farmer who owned it.

Partly from a laudable desire to rescue our natural resources from being plundered by private enterprise with effectively no benefit to the population at large, and partly to raise an issue that would destroy the coalition government, the resolutions calling for outright nationalization were pouring in for the conference in Cork in the spring of 1973.

There were a number of things that those who sent them in did not know, and which also seriously restricted my freedom of manoeuvre. Before my time,

---

6. See Appendix B for details of the licensing terms for oil and gas established by the author.

assurances were given that Tara Mines would be granted a lease. Later, when I became a minister, it so happened in this little country that the opposition spokesman on Industry and Commerce, Dessie O'Malley (who succeeded me in 1977), had a brother-in-law who was associated with companies related to Tara. Also, the secretary of the company, John Tully, so happened to be the son of my fellow deputy from Meath and fellow minister in the government, Jimmy Tully. The most serious constraint was this: if the state took possession of the whole ore body, there was legal advice that there was a very serious possibility that we would have to compensate the private owners at the full market value of their asset, a prodigious sum. My advice was that it would be foolish to enter litigation, which we would probably lose. Circumscribed as I was in regard to my freedom of action, there seemed to be a way out in the astute offer of Tom Roche, a vigorous entrepreneur who had built up Roadstone, one of the parts of which is now CRH. Roche offered to develop the part of the ore body where he and his associates owned both the land and the private mineral rights in a joint private/ state company, which would ensure for us a significant state take, even if it was less than I initially wanted.[7]

## MINISTERIAL ENDEAVOURS

The short-term crises passed, and we settled down to the longer-term drag of minimizing and then reversing the general economic downturn. And to that end, I got on the road. I found that in the Industrial Development Authority this state possessed a magnificent agency with a frenetic energy in promoting inward investment. My first encounter with its head, Michael Killeen, I recall with a certain wry amusement. Michael would have received the general information about me, namely that I was a dangerous red who had somehow strayed into being his political boss. And he would have been aware of my previous fulmi-nations against multinational corporations. What would I do? What would my political line be, and to what extent (with of course the utmost courtesy and correctness) would he have to circumvent or ignore it?

Dangerous red I may be, but also, I hope, a realist. I knew how desperately dangerously our economy was balanced. When I came to look at its heart, what-ever my feelings, I knew that I had no choice. Deciding to end the suspense, I said, 'Michael, at present there is only one thing worse than being exploited by

---

7. See Appendix B for details.

the multinationals, and that is being ignored by the multinationals.' He laughed; relieved, I think. We became fast friends, and I came to admire him very much. And I said to him, 'Michael, there are some doors around the world that will not open for your staff but which might open for a minister. Anywhere, anytime, if you think that such a situation exists, call my personal secretary and I'll go.' He did and I did.

He told a story about our being in Texas together a few years later. We were in Houston or Dallas (they merge in my memory) and there was a receiving line. I could muster 5' 5½" at my tallest, and with age and Paget's disease I have since shrunk. The Texans lined up to greet me were all about 6' 6" and wore high-heeled boots. I got a pain in the back of my neck looking up. My little hand disappeared into their great pink hands with golden hairs on the back. When it was over, Michael says that I said to him, 'How long do I have to go on prostituting myself like this?'

To relieve my feelings, while I was waiting with my set script to deliver my speech, I thought of an insult. I will introduce this, I said to myself, and start counting to see how long it takes to dawn on the audience. The insult was not original. It was purloined from the provost of Trinity College, who said, when Oscar Wilde moved to Oxford, that by doing so he had raised the intellectual level of both places. The Texans had been talking about the role of Irish immigrants in the development of their state. I thought I would say that when poverty and famine drove them from their troubled native land, and when they faced an angry ocean in frail barques to find a new life in freedom, that's when they made their way to Texas to participate in the upbuilding of that great state, and they thereby (wait for it) raised the intellectual level of both places. Of course, I didn't.

Those necessary travels, Japan and Australia and Canada too, gave rise to a bitter joke in Ireland, which cost me votes. Question: 'What is the difference between God and Justin Keating?' (There are unkind souls who suggest that that is a question that I might ask myself more often.) Answer: 'God is everywhere. Justin Keating is everywhere else.' But the years passed. The overseas investments flowed in, hastened by an extraordinarily favourable tax regime. It was worth it for a while, because foreign companies brought us expertise, a world vision and self-confidence. And best of all, employment – but they contributed very little in tax.

We used to have a standard Congested District Board cottage at a beautiful place at the end of the Ard peninsula near Carna in Connemara. Down the years I have always driven Peugeots – 'pour l'homme serieux'. Vets were fond of them because they were tough. Even when in government I drove myself as much as possible, and I insisted that I did not want the big Merc, the black car beloved by ministers in many countries. The Peugeot 504 was quite big enough for me, though probably my two Garda drivers hated their loss of status. So when we went to Connemara as a family, we were either in my own Peugeot or the state one. I like to go into a pub and have a Guinness by myself and look and listen. Or at least, I did before I became deaf. One evening I was having my half-pint (not a man's drink in much of Ireland; it should be a pint) in a pub in Carna. There was a man there, as I sat and sipped and listened, who clearly recognized me and was extremely angry with me. He was much bigger than me, and 'under the influence'. As a small opinionated man giving out unpopular opinions in public places, I have often been in danger of a 'belt in the gob' and, indeed, once or twice received one. So I have developed techniques for avoiding it. One is to get very close to your potential assailant. It is hard to hit a man who is trustingly close. A second is to stay serene and friendly. I kept eye contact and said, in the friendliest voice I could muster, 'It looks as if you are angry with me. I think I'm a reasonable man, so tell me what it is.' By this time I was too close in for him to hit me. 'You come here a lot,' he said. 'I do,' I replied, 'because I like it here. I could go lots of places but I choose to come here.' By this time relations were improving. After having a little think, with great vehemence but receding anger he said, 'All the years you are coming here, why do you never bring the black car?' (the minister's Mercedes with a Garda driver). I am still pondering what he said. Connemara is poor and since the days of the Congested Districts Board and later on Údarás na Gaeltachta, it has developed a culture of dependency. The thought was, 'If you have the run of a state car, why don't you flaunt it?' My effort at using the state's facilities in a modest way won me no brownie points at all.

## ARDMORE STUDIOS

My parents had been interested in film. They were members of the Irish Film Society, which had viewings on Saturday afternoons in the nearby Classic cinema in Terenure. One of the pioneers of film appreciation in Ireland, Edward Toner,[8] lived in Rathfarnham and was a family friend. Nothing for me in a cinema was ever equal to seeing a Bergman film at that time. So I was interested. And in TV, I saw an opportunity for a profitable activity.

---

8. The Irish Film Society (IFS) or Cumann na Scannán was formed in 1936 by Edward Toner with Liam O'Laoghaire.

It is a continuous source of delight that Ireland so loves and continues to produce great writers. For me, Joyce ranks with Cervantes and Tolstoy. I love some of Yeats' work while despising the man. Seán O'Casey, for an old socialist like me, is a continuous source of joy and optimism. Wilde and Shaw are not nothing. I love Synge, etc. and in recent times we have another splendid generation headed by Seamus Heaney. I have a special soft spot for a harsher, less charming, pawkier writer from the north-west, John Montague. And I think Friel is a great playwright. It keeps coming. Why this litany? It is because I thought that both for dramatizations for TV, and other background to a vibrant film industry, this wealth of writers was a bonus and that we had a flying start.

The family who owned the Theatre Royal, the Ellimans, built a film studio with excellent facilities in Bray, and some films were made there. It was always a struggle and by the early seventies it was up for sale, with the danger that the site would be used for housing. Early in my time as minister, I was able to rescue this film studio, Ardmore Studios. The site was valuable as building land, but as a new minister I called in all my favours in government to persuade the state to save a useful facility. There were very fine stages, a workshop where the best traditions of Dublin plasterwork were maintained, and a good store of scenery. It would have been a shame to let it all go. At the same time, a man whom I greatly admire was living up the road in Wicklow, at Annamoe. John Boorman was already a very successful and respected director of major feature films.[9] I allow myself the thought that if I had not made the initial purchase of Ardmore, this site might now be a suburban building estate, and some bits at least of the Irish film industry might never have come into existence. But a great regret is the fact that as the recession progressed I was unable to fund developments on the scale that I had hoped.


## UNA TROY AND SHE DIDN'T SAY NO!

There was an earlier family involvement in the nascent film industry; not by me, but by an aunt. The story is worth telling because it casts a shocking light on the activities of the Irish state on the extremely important issue of child sexual abuse in state institutions.

The story begins with a lovely man, District Justice Troy, who was based in Fermoy, Co. Cork. He had three daughters, and the only one to marry, Úna, had

---

9. In 1975 Justin Keating renamed Ardmore Studios as the National Film Studios of Ireland and appointed Boorman as chairman. Sheamus Smith became managing director.

the mixed fortune of marrying my mother's brother, Dr J.C. Walsh. He was very clever, a charmer, but a drinker who got into fistfights, though I never heard any suggestion that he struck his wife. Úna wrote a couple of novels under the name of Elizabeth Connor, *Mount Prospect* and *Dead Star's Light*; the first was turned into a play and was put on in the Abbey Theatre. Post-war, she turned to a different kind of writing; lighter, often amusing and, oddly, a great success in German lending libraries, from which a considerable income began and continued even after her death.

The most significant of her novels was called *We Are Seven*. It arose from a true incident in which her father was involved as a district justice. A case came before him concerning a handsome, unmarried woman in a small village who had seven children by seven different local men. It was reputed that some of the fathers had been persons of eminence in the local community. Local 'holy Willies' and worried wives made common cause with the clergy, and the state was called in. She was brought to court as an unfit person for the rearing of children. Had the authorities won the case, the children would have been taken into care – 'care' being the obscene, brutal system of reformatories run by the Catholic authorities. This provided a further source of pressure, because the Church was paid a capitation fee by the state for each child in its 'care'. They made a profit on this, so they beat the bushes all over the country trying to persuade district justices to give them kids. When the case came before District Justice Troy, he went to visit the house and have a look at the seven kids. And his judgement was that a very competent and loving mother was thoroughly caring for the children in a happy family environment, and that on no account would he break it up.

In 1958 *We Are Seven* was made into a film by the name of *She Didn't Say No!*, well written and directed to a very high professional standard by Cyril Frankel. There was a distinguished cast featuring many of the major actors in the Irish theatre at the time, and the whole enterprise was to be a significant development in the nascent Irish film industry. It views well now. But then it had very limited success. One of the problems is that the Irish state set its face against it.[10]

The historian Ann Butler uncovered an extraordinary (well, it is to me; perhaps it was normal) letter in the state papers; one that, as an exemplar of the spirit of the times, is worth quoting: 'As it was apparent on the basis of [newspaper] reports that [the film] would be the occasion of harmful publicity to Ireland [the

---

10. The Irish Film Institute notes that the film was scheduled for production in Ireland until permission was refused, upon which filming moved to Cornwall. Its first screening in Ireland did not take place until 2001, having been banned 'for moral reasons'.

Irish Minister in Brussels] was instructed to draw that fact to the attention of the authorities.' Two things are significant. One is that it was unhelpful to the Irish film industry. Much more important is that it expressed a not very vague hostility to anything which would raise questions about children in institutions under Catholic care.[11] The author from the Department of External Affairs is one Dr Conor Cruise O'Brien. At this time Conor was fighting a brave and very effective fight against CIA fronts in literary criticism, and against the magazine Encounter, and I cannot conceive that he believed the stuff in this letter. But in his diplomatic job, he was a hired gun untroubled by inconsistency.

## KILKENNY DESIGN

Very soon after taking up office, I received a request from the man who ran the Kilkenny Design Workshop to come and talk to me. As someone who had been ravished in my Scandinavian times by the beauty and quality (and indeed profitability) of the Danish design concept, I remember vividly my first visit to the permanent exhibition of Danish design in Copenhagen. For me it was an absolutely mind-altering experience, so I naturally felt warmly towards any organization that was trying to do the same thing in Ireland, even on a limited and underfunded scale. So I said, 'Yes, please come in.'

The man I met was a character – and I mean that in a positive sense – called Bill Walsh. The premises he worked from was itself inspirational. It was the mews of the old Kilkenny Castle,[12] and there a haven was provided for some remarkable craft workers from different countries, as well as homegrown ones. Bill told me the same old story. The centre had not been properly provided with adequate, regular and dependable funding. I told some member of my senior staff to beat the bushes to see if we had any underspending on my estimates, and to find out if we could give a significant sum then. I think we found £20,000 – chicken feed now, but not totally insignificant then. I was able, feeling rather smug, to tell

---

11. The film was described as an 'enjoyable piece of whimsy', but the story of the real-life woman visited by District Justice Troy had a sad and sordid end. Moll McCarthy was murdered with a shotgun in 1940, and the man who discovered and reported her body was hanged the following year in Mountjoy Prison for the crime. In 2014, Kieran Fagan's book *The Framing of Harry Gleeson* identified the fathers of Moll's children, causing uproar locally, and Harry Gleeson received the first posthumous pardon in the history of the Irish state.

12. Owned by the Butler family, built on the site of a motte and bailey constructed by Richard de Clare (Strongbow) in 1172 and the site of the Irish Confederate government in the 1640s.

Bill Walsh while he was still with me. But not a word of thanks; he immediately asked for more. I decided he was a good man and that I would be as helpful as I could. A state company was set up, the Kilkenny Design Workshop, and Bill was appointed manager. But budgets were still desperately tight, and every penny was fought over by different ministers. However, I was able to give positive answers to two important issues that arose in regard to the development of the centre. Could they refurbish a dower house of the castle, which adjoins the mews? The answer was yes. This was beautifully done and it serves today as the Butler House, which offers really pleasing accommodation in the city centre. And then: could they open a retail store in Dublin as a sister to their very successful Kilkenny shop? The answer again was yes, and the shop is a testimonial to this day, affirming that taste and design are improving and that Irish craftsmanship is alive and flourishing.

The new state had paid enormous attention and devoted serious money to promoting verbal and musical culture, often in pursuit of invented nationalist myths, but until people like Bill Walsh and my friend the very able Jim King, who succeeded him, and other passionate craft workers and administrators (Frank Sutton, for example), almost no attention had been paid to what the Scandinavians called 'material culture'. So I am very proud also of the Kilkenny Design Workshop, and of the little bit of help that I was able to give it at a crucial time. There is, however, a sad little footnote. A few years ago the centre celebrated an important anniversary and produced extensive and rather selfconsciously over-designed printed material. But neither Jim King nor I rated a mention.

## THE CIVIL SERVICE

There were other major themes – of course – in my time in government, but the vast majority of my strength and effort went into the economy. In Richie Ryan, I found a sympathetic colleague and, I thought, a good and courageous minister in desperate times. But I have a recollection of a meeting with his senior people and my senior people, which he and I attended. My line was that, in recession, the right thing to do was to borrow and spend. Stimulate the economy, prime the pump. Most of the senior finance people were more cautious. Their cast of mind was to estimate the tax revenues and then apportion them prudently. At some point in the course of the meeting, I snorted, 'You would think that Keynes had never lived.' When we were leaving I was drawn aside by Michael Murphy, an extraordinarily nice and decent and very senior person in finance. He said to me,

'Minister, I would not want you to think that we are anti-Keynes. Most of my staff has not read him.' Ironically, now that Keynes is the flavour of the year, it is a pity when we come to serve enormous debt that more of the old financial caution has not prevailed, but has been so completely swept away. In terms of decorum and courtesy, such meetings are not easy. The minister can say what he likes. The civil servant must be correct and polite ('Isn't that so?' 'Yes, Minister'). Of course, civil servants have the last say; ministers come and go fairly rapidly.

I am not going to discuss the Irish civil servants at length. Until fairly recently people were too poor for bribery to be a serious problem in public life. Their chief fault was their subservience to clerical control. So the departments I admire least are Justice and Education. In regard to my own department, which I know or knew best, I respect the decency of the people I met and their dedication to public service. But they are not good at management of the once-powerful Irish state sector. The generalization is that public servants do not understand business. In Ireland it is generally true, but it need not be so. France has a long tradition (back to the monarchy) of state participation in manufacturing and banking. The most successful motor company of the last half-century is Renault, a state company. The most successful aircraft company in the last quarter-century is Airbus Industrie, based in Toulouse. There are enormous advantages in this state overseeing important sectors of industry to minimize the social damage of untrammelled private enterprise (what George W. Bush calls 'democracy'). But in Ireland the civil service has not the skill to intervene profitably, nor the power to do so. No power goes unused.

The best advice, which I tried to give though it was often ignored, was to give the managers precise and clear instructions of their guidelines and their power, and then to stand aside and let the managers manage. Protect their liberty and power to act and don't starve them of capital. But otherwise leave them alone: 'Don't just do something, sit there.'

## BUDGETS, DEPARTMENTS AND STRATEGIC PLANNING

In my time, the process of making a budget was chaotic. Each department briefed its minister to go along to the budget meeting of government with a shopping list. You start with last year's budget and if you have new items, or whole new subheads, you argue for them, and then depending on the state of the economy and the state of the taxation revenues, you argue about the distribution of surplus (if there is any). I am sure it is more sophisticated now, and of course overtly and covertly the Department of Finance exercised enormous influence. But what worried me was that it was all so short-term. I can give an example. I was travelling the world trying to promote inward investment, about the tax regime. But inevitably, they asked about the communications system, and there is no point in such situations in telling a lie. Communications were awful. Garret with his good old economist's head knew this, and also how important it was. But we could not interest the Minister for Posts and Telegraphs.

Finally, in despair, though we were both enormously busy, we asked Conor would he mind if we met the top civil servants in his department to see what could be done, short term and long term. 'Delighted,' was the reply we got. 'Be my guest.' When we met, the first thing we did, obviously, was to ask about the existing situation. What were the investment plans, we asked? There were very few. Which sections of the service were the loss makers and which profitable? Essential, if a development budget was to be drawn. The extent to which the answer was 'we don't know' terrified both of us. I don't blame either the civil servants or the technical staff of Posts and Telegraphs; their riding orders were unclear and managers were not free to manage. But we completely lacked what I would call serious forward planning. Transport is another obvious example. Thus, the outcome of the budget was a bit hit and miss. It depended on the negotiating power and talent for forming alliances of individual ministers.

Both Garret and I were professionally involved in education at third level, and we recognized its importance at all levels. We were exercised that education had not done well in our first two budgets. So when we came round to our third budget, we decided we would wade in on the side of the Minister for Education. As it happened, the person in question was Dick Burke and he sat beside me. He had a brief on one sheet of paper, with a column of figures down the right margin and a tot at the bottom right corner. That was what he had to get. Gradually he realized that he had two unexpected allies in Garret and me, and that he might go back to his department with more than the basic total. He drew a ring around the essential total, and shoving it over in front of me, he asked in a whisper, 'What is 10 per cent of that?'

Readers may say that this story is a malicious invention of mine. My defence is that it would never ever have dawned on me that an adult, who I believe had been a teacher himself, could ever ask such a question. I tell this story to emphasize that in communication, education, transport and many other areas where government has a significant role to play, strategic planning on a much larger scale than existed in my time is essential.

# On Ireland's Future

'I have a dream.' How many years since Martin Luther King, Jr made that speech?[13] Sometimes, from the mouth of a great orator, words do make a difference. In the pale shadow of that great man, and in homage, may I speak his words – about the island of Ireland. Maybe if I knew the Celtic poets better, I could find a phrase. But we had no Shakespeare, so I must steal from him: 'This precious stone set in the silver sea.'[14] To me, Ireland is a precious stone, in part because that is where I drew breath and built my paradigm.

My dream is of a peaceful, reconciled island; brilliantly educated and extremely sensitive about issues of ecology – a green island with every spare square metre growing trees or other energy crops, on land and sea, and a developed energy policy that consumes, for all practical purposes, no hydrocarbons. An island where people can access all the information in the world on their laptops and our carbon footprint is tiny.

My dream – where did it get lost? As I write, the Irish economy is in desperate difficulty.[15] The failure to make provision during the Celtic Tiger years for a more difficult future almost surpasses belief in its shortsightedness. As somebody has remarked, we are Iceland with one different letter. Were it not for participating in the Eurozone, we would be in quite special difficulties. (Of course, it was in part the euro that caused the bubble, because we were inflating quite rapidly, but we still had money at low euro rates. Borrowing was almost free – so why not take a flyer?) But it is wider than that. Having had a turbulent history with a great deal of pain and exploitation, we have played 'the poor mouth' for so long that we have no idea of just how lucky we are.

Lots of places have too many people. We don't. Lots and lots of places are too hot and too dry. If global warming is coming, then we have a wonderful climate.

---

13. The famous 'I have a dream' speech was delivered at the Lincoln Memorial, Washington D.C. in 1963.

14. *Richard II,* William Shakespeare

15. The writing of this passage can be dated to October 2008.

All over the developed world, water is becoming a problem. Not for us; we have plenty. If the future, as I believe, depends on alternative energy, as we still burn our stored hydrocarbons in a most profligate way, we can build alternative energy on the tides and waves, which surround us, the winds, which blow over us, the biomass – in water and on land – of our wonderful growing environment, where conifers grow in mean annual increments that handsomely exceed those in major European timber-producing countries. We have wonderful harbours. We have wonderful fish and shellfish resources; we have wonderful land, which by world standards produces huge crops without vast inputs of fertilizer and water. None of that was very important in the past, but will be immensely important in the future.

About the level of organization one step below that of the state (I refer to local government) I have always been ignorant and have nothing worth saying to pass on. Except that as the power of the governments of nation states, situated and exercised within their boundaries, fades, weakens and becomes more and more irrelevant, so the importance of local government becomes greater and greater. The only way for the centre of supranational or 'quasi-supranational' governments to stay relevant and keep in touch with the populace is to devolve more and more power to the regions and smaller units. And in Ireland it seems to me that this calls for the most fundamental root-and-branch rethink, because in extremely important areas, such as transport, health, energy policy (at local level) and education, our performance under present systems is obviously seriously defective.

From the point of view of regional development, Ireland has extraordinary advantages. Geographically, we are a saucer. If Galway and Derry were developed to balance the larger cities around the periphery, we would have a planners' dream. And there is need and room for a central city – Athlone or Mullingar? Let others decide. But then we have the basis in wealth and population for an extremely efficient transportation system based on the railways. Because the winter temperature is so high, if our architects would wake up we could have houses based on passive solar heat, with proper insulation, solar panels and perhaps heat pumps. Great transport, practical energy-balanced comfortable houses, very very pure air by European standards.

So my dream is this. We cannot change the geography. Why should we? It is almost uniquely advantageous. We should, in the countryside, go right up the market to organic products developed for the special niche markets of the enormous industrial populations of the great nations of the European Union. We should abolish the town–country division by having information technology up every mountain of a quality at the very cutting edge. We should pay immense attention to every piece of our environment, making towns and villages both more user-friendly and more beautiful. We should have one of the best education systems in the world (and remember that while currently we get better slowly, much of the rest of the world is getting better very fast). When one looks at Ireland under a whole series of headings, we seem just incredibly lucky. But we have wasted a couple of decades on a stupid greedy Celtic Tiger, which made money but did not use it on the infrastructure or the disadvantaged. We have a pathetic health service, poor transport (because we bowed down before the motor-car lobby), mediocre education and a completely shortsighted and poorly educated rural policy headed by a largely non-functional Department of Agriculture.

There is a hope of rescue to stave off decades of hard times. It is oil and gas on the continental shelf. The Seven Sisters[16] and ourselves, I'm glad to say, did no business whatsoever. But I have no idea what deals, overt and covert, have been done since then. And this is important. If it has been given away at a very small return for our state, then that is a crime which will echo down the years.

States that possess oil and gas now are in a much better position than they were a third of a century ago. Peak oil (the moment when production turns down) has been passed. The wonderful success of Statoil in Norway has shown small nation states that they can avoid being ripped off if they have courage as well as clarity. There are new bidders in the market. China is there, with a great oil hunger. And the countries of what was the less developed world are rapidly coming on the scene. I hope that the existing contracts that have been signed have been drafted in a sufficiently prudent way to allow us to open up a totally fresh auction.

Because I've found a late taste for numbers – and because, as someone who became passionately green after my time in government, I follow world energy, production techniques, new alternative green sources, projections of need, promises of the stabilization of carbon emissions, etc. carefully – I am of the opinion that, while the world will respond, it will do so late and slowly.

As recently as the last part of the presidency of George W. Bush, there were heavily funded lobby campaigns in the United States aimed at convincing the population that there was no global warming crisis. The White House of Bush,

---

16. A term coined in the 1950s by Enrico Mattei, then head of the Italian state oil company Eni, to describe the seven oil companies which formed the 'Consortium for Iran' cartel and dominated the global petroleum industry from the mid 1940s to the 1970s. Two have since merged under the name of Chevron. The others are BP, Gulf Oil, Royal Dutch Shell, Esso/Exxon and Socony.

from an old Texas oil dynasty with links to Saudi Arabia amounting to a very serious conflict of interest, was listening to these siren voices. Fortunately for us all, Obama knows better. But the energy sellers will put up ferocious resistance. And though we possess the technology to make oil archaic, which we could do for the price of a few nuclear submarines, we won't. There will still be enormous demand for energy. We are lucky to have it. I hope we are wise in using it to repair the economy for our past mistakes.

As I read back over these paragraphs, I am convinced that it is not an impossible utopia, but something that we can do relatively easily and relatively quickly. The fundamentals are so good. So, what more do we want? The wit to plan long; the wit to heal old wounds, to forget and let go; the wit to build a really superb educational system. None of this is beyond us now.

# 6. Northern Ireland and Other Politics

There were other continuing themes while we were in office, of course. Northern Ireland was one. And there I took a personal line, which was not important because I had no input into policy, and I did not leak my doubts and disagreements.

There was a widespread feeling among politicians at the time that this crisis could escalate to the point that it would threaten the security of the state and precipitate a physical confrontation between North and South. I never believed this, though there were some developments that worried me very much. One was that there was appointed a semi-official Security Committee that must have reported to someone, presumably the Taoiseach. But the government at large knew nothing of their deliberations, and they made no report to us. Its members, I think, were Pat Cooney (Fine Gael, Justice); Paddy Donegan (Fine Gael, Defence); James Tully (Labour, Local Government); and Conor Cruise O'Brien (Labour, Posts and Telegraphs). What was very serious and potentially destructive was that Garret FitzGerald (Fine Gael, Foreign Affairs) was not a member.[1] Nonetheless, from conversation, it was possible to form an idea of what their basic approach was. The government was split: on one hand the common sense and realistic skills of Foreign Affairs; on the other hand the people (not, alas,

---

1. Nor was FitzGerald a member of the Cabinet Committee (which dealt with Northern Ireland) during this period.

without influence) who were convinced that the sky was falling or, put another way, that civil war was a grave threat to the whole island.

The reference back was to the men of the War of Independence, and the subsequent Civil War. The difference in my mind was that most of the combatants were men of no (or very little) property. The Ireland of 1970, on the way (with the interruption of the oil shock in 1973) to becoming the Celtic Tiger, was a very different nationalist place from the Ireland of the late 1910s and early 1920s, when the men of no property were in the ascendant. But since then, in the South, a new Catholic bourgeoisie had developed, much less inclined to risk their assets in civil conflagration. The menfolk represented what a Danish friend of mine called 'Cliffs of Mohair'. If it were a case of my daughter (Kathleen Ní Houlihan[2]) or my ducats, the ducats would surely win. I never believed that civil war was a serious threat, whatever a minister from Donegal (Neil Blaney) or an old unreconstructed nationalist (Kevin Boland) might say or endeavour to do. The thought of an Irish military force entering Northern Ireland in conflict with the British army protecting a portion of the United Kingdom was simply preposterous. The other thing I think it is fair to say is that the British army behaved less stupidly and brutally than they had in the recent past in Malaya (as it then was) and in Kenya. However crassly, and Bloody Sunday notwithstanding, they behaved better than they had elsewhere.

Essentially, the Northern Irish population supported four political groupings, two unionist and two nationalist (the SDLP, successors to the old Nationalist Party, and Sinn Féin). This was not the traditional position, where for decades orange supported the Unionist Party and green the Nationalist Party. In times of intense conflict, regression is the norm. Around Ian Paisley a large part, ultimately the majority, of Northern unionists regressed to support him, while an ultimate majority of nationalists regressed into the simplistic physical force tradition of Sinn Féin/the IRA, from which, after decades of needless slaughter, misery and economic destruction, they have finally rescued themselves.

I was always absolutely certain, because the population was then divided, two-thirds Protestant and one-third Catholic, and because the separation of the two groups in geographical terms (ethnic cleansing) was impossible, that in the end there was no alternative but peace. Distrustful, bitter, more separate in feeling than before the violence started, but a kind of minimalist peace was inevitable.

---

2. A symbolic figure in literature and art; a personification of Ireland as an impoverished, dispossessed old woman calling for aid. Most often encountered as an emblem of nationalist discourse, notably in the play *Cathleen Ní Houlihan* (1902) by Yeats and Lady Gregory.

Very few people were nasty enough to point it out, but the whole of the IRA violence campaign produced less than nothing. For a government in Dublin, the question was who to support and how to do it effectively. To me, the core of policy for us should have been to aid the non-IRA section of Catholic nationalist opinion in holding off the men of violence.

My principal disagreement with Dr Cruise O'Brien antedated our presence in government. I loathe terrorism only a little more than I loathe nationalism. But I was realistic enough to believe that execrating the SDLP was exactly what the IRA wanted. Or, to try and turn the other way, the only policy that would keep Northern Catholic nationalists out of the arms of the terrorists was to aid constitutional nationalists. It did not in the least matter that my personal opinion was hostile to all nationalism.

There was a real and important choice, and Conor and I were on opposite sides. In August of 1969 Conor, [Frank] Cluskey, [Michael] O'Leary and I drove north. After a slightly fraught visit to the Cardinal Archbishop[3] in Armagh, we went on to Belfast and called on Gerry Fitt. It is impossible to overstate the wonderful courage and persistence that he and people like Paddy Devlin showed at this terrible time in Belfast. We were in Gerry's house one day when the phone rang and an anonymous caller spoke to Gerry's wife: 'We saw that you were at the clinic this morning and we hear that your asthma is worse' – you probably know that stress and worry are an important influence on those attacks – 'but you can stop worrying, Mrs Fitt, you will soon be a widow.' I saw at first hand the wonderful courage of those nationalists who stood against all terrorism, be it orange or green. But Gerry was a city man, a seaman in the British merchant marine for part of his life. I marvelled at his courage and resolution in the face of the most shameful Loyalist intimidation. But not for a moment did I think that he was the man who could lead a sufficiently powerful section of Catholic nationalist opinion to prevent the complete victory of the IRA among Catholics. I felt that he simply did not understand what it was like in the countryside as you moved west. So I was pleased when John Hume succeeded him as leader of the SDLP. Gerry ended up in the British House of Lords as Lord Fitt, which I regret – and I said so, which earned me a rebuke from Paddy Devlin.

It became fashionable and has almost passed into the language to describe Catholic nationalists as behaving in a 'tribal' way. I dislike this for a number of reasons. Firstly, it is a put-down. Secondly, and more importantly if one cares about rigour, is that in my understanding of the evolution of structure in human

---

3. Cardinal William Conway was Archbishop of Armagh and Primate of All Ireland from 1963 to 1977.

society, the structures which preceded the Elizabethan conflicts in northwest Ulster and the beginning of the Ulster Plantations were chiefdoms[4] and not tribes, and in the intervening three hundred years modern society had developed to the point where the motives for Catholic disaffection were inequality before the state, the law, the local social structures like housing, and the jobs market. A fairly abusive term like 'tribalism' explained nothing, offered no policy or action programme, and avoided serious thought about serious solutions.

The job Conor had wanted was Foreign Affairs, which fortunately he was not given – though without any decision that I am aware of, and in my view totally improperly, when we did form an administration Conor often acted as the Foreign Minister, and established by use a certain sort of authority as unofficial spokesman on 'the Troubles' in Northern Ireland. I know of no decision, either by the government as a whole or by the Labour Party, to let him function in this role – though it is possible that such a decision was taken, as my job required that I be absent from government meetings a lot. Had I been present, I would have opposed it vigorously; having a second spokesman, separate from the responsible minister but as a full member of government and not subordinate to him, seemed to me potentially disastrous. It took all the skill and patience of character of Foreign Minister Garret FitzGerald and of the senior staff of the Department of Foreign Affairs, who had plenty of experience of old of what Conor could get up to, to ensure that this did not happen. This was a nuisance, but one which they were able to contain.

Conor had written a book called *States of Ireland*.[5] It was clear to me from reading it that it could not be reconciled with the policy of the Labour Party. (It was consequently not a surprise when Dr Cruise O'Brien ended in Bob McCartney's UK Unionist Party.)[6] I had the greatest love and sympathy for the stalwarts of the Labour Party, spread out all over the country, often in desperately

---

4. Jared Diamond offers politico-anthropological definitions of tribes and chiefdoms: the political unit of a tribe 'was a village or a close-knit cluster of villages' (far smaller than common definitions), while chiefdoms might encompass 'several thousand to several tens of thousands of people. That size created serious potential for internal conflict because … the vast majority of other people in the chiefdom were neither closely related by blood or marriage nor known by name … People had to learn, for the first time in history, how to encounter strangers regularly without attempting to kill them' (*Guns, Germs and Steel*, pp. 270–3).

5. Published in 1972 by Hutchinson.

6. Having supported unionist objections to the Anglo-Irish Agreement in 1985, Cruise O'Brien officially joined the UK Unionist Party in 1996. He opposed the 1998 Good Friday Agreement and later resigned from the UKUP when his memoir was published, which advised unionists to consider uniting Ireland in order to thwart Sinn Féin.

difficult circumstances, who would be deeply embarrassed by his beliefs becoming our policy. So I supported a move that the [shadow] spokesmanship on Northern Ireland be removed from him.[7] Deeply insulted, he described my action in a newspaper article as 'stabbing him in the back'.

Conor very much disliked and worked against John Hume, which I thought disgraceful. More importantly, under Conor's influence the Dublin government initially didn't like him, thus handing another advantage to the IRA's 'no other way' argument. John Hume was relentless, brave (you had to be, to continue) and a natural leader of the SDLP. He is a sincere and profound nationalist and a sincere Catholic (who spent some time in a seminary), those things which I keep saying I am not, but he contributed more to a valid resistance to IRA dominance of northern nationalism and more to the ultimate (partial) victory of peace than anybody else in Ireland in the last century. I am an anti-nationalist atheist and I believe that, at the time, Conor was also both of these things; yet I believe that Conor has done great harm to the broad policy of sincere reconciliation of both communities and has, against his own wishes, borne great aid to the IRA. I think the core of the various mistakes that he made related to his sense of imminent catastrophe. The sky was always falling.

In those times it seemed to me that, for all his brilliance, he often produced the opposite result to the one he intended. So we were at loggerheads, but in a civil way. I stuck to my last, and left him off. But later there was an event I took very seriously indeed. In fact, in my eyes it completed the rift.

## THE ARMS CRISIS

How the Arms Crisis really came about may never be exactly known. In Kurasawa's film *Rashomon*, the same event experienced by seven different people is seven different events. I don't mean that I am a post-modernist. There is a truth out there, but in politics it is hard, in the prudent absence of documents, to find it. 'I know', says the subtle politician, 'that you think that you understand what you believe that I meant, but what I intended to utter is not what you suppose that I said.' Or words to that effect – there are many versions of the best bits in government in the discussion which takes place after the secretary to the government (a civil servant and, in

---

7. On 11 October 1972, David Thornley brought a motion before the Labour Parliamentary Party to remove the shadow spokesmanship on foreign affairs and Northern Ireland from Cruise O'Brien. Justin Keating called on him to resign for the good of the party. According to Akenson (Cruise O'Brien's biographer) the vote was close, but the motion was not passed.

my experience, someone upright, honest and patriotic) has left. The government ministers, such as they are, tell very little. The real action is elsewhere.

So what did I, from my jaundiced viewpoint in opposition and my subsequent membership of the Committee of Public Accounts investigation, think actually happened? Remember, this is guesswork. And it involves judgements about individual personalities, which are necessary in politics (what will so-and-so do in such and such a circumstance?) but notoriously unreliable. You may make them, provided you don't trust them.

At that time I was the Irish representative of the only effectively functioning branch of the Socialist International. Our meeting in May 1970 took place in London and coincided with a meeting of the Inter-Parliamentary Union.[8] At the 'cocktail' at the end of the Socialist International meeting I came into contact with a man from the Foreign Office. He was very friendly and said that he came from Kildare, that (in so far as I recall) his surname was Neville, and would I like to come back to the Foreign Office for a chat and a drink. Curious as usual, and a new boy in these surroundings, I went and the gin bottle was the source of large drinks. After friendly preliminaries lasting a little while, it became clear that there was something on his mind about Ireland and he wanted to pump me as to what I knew about what was going on. I had no experience whatsoever of this kind of situation, but I had bought and sold a few horses in different places and I think that it is a fair training for many political transactions. I knew absolutely nothing about anything special going on, but I spun out my ignorance a bit in the hope that *I* might pump *him*.

Of course, I got absolutely no detail, but I did form the conclusion that something very important was going on at home, whatever it was. A British diplomat (let us assume that that is what he was) knew something big about the Irish government that I did not know. I was convinced enough and worried enough to do something about my conviction and try to get home at once. The Aer Lingus office in London was, I think, in High Street, Kensington. I went there, asked for the next Dublin flight, and perhaps helped by the gin sloshing around in my belly and the bucket of canapés that I had eaten to keep sober, I settled on a seat. Nobody disturbed me; I spent the night there and got the first flight early in the morning. I was home first. Nobody among my contacts knew anything.

---

8. The Inter-Parliamentary Union is an international assembly of national parliaments and meets once a year. The European regional body is the Council of Europe. The author was appointed by the parliamentary Labour Party as its representative in the Irish delegation.

The Fianna Fáil deputies and senators attending the Inter-Parliamentary Union were hastily summoned and got home by mid afternoon. So something was afoot. Their Fine Gael colleagues only got in late. And the next day, the balloon went up. Jack Lynch dismissed Blaney, and – surprisingly to me, anyway – Haughey and Kevin Boland resigned in sympathy.

Why do I tell this personal story? It strengthened a suspicion that I had long been developing, that the penetration of British intelligence into all aspects of Irish life was long-standing and pervasive. This, again, falls into the 'I think' category and not into the 'I know', or even 'I believe'. My original reasoning was this. As an empire, Britain had possessed a large intelligence system – at least since the East India Company was superseded by the King in control of the Pearl of the Orient.[9] Ireland, of course, is much less important; but for a country that had built its supremacy in the world on its control of the seas, the possibility of naval bases in foreign hands to the west of the home island must have seemed terrifying. Leaving three-quarters of Ireland must have hurt. To me it was (and is) unthinkable that upon British withdrawal in 1921 they did not leave a whole cohort of intelligence 'sleepers' in every aspect of life, like currants in a cake – including within the Gardaí (many old Royal Irish Constabulary men) and the army (ex-Great War veterans whose military expertise was welcome in the hasty building of an effective force in the circumstances of the Civil War). I am not writing this in anger or disgust; it is perfectly normal. Any self-respecting empire would do exactly the same thing. I think that Britain and the other European empires did it all over the world at the end of World War II.

I cannot remember where I first heard it, but I remember my surprise at learning that it had long been the custom for the Irish army to send a bunch of its bright cadets for a military education in British institutions at regular intervals. I assume that about one man in ten is gay. And I can at least surmise a conversation where someone from UK military intelligence says to an Irish cadet: 'You are a promising young man. And lots of people are gay, but it is very damaging if it is made public. So we will say nothing if you co-operate with us. We would like a conversation – confidential, of course – with you now and then.' (I must make it clear that I am not homophobic; in fact, I think that in a sane world there would be no problem with homosexuality. It is straight people in our present, Christian society who are the problem.) In the light of their treatment of Roger Casement's diaries, this was a credible and terrifying threat.

---

9. The term 'Pearl of the Orient' has been used variously to refer to Hong Kong, Sri Lanka, Manila and the Malaysian state of Penang; here, Hong Kong is the most likely intention.

There is a hidden world of serious professional spying (every country does it) that does not leak or become public. The few people I have ever met whom I knew to be spies (with one honourable exception, Col. Heffernan) struck me as living in a cocoon of misunderstanding and fantasy of their own construction. It does not mean, alas, that they are powerless.

To sum it up, I don't think any important Irish person in any walk of life can ever fart without British intelligence, if they want or need to, hearing about it. So from my meeting with the man from the Foreign Office in London, I am convinced that the British knew about the Irish government's plan to import arms for the IRA. In the circumstances (I had been in Belfast and Derry in 1969) and from their point of view, they had a perfect right to. And indeed, the intelligence apparatus would, properly, be considered derelict in its duty if it had failed to know about such a conspiracy. Looked at from that point of view, the decision to import and pass on arms to support an insurrection inside a neighbouring friendly country was almost unbelievably dangerous, irresponsible and mindless, because it was certain to be found out.

Anyway, here is my version. After the August events in Belfast and Derry, the blood of the nationalist community, North and South, was roused.[10] The demand was out that the Dublin government should 'do something'. As usual (see 1916) the stupidities and misbehaviour of the British army was the greatest recruiting gift for the IRA. They have done similar elsewhere, most recently with their US big brother in Iraq.

But do what? It never ever was simple. There were one million (give or take a few) unionists on an island of five million, sandwiched between nationalists and the British authorities – fellow Irish men and women, whom we purported to love and cherish and with whom we purport to want to be united, though our ways of demonstrating our love have at times been a little odd. When a delegation of Irish Labour deputies visited Derry in August 1969, the defence committee told us that in a doomsday situation the Dublin government had promised them arms. We told them that they might have been promised, but they would not get them.

What could we do? Land army against land army? Don't pull my leg. And when it comes to navy against navy, and air force against air force, the proposition becomes even more preposterous. It was a situation where the appropriate policy was 'Don't just do something – stand there!' But what about the constituents?

---

10. During 12–17 August 1969, Northern Ireland experienced intense political and sectarian rioting, particularly in Belfast and at the three-day Battle of the Bogside in Derry. Violence escalated sharply afterwards; this period is deemed to have marked the start of 'the Troubles'.

What about half a century of imbecilic and nationalist rhetoric, culminating in our young TV station celebrating the 1916 rising half a century later? There was an obvious way out. The government must be seen to *appear* to be doing something. Give some arms to the IRA. Not large arms. Not much of them (£100,000 for brave Captain James Kelly to pass on would not buy fly buttons for a serious military force). But the gesture – a bit 'comic opera' as it was – was all. In secret, of course. What were they thinking? Did they really believe that it could be done in secret? It was imbecilic, because the British knew. But it was a decision of government.

Later I was a member of the Oireachtas Committee of Public Accounts, which had the task of investigating the history of the famous £100,000 provided by the government to aid the Republicans of Northern Ireland. We interviewed Captain Kelly of Irish army intelligence and his boss, Colonel Heffernan. In my encounters with Captain Kelly, he struck me as a decent, somewhat hysterical, ignorant and misguided man.

I was widely accused of being a 'Provo' by my political opponents, some even within my own party, because I was seen to be soft on them. I was. Not because I agreed with the comic-opera but potentially very dangerous enterprise in which they were engaged, but because they were honourably carrying out policy decisions that came from higher up, and I did not wish to see honest people scapegoated for carrying out orders, however stupid, that came from their seniors. But after a while I resigned. It was a total waste of time. In Marx's famous phrase, 'History repeats itself, first as tragedy and then as farce.' For the Catholics of Belfast and Derry it was a tragedy, but for the larger world it was farce. In fact, the paradigm that questioning revealed frightened the life out of me. It was anti-British in a simplistic, traditional way. It was based on a whole series of nationalist myths that even now enjoy widespread currency. The only consolation was that, unless by accident, they would do no harm; the British knew too much. But there is always Murphy's Law. They frightened me.

Jack Lynch was, as Taoiseach, the kingpin. As a great hurler, he had a flying start in politics, of course. He was soft-spoken, charming and, I think, a decent man inside, carried a bit out of his depth by politics and the happenstance of the times. And he was a brilliant opportunist in the short term, much tougher than his pipe-smoking kindly image would lead you to believe. But as for strategy, anything beyond a month or so was not his forte. He had a variety of conflicting pressures to contend with. The 'Republican' ministers, led by Neil Blaney, were clamouring for action. Mixed up with their policy dilemma and influencing its outcome was the battle for leadership within the party. In fact, he owed his position to the seeming compromise between the rival claimants, Haughey and Colley.

I got to know Neil Blaney quite well when we were both members of the European Parliament, and as we got closer I came to respect him and even to like him. I am convinced that he believed in the justification of an oracular government decision, which could be interpreted in many ways. He interpreted it, naturally, within the framework of a Donegal homeplace and a Republican background. The paradigm of his childhood was unrevised. He was anti-British/anti-unionist in an utterly, and I would think unchangeably, visceral way. He was a realist, well aware of the moral deterioration in his own party. I recall his memorable definition of an honest politician as one who, when bought, stays bought. I can well believe that in his fantasy world, harking back to the death-dealing heroism of 1916, he could well believe that Irish state arms had not only a place (that was easy), but a significant or relevant place. Blaney was unstoppable. He believed that he was acting within a decision of the government and that it was his colleagues who had betrayed Irish nationalism. This may have been naïve, foolish and dangerous, but it was not dishonest. The downside risk of this adventure: enormous. The upside possibility: none whatsoever. That Kevin Boland supported an adventure surprises me not at all. He was a physically violent punch-up merchant who lived still in the romantic myths of the War of Independence. He was a loose cannon who had outstayed his time.

The mystery, however – the enigma – is C.J. Haughey, 'the Boss'. Seriously able and wildly ambitious, with an intense hunger for the goodies of the nouveau riche. An important period house, an island, a motor yacht, the best restaurants, horses (what O'Eochaid means),[11] Charvet shirts, Cristal champagne, a fashionable partner outside marriage as well as the comfortable feeling that he could always go home to his wife: he wanted it all. And he got almost all of what he wanted. (The point about his kind of wanting is that it is insatiable.) I think everything he did was governed by opportunist self-serving. He believed in nothing except C.J. Haughey, the means of C.J. Haughey's conspicuous consumption, and how to find the wherewithal to service the lifestyle far beyond his means.

What was he doing, involving himself in the somewhat comic-opera enterprise of arms for the North? He had, of course, a background both Republican and Northern, but coupled with a slight rush of blood to the head was the chance of the much greater prize of ousting Jack Lynch – and, as he ultimately did when

11. The surname Haughey, from the Old Irish *ech*, or 'horse'.

all was forgiven, leading Fianna Fáil from the Taoiseach's chair. The Irish people, it seems, love a rogue.

My answer is that I don't think he was involved. What he was doing was sitting on the fence, without any commitment to the Blaney/Boland camp, to see if a situation would arise where he could discomfit Lynch.

So, in my version of events, Lynch permitted and presided over the discussion in government, the judge who seems to satisfy both sides. Imprecise in its conclusions, it could seem to satisfy the realists, but also simultaneously (and impossibly) threw a sop to the activists, even if it was a tiny one and a secret one. And I think that what precipitated the dramatic dismissals of his most troublesome ministers was a British intervention. They said to him, in effect, 'This is a preposterous provocation. Stop it now, sonny.' Not those words, of course. Just an icily correct warning by a senior source. I suspect that either senior Gardaí or British intelligence had put Liam Cosgrave, the leader of the opposition, into the picture. He wanted Haughey out too. Liam, who is well and strong as I write, will perhaps chew his moustache a little and tell us nothing. I wish he would. I think he knows a lot.

Opportunistically, Haughey went along with the charade. And Lynch saw the chance to be rid of him. He may not have had a long vision. He may not have been a great strategist, but he had an instant, courageous and brilliant tactical sense. He saw that Haughey, his bane, was offside. I think Lynch deliberately left ambiguity at government discussions as to the extent of the support of the adventure. With a majority of the government on his side, he reversed the imprecise, unrecorded quasi-decision to stage the comic opera and forced the resignation of those who believed they were acting honourably. For the moment the expendable Blaney and Boland (he resigned in disgust) were going, and they had nailed Charlie. Lynch hung them out to dry, which of course was right and necessary – but what was neither right nor necessary, and was bad for the morale of the public service, is that honourable civil servants who believed that they were acting within the legitimacy of the government decision were also hung out to dry and had their careers destroyed.

When, a few months later, the government tried to prove in court that the dismissed ministers had betrayed their trust, they were unable to do so. The charges were dismissed and Haughey began the long and, one would think, loathsome 'chicken and ham or salmon' pilgrimage of eating his way back into power. Blaney remained outside, but voted 'the right way' as an independent, and as I write his nephew is being wooed back into the fold. Reconciliation is beautiful. Now is the time for all good men to come to the aid of the party. Mind you, I said nothing.

## ADVICE TO ASPIRING POLITICIANS

Here I will digress slightly to offer some advice to young politicians: you must never expect any sort of subtlety or nuance in the judgment of what you do. I suffered because I presented a sort of contradiction, which nobody took the time to ponder, and which my opponents were happy to use as a simplistic stick with which to belabour me. The contradiction was this. I was clearly and outspokenly anti-imperialist. I had read my John A. Hobson and my Lenin. I think that the social trauma to any society and culture of domination by a hostile and often coarse and ignorant set of imperialist rulers corrupts those who exercise power, and those who opportunistically decide that the best individual policy for them is to co-operate with it. Social revolution is halted. Cynical corruption proliferates. Everyone suffers.

While having a very poor view of all of them, I thought the cute hoor Charlie had been hard done by, and I let this thought emerge. A mistake again: never offer complex or delicate explanations. Simplistically, therefore, I must be a covert Provo. Those who are not for us are against us. 'Either/or', in this baby-talk way. So when I said that I was simultaneously anti-imperialist and anti-IRA (describing them long ago as 'mendacious, murderous and mindless'), I was misunderstood and misrepresented. So, aspiring politician – don't tax the minds of your political opponents or of the chattering classes. You may do vastly subtle and complex things (politicians do, all the time), but never let it show. The Peter Principle is true; people do rise to the level of their incompetence.[12] Keep it simple.

## NOËL BROWNE

Of the various people I knew well over seventy years, I think Noël is worth writing about. He was 'difficult'; I notice that when I write about people I loved (yes – loved) and whose memory I revere, there is always a niggle. I'm afraid that is true. But I am trying to tell the story as I really recall it, and very good and remarkable people in my experience do not always behave impeccably.

---

12. The 'Peter Principle' is a concept in management theory formulated in 1969 by Laurence J. Peter which claims that 'managers rise to the level of their incompetence'.

My knowledge of him goes back a long way, to 1948. Fianna Fáil had been in office since 1932 and the feeling was abroad that it was time for a change. In 1947 there was the beginning of a coalition (Fine Gael and Labour, the small farmers' party called Clann na Talmhan[13] and the untested but newsworthy Clann na Poblachta) that might challenge the monolith. To a large degree Clann na Poblachta was the brainchild of Seán MacBride, a striking-looking man (it is suggested that he was the inspiration for the Mr Gentleman character in Edna O'Brien's wonderful novel *The Country Girls*) and the son of Maud Gonne and Col. John MacBride. His new party was distinct from Labour but more or less to the Left depending on who you were talking to. I don't like Irish names for political parties that give no indication of the presence or absence of a political philosophy. MacBride's new group Clann na Poblachta presented itself as socialist as well as nationalist, and it quickly attracted the adherence of a passionate and charismatic young doctor, Noël Browne.

In the summer of 1942 (I think; I was 12 years old) while helping to cut turf on Glencree bog, I met Muriel MacSwiney, the widow of Terence MacSwiney, among the group of helpers. Muriel told me and others that in the late 1920s and early 1930s Seán MacBride was in contact with senior Communists in Europe. He had grown up in France, spoke perfect French and retained a strong French accent – and was presenting himself as a Communist. But he was also anti-abortion and a defender of Catholic family values. Whatever he was (perhaps more than one thing), he was secondly scheming and devious. Even then, he was distrusted as being too complicated by half and untrustworthy. Much later I was invited to lunch by MacBride, perhaps to try to enlist my support. Since I had an almost instant feeling of distrust and was not very forthcoming, no clear proposition emerged. But with the coalition government he went along with the most handsome, talented and charismatic young Dr Noël Browne. I'm afraid it was a formula for chaos.

## NOËL BROWNE THE MEDIC

At that time Noël Browne worked with a brilliant and underestimated Kerry barrister, Noel Hartnett, who remained in his shadow – to my regret, as I thought very well of Hartnett. My mother fell under Browne's political spell and became a follower, and Browne and Hartnett used to meet often in my parents' house,

---

13. Translated: 'Family of the Land'. Active 1939–65.

just beyond Rathfarnham. Himself a sufferer from tuberculosis, Browne saw the scourge that disease represented for the whole population, but of course most seriously for the poorest and weakest. In his own family he knew at first hand what a terrible disease tuberculosis was. He has written an excellent autobiography in which all of these events, as well as his own traumatic childhood, are movingly and graphically described. Every family knew such experiences. I recall the deaths of intimate friends among my own circle in the late 1940s, and Mike and I grew up drinking goat's milk on top of a mountain because my parents were so scared of it.

The terrible ravages were soon to end, though in circumstances of poverty, overcrowding and poor nutrition it still remains a threat. But two things broke the back of TB in Ireland in the decade after World War II. A pair of French scientists, shortly before the outbreak of war, had developed a successful vaccine. Named after them, it is the famous BCG – 'bacille Calmette-Guerin'. A great radical doctor (and intimate friend of my mother), Kathleen Lynn, was interested in its use here. So was another hero of mine, who was Chief Medical Officer and has written a splendid autobiography, Dr James Deeny. In 1928 Dr Alex Fleming had had the first insight into the action of chemicals produced by bacteria that killed other bacteria. The concept was one of the milestones in the development of ecology; once the idea of antibiotics was abroad among scientists, both in the pharmaceutical industry and state labs, a furious search began. Dr Howard Florey in Oxford made possible the industrial production of commercial quantities of penicillin. But among the killer diseases against which penicillin was useless was tuberculosis. The other great relevant medical development was the commercial availability of streptomycin, which *was* effective against tuberculosis. If one looks at the incidence of tuberculosis in many developed countries in the decade after the war, the graph of infections falls over a cliff. The privations of war were ending, and that had something to do with the decline, but mostly it was due to BCG and streptomycin.

In the dramatic election of 1948, Browne became a deputy at the age of thirty-two, and the other Noel a candidate for the Senate. Practically on the first day of his presence in the Dáil, a new government was formed – a potentially fragile coalition. Browne went from being a medical doctor specializing in tuberculosis to being not just a deputy, but on the same day Minister for Health. He had control of a fairly substantial sum of money accumulated from the activities of the Irish Hospital sweepstakes, and this he spent on a crash course of building TB hospitals. Their availability coincided with the conquering of TB.

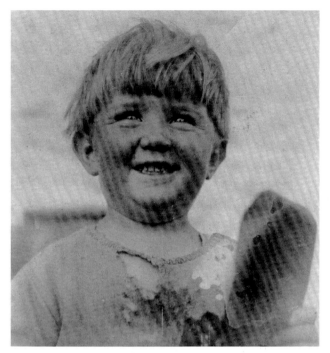

Justin holding a sod of turf, 1933. © *Estate of Seán Keating,*
*IVARO Dublin, 2017.*

Michael, Seán and Justin Keating on the Aran Islands, 1934.

Outside the Dalton Tutorial School: Norman Lecky, Liam Dalton, Justin Keating, Peter Lennon, Joseph Teller, unknown and Jackson, 1946. *Photograph by Otto Falk.*

Justin and Desmond Greaves just back from Belfast,
December 1949.

Drawing of Justin by his father Seán, 1950. Studio photograph of Justin, January 1952.
© *Estate of Seán Keating, IVARO Dublin, 2017.* *Courtesy of Edmund Ross Photography.*

Carla, cousin Masha, Eilis and David at the house in Bolbrook, 1965.

Justin and Laura outside the house in Bishopland, 1970.

In the Tivoli Gardens, Copenhagen, 1970:
centre, Justin; left, Hans-Henrik Krause
with his wife Marianne; right, Lelia Doolan.

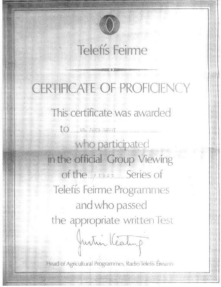

Certificate issued on completion
of the *Telefís Feirme* course, 1967.
*Courtesy of James Conway.*

Justin in contemplation.  Justin laughing. *Courtesy of Tony O'Malley Pictures Ltd.*

The 'shotgun wedding' coalition, 1973. Ireland as the priest, Liam Cosgrave as the groom, Brendan Corish as the bride, Garret FitzGerald and Justin Keating as witnesses. In the window, a shotgun-bearing Jack Lynch. *Cartoon by Warner.*

The New Cabinet, March 1973. Seated, left to right: James Tully, Patrick Donegan, Liam Cosgrave, President de Valera, Brendan Corish, Richie Ryan, Mark Clinton. Standing, left to right: Tom Fitzpatrick, Michael O'Leary, Tom O'Donnell, Garret FitzGerald, Conor Cruise O'Brien, Richard Burke, Peter Barry, Justin Keating, Patrick Cooney, Declan Costello. *Courtesy of The Irish Times.*

Mervyn Taylor, Seán Keating and Justin in the house at Ballyboden, 1973. *Courtesy of Tony O'Malley Pictures Ltd.*

The signing of the oil agreement, 1976. At the table are Justin and Pierre Guillaumat, Chairman of Elf Aquitaine. Far left: J.C. Holloway, Assistant Secretary, Dept. of Industry and Commerce; far right: Padraig O'Slatarra, Secretary, Dept. of Industry and Commerce. Others present are members of Elf Aquitaine Group. *Courtesy of Irish Photo Archive.*

Justin on board ship, 1977. *Courtesy of The Irish Times.*

Seán and Justin Keating at Galway docks on their way to the Aran Islands, 1977.
*Courtesy of Stan Shields.*

Carla and Justin at the National Co-Operative Conference, 1982.

Hans-Henrik Krause making a point to Justin, France, 1993.

Justin and Barbara on holidays in Saint-Mamert-du-Gard, France, 1993.

Justin in front of his father's portrait of May Keating, 1994.
© *Estate of Seán Keating, IVARO Dublin, 2017.*

Eilis with her mother and father at the opening of her offices in Naas, Co. Kildare, 2000.

Justin and David Keating on the set of *The Last of the High Kings* in Howth, 1995.

Celebrating Granny (Claire) Wine's ninetieth birthday: Justin's grandchildren Jonah, Seán, their cousin Julia, Wendy and Justin, 1997.

Justin and Barbara at Grand Canal Dock. *Courtesy of David Keating.*

Justin feeding his first great-grandchild (Ana), 2007.

In fact, many of these sanatoria rapidly became redundant, but of course they were put to good use to meet different needs, and the money was not wasted. Noël – and more vociferously, his supporters – hailed the initial disappearance of TB as his doing. He was the man who conquered tuberculosis. In my opinion, stating it bluntly, this was not true. But it cemented his reputation at the time.

## THE MOTHER AND CHILD SCHEME

The seeds of it may have been hatched years before, but in passionate discussions, some of them in my parents' house and often with Noel Hartnett, he hammered out the famous Mother and Child Scheme, to protect the health of mothers and their children. By modern European standards, there was nothing radical in it. Ireland sixty years ago was a country where the medical profession and the politicians (with what Noël called his Holy Mother Church in the background) vied with each other in defending family values. Noël Browne's Mother and Child Scheme was the most serious effort at the application of some family values in the life of the state, and it rallied an incredible coalition of opposition.

My father painted Noël at the time of the Mother and Child Crisis. My father was a keen political observer with a sharp tongue. At the time he said that Noël's posture reminded him of the Dublin slattern who was accustomed to being beaten up by a drunken husband on a Saturday night. She would grab up the baby out of the cot and shout, 'Strike me now, with the mother and child in my arms!'

Though Noël failed at that time to have his scheme implemented, and though it did not usher in the development of the new Ireland, it nonetheless certainly marked the beginning of the demolition of the old one, and most importantly, of the stifling stranglehold of the Roman Catholic Church. Often, glorious defeat is more effective in the long run than victory. I don't know why Noël Browne adopted the tactics he did. It may have been some such thought. I had my conflicts with him in subsequent years, and I am sorry to be critical of him but I'm afraid that, perhaps understandably, he was suspicious to the point of paranoia. The secret of getting things done in the short run is, in my experience, to gather as many allies and as few enemies as possible, to adopt a low profile and let everybody share the credit. With the Mother and Child Scheme, as I see it, Noël did the opposite.

First, he upset his own profession. The doctors at that time, with a handful of honourable exceptions, were an extraordinarily conservative bunch of people, and hand in glove with the hierarchy. Of course, there were a few Protestants and Jews in some very senior positions, but the great serried ranks were Catholic. In the Mother and Child Scheme they saw 'socialized medicine' and less money for them. I had done UCD pre-med a few years earlier and I was terrified then, and remain so in retrospect, at how ignorant the students were and how out-of-date the syllabus. But in this they were not unique. Reading even a little of the history of mid-nineteenth-century medicine, the medical profession held ridiculous beliefs and did more harm than good. But they still demanded and got enormous public respect. When the Cold War was raging, the doctors called it 'socialized medicine'. The Church was equally disapproving (the loathsome Archbishop John Charles McQuaid was then at the top of his power).

The opposition within the government rallied too. Faced with the alliance of medicine and the Church, Noël developed an extremely strained relationship with Seán MacBride, the leader of his own party. Noël was solitary and proud and maybe a bit paranoid. But in my experience 'Mac B', as Noël called him, was one of the most devious, tricky, complicated people I ever knew, whom I never trusted an inch. In that particular conflict, I think that the villain was Mac B. But the end was inevitable before the coalition fell.[14] The other parties in the coalition took fright, most notably the old Fine Gael, led by Taoiseach Costello. Fianna Fáil made 'no coalition' a core value, and since they then had enough votes to rule alone, a failed coalition simply copperfastened them in power, with a short break, until 1973.

I was very busy with my studies and preparing to go to England for postgraduate study. I can add nothing personal to a controversy that became a *cause célèbre* and has been extensively analysed. However, the wreckage that ensued from the collapse of the first coalition proved (in the words of the cliché) if not the beginning of the end, at least the end of the beginning, of the 'holy Catholic Ireland' that the state's founding fathers and most especially Éamon de Valera had built. Noël was a hero in our house. Subsequently, the Mother and Child Scheme, under the auspices of a new streetwise Fianna Fáil government, passed into law with a few small cosmetic changes. At that time Browne actually joined Fianna Fáil (into which, I am ashamed to say, my mother followed him for a brief period).

---

14. In 1951, MacBride controversially ordered Browne to resign as a minister after the Mother and Child Scheme was attacked by the Irish Catholic hierarchy and the Irish medical establishment.

## BROWNE IN THE COALITION GOVERNMENT

Noël could not find what he wanted in Fianna Fáil and founded the National Progressive Democrats with the admirable Roscommon man Jack McQuillan. They were quite effective in the Dáil for a very small party. They often fought the Left issues on which the Labour Party, not at one of its high points, should have been campaigning but wasn't.

By the time I entered the Dáil in 1969, Noël had joined the Labour Party and had a Dáil seat, so I saw plenty of him. He was *in* the Labour Party but not *of* it. It was what you might call an external association. At that time he wrote occasional articles for the high-circulating *Sunday Press*. In them, it looked as if he had made a list of all of Ireland's psychological corns and was determined to stamp on them all. That caused considerable grief among those deputies who were hanging onto difficult rural seats. I am thinking of the likes of Dan Spring, John Ryan, Tom Kyne or Liam Kavanagh (I do not include Steve Coughlan or Michael Pat Murphy). I considered these deputies the salt of the earth. I very often disagreed with them, but they hung on and kept a Labour presence alive under very difficult circumstances. Their survival ensured the survival of the party and laid the foundation for subsequent growth, and I often restrained myself with their wellbeing in mind. Not so Noël. You could hear the votes ticking away. Whenever Noël got into full spate, it was then that Brendan Corish used to take out his diary to ostentatiously consult the phases of the moon. That action was more than just a put-down. There were brief intermissions when I felt that Noël was not quite sane.

One such involved me. We had a meeting of the Dublin Regional Council in the afternoon and a meeting of the parliamentary party in the evening. At the latter, Noël told the assembled members that at the afternoon meeting I had tried to have him expelled from the Labour Party. The chairman turned to me. I said (approximately), 'Really, this is quite simple. There are at least half a dozen people in this room who were there. I say that I made no such effort. Now I call on them to say which one is telling the truth.' They said that I was. Then I said, 'Noël, one of two things: either validate your charge, or withdraw it.' Amid a continuously growing sense of embarrassment, Noël put his arm on the table in front of him and rested his head on it, making no eye contact and saying nothing. After an awful minute the chairman moved on to the next business.

Later I was the occasion of humiliating him again, in a way that caused me more pain than any other event in my political life. We had our 1973 annual conference in Cork.[15] The Left opposition in the party was powerful and well organized at the time, with Noël as the figurehead. Noël was a splendid public speaker. His speech in the morning session was a huge success. Handsome, charismatic, suffering, dropping his voice to a whisper, he completely captured the delegates. The audience gave him a standing ovation. If the vote had been taken at that moment, his resolution would have been passed overwhelmingly. But fortunately for the platform, the debate was scheduled to last all day, without the conference managers having to fiddle standing orders. Lots of delegates wanted and had their 'spake'. The leadership recognized a crisis when they saw one.[16]

What to do? They did something clever. The consensus over a panicky lunch was that I should be the person to try to win over the delegates. This decision I accepted, but I knew that it was precisely because, of all the party leadership, I was the most Left, and also that I enjoyed some goodwill and trust from the members. So the plan had a double edge. With all the people who loved and revered Noël, I would be destroyed, win or lose. If the platform lost, it would be my fault. And if we won, we were back on course. Beautiful. I accepted because I believed that it was the right thing to do, and bloody fool that I was, I believed that I was the only person who could do it. Ruairí Quinn has described in his autobiography *Straight Left* the drama of the afternoon from the viewpoint of a delegate, and he tells it as I recall it – but then it is friendly to me, so I would say that, wouldn't I?

The time ticked around. The first intensity of Noël's speech had faded. As a teacher and broadcaster, I had learned to feel the mood of an audience. When I got up, the hall was hostile. All I did was to take it slowly. I knew the chairman would give me as much time as I wanted. I took it very low-key at first. I teased out the consequences of Noël's resolution in reality. Their response was stony. I passed on to my second point: were those the consequences they wanted? They

---

15. The 1973 Labour Party conference took place at Cork City Hall from 12–14 October.

16. Brendan Halligan's account: 'Arguably [Keating's] most significant [contribution was] evolving a policy on the development of our oil and mineral resources which protected the national interest while encouraging private sector engagement. This last achievement did not come easy. It was opposed by right-wing elements outside the party and left-wing factions within. It gave rise to probably the best Labour Party debate in modern times at the 1973 Annual Conference held in Cork. Coming in the wake of a succession of highly charged speeches opposing his policy, his performance at the rostrum was a masterpiece in oratory and political psychology. It was a mesmeric exposition in matching the ideal with the realistic, a combination of reason and passion. It was the apogee of his career and it won the day and thereby cemented the party in power until the general election defeat of 1977.' (*Justin Keating: A Tribute*).

began to listen. I began to pile on the arguments and the feeling. They began to shift. Rather low-key but gradually and slowly raising the intensity through the whole of Noël's resolution, I repeated that they the delegates were sovereign, and that if the consequences were what they really wanted then they must pass the resolution. Gradually, I got a faint supportive murmur. Gradually, it grew. I began to see hope and I kept relentlessly at it, until it was perfectly clear, even from the platform, that our side would win the vote.

At a conference there is usually a lot of socializing and a bit of 'jar' at the end of the day. But I left the hall before the vote was announced. I knew the result. High drama, you would think, and I would have been feeling great. No. I knew what I had been chosen to do and I could not refuse, but I was defeating someone – beyond his 'impossibleness' – whose passion for equality and for the weakest in society I knew was not mirrored in the minds of the 'realists' on 'my side'.

I drove straight from Cork to my home in Ballymore Eustace, deeply troubled and psychologically exhausted – it is a wonder that I got home safely. My teenage son David was sitting by the stove in our old warm, well-used farmhouse kitchen and, tired from the road, I asked him to make me a cup of tea. I told him what I had done and why. I told him that I had been trapped, but I believed that I had to do what I did; that it was the right thing but I was miserable about it; and that it had strengthened that feeling I had prior to my first election – that I had made a mistake by going into politics. Not long afterwards, my experience in government confirmed that feeling, and my subsequent withdrawal. But that conviction took a little more time to develop fully. Of course my Paget's disease, which made the decision inescapable, lay in the future. But the doubt started then.

If rumour is a lying jade, memory is twice as bad. Concerning immensely emotional events, every time one replays one's tapes of memory, one tweaks them a little. The weaknesses, the dishonesties, the downright stupidities are gradually edited out, like the images of the old Bolsheviks in Stalinist propaganda. So recently, for confirmation or otherwise, I checked with David, who a third of a century later recalls the events as I do.

I have said and recounted some awful things about Noël Browne. But I said at the beginning that I loved him. Were he alive, I can hear him saying, 'You could have fooled me!' But it's true, and I admired him as well. Why? I think I know the answer. I love and respect his memory more than that of, say, Conor Cruise O'Brien because of the depth, passion and – whatever his other inconsistencies – utter consistency of his love of the weakest and most exploited people. Of all the people I have ever been close to, he had the greatest sense of the injustice of the world, and of anger against that injustice and inequality. His socialism arose, I think, because he realized (correctly, I believe) that an unregulated market could never provide equality, fairness and justice. He felt intensely the pain and hurt of the disadvantaged, whether by ill health or needless poverty. And they knew that he felt it, and they loved him for this empathy. I think that that characteristic is the most beautiful one in that contradictory entity one calls human nature. I loved Noël because he possessed it so abundantly.

The Scottish poet Ronald Campbell MacFie catches my feeling perfectly:

> 'We blame thee not, thy failures we forget,
> Forget the seeming-weak, the seeming-wrong;
> But in our hearts there blooms and blossoms yet
> The wild sweet passion of his song.'[17]

## THE DUBLIN BOMBING AND THE BARRON REPORT

I don't believe in the concept of an 'objective truth'. One's perceptions are always influenced by time, place and one's paradigm. But I think that a great deal of postmodern criticism of the 'objective' position has thrown out the baby (a fair shot at what actually happened) with the bathwater of bias. It is fair, therefore, that I make it clear where I am coming from when I write about the 1974 Dublin Bombing – which, remember, killed 27 people on the spot and injured 137 others, a few so seriously as to cause their deaths later on. It was not nothing. It was a major outrage. One of my daughters, who was a student at the Royal Irish Academy of Music around the corner on Westland Row, was there at the time and place of the South Leinster Street bomb. And I visited both sites. There has been a long debate about who did it. In his book, Garret FitzGerald says simply, 'Bombs set off in Dublin by Loyalist paramilitaries.' I think that is too simple. It was a time of crisis: the Loyalist strike and the collapse of the Sunningdale Agreement.

I hope I always make a distinction between 'I know' and 'I believe'. The former indicates evidence exists that I find convincing, strong enough to stand up in a court of law. But one cannot live life like that. I have many important beliefs, which cannot be so validated, but on which I am willing to base actions. In the latter case, I hope I will always say 'I think' and 'I believe' rather than 'I know'. The Dublin Bombing is like that.

---

17. Ronald Campbell MacFie: 'In Memoriam: John Davidson'

I came to the conclusion that there was some collusion between Loyalist para-militaries and British military intelligence (the last two words are oxymoronic), and I said so. There are lunatics and mountebanks in all intelligence services, in my very limited experience, as well of course as decent people doing their duty. But I have no doubt that the policy was to soft-pedal investigations, though they had killed a lot of innocent people. We must not offend the British; we must not give comfort to the IRA. But again it seems to me that not pursuing the matter was precisely the sort of weakness that validated the IRA's physical force policy: 'If the government in Dublin won't protect us from Loyalist and British thugs, we have to do it ourselves.' Quite a powerful argument in a nationalist ghetto. We left a couple of decades of nationalists feeling that the government in Dublin had betrayed them.

The outcome of long agitation was the eventual setting up of a tribunal under a very distinguished Supreme Court judge, Mr Justice Barron. In the conclusions of the Barron Report,[18] he deals mainly in what he can prove. But the doubts remaining, which he also expresses with impeccable fairness, I believe to be terrifying. The consequences are alarming. I think this was an example of state terrorism by the British. I believe that my country, at a time when I was part of the government, also practised state terrorism, and though unaware of this at the time, I am deeply ashamed. All this I feel is worth saying because I believe that state terrorism is widespread, and I hate all terrorism, wherever it is coming from. The argument that 'we' are nice and therefore don't do it, while 'they' are nasty so they do it all the time, simply does not convince. Consistency is important. To have two standards is bad: 'What is sauce for the goose is sauce for the gander'.

## NODS AND WINKS

Ireland is a physical country. Men strike each other, teachers strike children, etc. in a way which in more civilized European countries would be unthinkable. Falling off the tightrope into violence is therefore a constant threat to correct behaviour by the police. It calls for immense discipline and restraint to behave well in all situations. And it is natural for senior Gardaí to demand more power. But for society as a whole and for their own sake, it is essential that they behave correctly. With great regret I say that I think that in my time, encouraged by nods and winks from above, the Gardaí fell off the tightrope.

---

18. The Barron Report was published in 2003. 'Barron is right about 1974 bombs', an *Irish Times* article by Justin Keating, is reproduced in full in Appendix C.

This is not an anti-Gardaí diatribe. The Gardaí are numerous enough to contain a spectrum of humankind, from the very worst to the very best, with most somewhere in the middle. There may be a bit of a skew, because the power and local social authority that the job holds out may be an improper inducement. But I have known a lot of Gardaí in my time and the vast majority have been decent, upright, proud of their work and humane. I was proud of them and felt that our state was well policed. Also, let nobody underestimate how difficult and unpleasant the job can be. A violent drunk will spit and shit and piss on those trying to restrain him. A good thump, if wrong, is the most natural response in the world.

And again, it is entirely normal that in circumstances like the state's battle against the IRA, the Gardaí should wish to use more force than was strictly in the rulebook. What is not normal or permissible is that they should get the nod from ministers of the government that it was okay to do so. They got that nod during my time in government.

The initial event arose from the IRA kidnapping of an extremely strong, resolute, decent and well-liked Dutch industrial manager, Tiede Herrema. He was held captive and initially an intensive hunt turned up nothing. And then he was found in a house in Monasterevin, safe and as well as could be expected.[19] But *how* was he found? I quote Dr Cruise O'Brien, presumably party to knowledge available to the Security Committee but not to the government. In his book *My Life and Themes* he recalls a conversation with a Special Branch detective who told him how the Gardaí had found out the location of Tiede Herrema from a suspect:

> So this man was being transferred under Branch escort from a prison in the country to a prison in Dublin, and on the way the car stopped. Then the escort started asking him questions and when at first he refused to answer, they beat the shit out of him. Then he told them where Herrema was. I refrained from telling the story to Garret (FitzGerald) or Justin (Keating), because I thought it would worry them. It didn't worry me.[20]

Well thanks a bunch, comrade. Same party. Same government. Same shared collective responsibility, but you don't tell a colleague. I looked on that silence as a personal betrayal, because as a former senior diplomat Conor knew that there was such a thing as cabinet responsibility. I did not know about this piece of

---

19. The kidnap took place on 3 October 1975 and the initial manhunt lasted eighteen days before Herrema was located. A stand-off of eighteen more days ensued before the kidnappers surrendered.
20. *My Life and Themes*, p.355.

state terrorism, but I inhere in the collective responsibility for it and I am deeply ashamed. Had I known, this was for me certainly a resigning issue.

It was all a sorry episode, and it is to the eternal credit of the senior people in the Gardaí that they were the people who brought the actions of the Heavy Gang to the attention of senior political people.[21] Our Gardaí should be loved and trusted by the public, but they must earn that love and trust. The Herrema case and the Heavy Gang had the opposite effect, so I'm not really surprised that in recent years they have slipped a little in public esteem.

## THE 'THUNDERING DISGRACE'

In the autumn of 1976 a crisis arose involving the Minister for Defence, Paddy Donegan, who might euphemistically be described as a 'colourful character'. An alcoholic publican from Co. Louth, he achieved some publicity by firing his shotgun at some travelling people, and in my hearing, expressed admiration for the proto-fascist Blueshirts. The President of Ireland Cearbhall Ó Dálaigh, himself a distinguished lawyer, while acting perfectly within his authority referred a bill to the Supreme Court before signing it into law. The bill, and the President's referral, incensed the Minister for Defence. At a public ceremony in a midlands barracks he indulged in an abusive attack, including a phrase about the President which included the word 'fucking'. It was rendered by the only journalist there as 'thundering disgrace' but (behind my hand – and mind you, I said nothing) everyone knew the actual word.[22] We may try to excuse him by using the common politicians' excuse, which is that he was 'tired and emotional' (i.e., drunk) but it was more serious than that. That a president, even if acting perfectly legally, who

---

21. An author's note reads 'Check Garret's take on this'. In *All in a Life*, FitzGerald recounts: 'In mid-February 1977 I was asked by two responsible members of the Garda Síochána if I could see them privately ... Many of the allegations were false, they said, concocted by subversives to undermine the Gardaí and in the hope of avoiding conviction for offences of which they were guilty... But in some pending cases it was believed by some that confessions had been extracted by improper methods, and Garda morale would be seriously damaged if those cases went ahead and some Gardaí were persuaded to perjure themselves in the process.' FitzGerald determined to raise the matter in government; by threatening resignation, if needed.

22. That journalist, Don Lavery, later recalled the evening's events in an *Irish Independent* article dated 6 January 2007. Contrary to common belief, Lavery maintains that the words were indeed 'thundering disgrace', not any of the other rumoured permutations, and that the minister (though a known alcoholic) had not been drunk then: 'He did not slur his words, and he did not stagger or sway. He had been quite definite in what he wanted to say.'

had previously been associated with the major opposition party should be subject to abuse by a minister in our government is in my view not acceptable. When all this blew up I was out of the country, trying to promote exports and inward investment. The Taoiseach decided to stand behind his minister and persuaded the government to go along. When I got back, it was a fait accompli and none of my party colleagues had thought it worthwhile to tell me of the crisis.[23] I was isolated. Collective responsibility applies to government, and to my shame, I did not resign.

I already felt that I had made a mistake in entering politics. I never asked anything of, or offered anything to, Brendan Corish. I had absolutely no aspirations to lead the Labour Party, as I love the party and wished it success and believed that my atheism, which I never ever concealed, debarred me. Perhaps that is not true a third of a century later, but I believe it was then. But there were three other Labour ministers who were united in believing that I was a contender and that they should oppose me. Two of them wanted the job themselves. Michael O'Leary ultimately got it, and ended up in Fine Gael.[24]

## A JOURNALIST'S DUTY

When the election and my Dáil seat were lost, I stood for the Senate and got elected. I became the leader of the Labour Party in the Senate, trying to keep a credible opposition going with small numbers, among them notably Mary Robinson. The leadership of the Senate as a whole belonged to Fianna Fáil as election winners, and the post was occupied by Eoin Ryan, whom I found a decent and straightforward man in his personal dealings.

Conor Cruise O'Brien was also elected a member. He soon went to London in a major executive position at *The Observer* newspaper and did not take much part in the Senate. He retired in June 1979, justifying his resignation in that there had been no facilitating response to his request to have a particular piece of Senate business rescheduled to fit in with his timetable. But he certainly made no request to me, and I asked Eoin Ryan if Conor had made the request directly

---

23. Following the July 1976 assassination of Ewart-Biggs by the Provisional IRA, President Ó Dálaigh referrred the Emergency Powers Bill to the Supreme Court. The same day that it was signed into law, that October, an IRA bomb killed a Garda. Some government members considered the referral to have prompted this; Donegan's outburst occurred the next day. Taoiseach Cosgrave rejected Donegan's resignation. Ó Dálaigh resigned 'to protect the dignity and independence of the presidency as an institution'.

24. Frank Cluskey succeeded Corish as leader in 1977 and O'Leary took over in 1981.

to him. 'No', he said. If I have to choose between these two opposite versions, I am afraid I'd choose Eoin Ryan's. And then came what seems to me a particularly awful event.

Mary Holland was an English journalist whom I knew quite well. Painfully honest and meticulously professional, she fell in love with a Derry socialist who was absolutely not a terrorist, Eamon McCann, and she came in due course to know and understand the nationalist population very well. In *The Observer* she wrote a piece about the plight of the Catholic Sinn Féin-supporting women of Derry. It was sympathetic and explained the awful dilemma they faced. Conor, using his editorial power, fired her.[25] There was public outcry; in my view, quite rightly. Is it not a journalist's job to get inside the minds of embattled groups to explain to readers how they experience a situation and how they reach the conclusions they do? It helps to understand the mindset of those we consider opponents. A journalist's duty, I would have said. But she lost her job. Again, consider the consequences. An ex-minister of the Dublin government, who had been very recently playing a significant role in the formation of Northern policy, penalizes the journalist who was trying to explain the IRA viewpoint. It must not be explained or discussed or even touched. Another victory, I would have said, for the IRA. Another justification of 'They only understand force.' I think that such arbitrary (and in my view unjust) use of power must have upset John Hume and pleased Gerry Adams in equal measure.

After my stay in the Senate I did not contest either chamber again, so I did not come across Conor again, but of course I read the papers. I hope the reality was more nuanced than came out in the media (it often is) but it appears that he espoused the cause of Bob McCartney of the United Kingdom Unionist Party whose policy, as the name indicates, was the full integration of Northern Ireland into the United Kingdom.

For someone of Conor's background, which to a degree I shared and under-stood quite well, this was an amazing shift. The problem of Northern Ireland

---

25. In clarification: Holland, whose coverage had won the Journalist of the Year Award, was not technically fired by Cruise O'Brien, although she lost her position due to his influence. He penned a memo that read: 'It is a very serious weakness of your coverage of Irish affairs that you are a very poor judge of Irish Catholics. That gifted and talkative community includes some of the most expert conmen and conwomen in the world and I believe you have been conned.' Her article was pulped on his orders; when her contract came up for renewal shortly afterwards, Donald Trelford deferred to Cruise O'Brien and did not renew it. Holland was rehired soon after Cruise O'Brien left the newspaper.

obviously was that two hostile populations lived intermingled in the same space. One was obviously, and to its great advantage historically, allied to the occupying power and – indeed, more than allied – *was* its upper class, with a shared religion and often even shared education, and an almost identical culture. Though this of course did not apply to the Belfast Protestant working class; McCartney's party was the political expression of this small section of Protestant opinion. But over the centuries it was the Catholic nationalists who were oppressed even more than Protestant workers. And the Northern Ireland state was set up to put them in a permanent minority. Of course, differential rates of reproduction and emigration have changed all that. There is now no solution except the one being found after terrible pain and turmoil over many decades. Both sides have rights that are equal. Neither side chose where to be born. Each has the right to remain and live a decent life. It seems to me that the policies of John Hume and the reformed unionism of David Trimble offered this. The policy of Robert McCartney did not. If one side wins the other must lose. And if either wins, there can be no solution.

From Conor, the espousing of McCartney's party was a bizarre piece of irresponsible buffoonery, motivated in part – as I have felt about some of his wilder actions – by the desire to shock. But, having helped to validate the most intransigent unionists' conviction that they were right all along, having marched them up to the top of the hill (from which in their covenant they could see the promised land) he proceeded to march them down again. The next *volte face* was to tell them that that hope was a chimera and their best hope of survival as an ethnic and cultural entity was to make common cause with the nationalist tradition and join the Republic. Another piece of irrelevant quixotic nonsense.

### A CURATE'S EGG

Conor is alive as I write; in his early nineties, but able to enjoy life, with an active mind. Before I end this chapter (this assault, one might say, because I recognize that that is what it is), I want to touch on one other topic. In 1986 Conor wrote a book about Israel and Palestine called *The Siege*, the metaphor of the title referring *not* to the Palestinian people, but to Israel. Conor writes extremely fast, as well as uniquely beautifully, but even with his force of mind, it was a huge labour in a short time. It is still so utterly (yes, I know, in my opinion) skewed in the Zionists' direction that I allow myself to speculate as to whether he accepted research assistance from Zionist people with an axe to grind. Before it was written, he and I used to argue about it, as I had a growing disenchantment with Zionism.

Perhaps he was simply frivolously declining the argument, but he said to me that in his time at the United Nations (he was a senior Irish diplomat at the time), when the seating was in alphabetical order he fetched up beside the Israelis, and they were charming and funny and able people. Much nicer than the Arab representatives. It may just have been his way of telling me to get lost. But I feel it was revealing, all the same.

In all of what is now, I am glad to say, a long life, Conor was the best talker and the worst listener I have ever met. It has been a long road, with many bends, from the young socialist student that I met in Glencree before World War II. In 1681 Dryden wrote a famous put-down poem, *Absalom and Achitophel,* in an exaggeratedly angry vein, and it kept coming into my head during the writing of this chapter:

> Stiff in opinions, always in the wrong;
> Was everything by starts, and nothing long:
> But in the course of one revolving moon,
> Was chemist, fiddler, statesman and buffoon.[26]

Conor had no interest in music that I ever heard, and alas, I think it shows in his way of thought. In the false and harmful split of arts versus science, he was a very pure arts man. So not a fiddler, nor a chemist. On his best days, certainly a statesman; on his worst, which were not infrequent, a buffoon. I have known him as a brilliant man, and the best company you would ever spend time with, but a curate's egg – the best is wonderful, the worst is awful.

---

26. John Dryden (1661–1700). *Absalom and Achitophel* is a satirical allegory that uses the biblical Absalom's rebellion against his father, King David, as commentary on the contemporary dilemma of legitimate succession to the throne of Charles II. These lines are said of the character Zimri, who represents George Villiers, second Duke of Buckingham (1628–87).

# On the Perils of Nationalism

## NATIONALISM IN EUROPE

The most important point about the nationalism that has been rending Europe for one-and-a-half centuries is that, historically, nations are extraordinarily recent things.[27] Etymologically, the word shares a route with 'natal'. Where were you born? Quite recently, people could speak of the 'nation of students' in Paris, or of the 'nation of merchants' in some trading city. And if one looks, as Hobsbawm did, at the states of Europe, one finds that language, ethnicity and natural boundaries are not coextensive. Much of the false nationalist ideology about nations goes back to Herder in Germany. Though he himself was not a racist or a proto-fascist, it was a short step from his ideas to racism and the Nazis.[28] The racist aspect of the nation ended in the Holocaust. In Ireland, the racist aspect ended in the burning of Protestant landlords' houses during and after the Civil War. This is an episode that, until recently, sanitized nationalist history had chosen to ignore.

Those who want to check out the source of these ideas could start with two books: Eric Hobsbawm's *Nations and Nationalism* and Eugen (not Max) Weber's book, now translated into English as *Peasants into Frenchmen,* which shows how very recent these feelings of nationhood are in rural France. Remember: Chauvin was a Frenchman.[29] Following these and other now widely researched works, I

---

27. Eric Hobsbawm, *Nations and Nationalism Since 1780*, p.16.
28. Johann Gottfried von Herder (1744–1803) was a philosopher, theologian and literary critic whose theories on the value of the cultural traditions and language of the ordinary people or *Volk* were seminal in conceptualizing 'the nation'. In his time, German-speaking Europe encompassed over 300 political entities; Herder's pride in their common origins, language and folk culture galvanized patriotic feeling, though he also warned of the perils of extremism. He collaborated with Goethe and inspired the Grimm brothers to their pursuit of folk tales.
29. The term 'chauvinism' originally connoted an exaggerated and aggressive patriotism and derived from the figure of Nicolas Chauvin, a possibly apocryphal French soldier said to have been wounded and severely maimed in his country's service and later rewarded by Napoleon.

simply state bluntly that there was never, is not now, and in my estimation never will be, an Irish nation, using the definition of 'Irish nation' above. Nation states, as they have evolved, do not in most cases exhibit ethnic, linguistic or religious unity. What they do have is: a single territory, a single administration and, until recently, a single currency.

Marx saw the dangers for effective working-class and majority (including small landholder) action when it was beginning to flex its muscles. He was consciously internationalist: 'The workers have no country.' And the anthem of the international Socialist movement is not the emotional 'Red Flag', written by an Irishman and which even current British Labour Party members find it possible to sing, but 'the Internationale'.

One of the most awful moments in twentieth-century European history (which contained plenty of them) was the summer of 1914. The growing, confident left-wing parties met at their various conferences and renewed their vows of fraternal solidarity. Within months, they were at war and killing each other. At the war's end, the rulers of even the defeated countries enjoyed an unchanged lifestyle, while as usual the ordinary people paid – in lives, in grief, in widowhood, in the destruction of what little they owned. How can they have been so stupid as to endure this and the subsequent economic upheavals? No question of this kind ever has a simple answer, but the siren charms of nationalism form part of the answer: 'For God and Kaiser', 'For King and Country', and later on, '*Ein Volk, Ein Reich, Ein Führer*'.

A significant turning point came within the world Communist movement in the middle and late thirties. When I was a very young Communist, I used to think in my out-of-date way that Communism would provide the antidote to this foolishness that rendered the workers helpless and set them in conflict with each other. But feeling the threat of a developed world getting ready to destroy the Soviet Union, they advanced the policy of the Popular Front. They embraced other working-class movements, and even some liberals. But it is my heretical view that in the shotgun marriage, the nationalists won.

I encountered the internationalist/nationalist tug of war when I went to London in 1951 and became active in the Connolly Association. Connolly had dramatically thrown in his lot and that of his followers with the nationalists planning the 1916 rebellion. (It is worth remembering that some aspects of the relevant movements were pretty nasty, including Pádraig Pearse's affirmation that it takes the shedding of blood 'to make a right red rose'.) It is a valid question, when one looks at the island that grew out of these events, as to whether that was the right thing to do.

But the name of the Connolly Association was not idly chosen. And I infer that in my time in Britain (1951–4) there was a debate within the Irish committee of the Communist Party, to which I was not party, and which I was never told about, between what I might call the 'Greavesites' on one side and the more internationalist 'Hobsbawmites' on the other. But in the last half-century the Greavesites have proven themselves the winners – not that victory is worth much.

The Irish successors of my comrades of that time are Communist with a small c – nationalists. But without clout. They are a testament to a dangerous human weakness after a certain age: the inability to grow and learn and change.

## MYTHS OF IRISH NATIONALISM

From the middle of the nineteenth century until just recently (you see, it is recent), Ireland lived in a fever of nationalism. It was the flavour of that century and of most of the twentieth, and I use the word 'fever' advisedly because it was characterized by a series of hallucinations, of wonderful, pervasive, charming nationalist myths, which did us terrible harm and which I hope and believe we are outgrowing. Born at the time of rampant Irish nationalism following the establishment of the new state, my paradigm as a child coming to awareness of the world was Irish nationalism – until the moment, I think, when the IRA shot my friend Dinny O'Brien in September 1942. There were certain political assumptions that were practically universal (except amongst the small and diminishing unreconstructed unionists, almost entirely Protestant).

### The myth of nationhood

When I was a kid, before World War II, we sang 'A Nation Once Again' ('… and Ireland, long a province, be a nation once again'). Implication: a long, long time ago, without saying exactly when, Ireland was a nation, and after a long period of occupation (often stated to be 1000 years) we were reclaiming that nationhood. But this is terrible nonsense. Among the assumptions were that a nation was a very ancient and precious thing that enshrined the soul of its population and that the national territory was everything on the island, from the centre to the sea (the definition of 'national territory' was equally unhistorical, divisive and meaningless).

Our largest political party for the whole of my lifetime calls itself Fianna Fáil after the wonderful mythological cycle that developed here 2000 years ago. But there never was such a coherent 'Irish nation' at that time. I gave a lecture (not well received, I regret to say) to a third-level audience in Dublin entitled 'When Was Ireland?' I affirmed that nothing faintly resembling a modern nation ever existed in Ireland prior to the establishment of the present state. I liked the two-nation theorists[30] for the baggage they threw out, but the replacement does not stand up to scrutiny, in my view.

## The myth of the first national language

In a preposterous preamble to our 1937 constitution, Gaelic – or in current speech, Irish – is described as the 'first national language', whatever that means. Even the circumlocution is revealing. This assumes that 'nation', people and language are somehow coextensive and have evolved over a very long time – that Gaelic was of great antiquity, and that it had been spoken by the majority of the population since time immemorial. But this, again, is patently not true. The military ruling caste who conquered Ireland and installed the Gaelic language came very recently: after 1000 BCE. In many ways, the most exciting ancestors we possess were the people who built Newgrange, the other monuments of the Boyne, and the Céide Fields in north Mayo. Of their language, technology or origins (from Spain or Middle Europe or Scandinavia) we know nothing, alas. As my friend David Greene (Daithí Ó hUaithne), Senior Professor of Celtic Studies at the Dublin Institute of Advanced Studies, used to mischievously remark: 'There has been a chair in Celtic archaeology for a hundred years; but the difficulty is that there is no Celtic archaeology.' He exaggerated to provoke, but he was basically right.

Our island has always contained different populations. It seems that on a small scale the Romans were here. From quite early on in their extraordinary eruption, the Vikings were here; witness the extent of Viking place names. Having colonized Scotland, the reverse subsequently took place. Since the Norman invasion, large numbers of English (and others who were Anglophone) have come here. The administration (until the efforts of the twentieth century) has never been in Gaelic. The major cultural centres in the towns have never spoken Gaelic; the 'Irish town' was outside the walls.[31] Statistics of population before the censuses

---

30. The Two Nations theory posited that Ulster Protestants had the potential to form a nation in their own right, and that the Southern government's refusal to accept their right of self-determination was the cause of 'the Troubles'.

31. In *Reflections on the Irish State* Garret FitzGerald writes: 'By the end of the seventeenth century the Irish population throughout the island had been left absolutely leaderless, control of both administration and commerce being in the hands of the relatively small minority of colonists. From about 1700 onwards that indigenous population began gradually to adopt English as their language ... by 1800 up to one half of the population was English-speaking' (p.171).

of the nineteenth century [are unreliable];[32] it is no more than an educated guess that the great expansion of an Irish-speaking rural population depended on the potato and was made up of very poor people with a relatively low cultural level.

The claim for Irish as the first national language marginalizes – indeed, externalizes – a very significant section of our population. I think it shows how very stupid very clever people can be. De Valera was, as well as being longsighted and devious, very clever. He claimed that the passion of his life was national unity. And yet his language claim made unity impossible. Clever and all as he was, he does not seem to have noticed a contradiction, and neither did those who followed him. That same contradiction is more obvious in the IRA/Sinn Féin. Having spent nearly four decades in murderous, sectarian, divisive civil war they pose as the champions of 'national unity' and 'the rule of law'. One is tempted to the cliché, 'How stupid can we be?' But this nationalist Celtic fantasy world has long lost touch with reality.

'*Gan teanga, gan tír*', they say: no country without a language. A dangerous myth. I wish they knew the history of German nationalism and of fascism. The Irish language pioneers seem to have swallowed Herder's ideas uncritically but wrongly. I have seen the claim that there are 6000 languages, though obviously this is a soft figure depending on definition and on difficult questions of patois and pidgins. Apparently, sophisticated robots develop language quite quickly and easily. Languages are born and evolve rapidly – *pace* the French Academy and what I think is their foolish effort to freeze French like a fly in amber. The language of the kids, slang-based, is difficult for people of my age. The language of the text message is new, rapidly evolving and perfectly valid. Purists may rail against it. They cannot stop it.

In the light of all this, a 1937 description of Irish as 'the first national language' is as preposterous as it would be funny, had it not caused so much pain and damage to the educational system. Irish has been taught as a compulsory subject in primary and secondary schools during most of the life of the state. This has had a terrible effect on other school subjects. (To me, the queen of all studies is mathematics, and in the world league tables of the late school levels of mathematics, our record is really very poor. In our globalizing world, this matters.) Another effect of the compulsion policy, perfectly predictable if its perpetrators had known any history, is to make it hated. I know that the movement of *gaelscoileanna* is having

---

32. The author left a gap here. From the context, his meaning is inferred: as the first census of Ireland took place in 1821, any so-called statistics predating that time, or assertions based on them, are unreliable at best.

some dramatic growth. But for society as a whole, a subtle and beautiful language has been practically destroyed.

I carry in my wallet a card that defines me as a person who has been a member of the houses of parliament (in my case, both Dáil and Senate). It carries the harp and the words '*Tithe an Oireachtais*' and, underneath, 'Former Member' in English. In Ireland, this card is unnecessary; outside Ireland, given to a French gendarme, for example, it is perfectly useless. In other words, it is another piece of foolishness rooted in the Celtic fantasy world that we have invented.

## The myth of a Celtic identity

The deepest and most dangerous myth is racist. It is the myth of the two races in the British Isles: Celts and Saxons – that the population (except for that pejorative word 'planter') was predominantly Celtic, possessing a distinct ethnic identity, while the 'old enemy' (not the British Empire, but England) was ethnically different: the 'Saxon foe'. We needn't argue about it, because DNA studies have destroyed it. Modern genetic analysis both of nuclear and mitochondrial DNA has indicated that the population of the British Isles has a mixture of genes from various sources and that, while there are gradients from north to south and from east to west, there *are* no 'ethnic Celts'. So the 'Celtic race' is without scientific meaning, though in the minds of those living the myth it has a very harmful meaning. Likewise, 'Saxon' has no meaning. In regard to the mindset that George Bernard Shaw was mocking a century ago in *John Bull's Other Island* and which James Joyce never ceased to mock: the pragmatic, efficient, ruthless, soulless Saxon versus the sensitive, spiritual Celt is as mythical as the Celts and Saxons themselves.

But merely destroying a myth intellectually does not remove it from the minds of a population. The Celtic thing is still around. This myth was extremely divisive of the population living in these islands, validating the obscenities of both the IRA and Loyalist paramilitaries. It has taken the phenomenon of the Celtic Tiger to dent these misconceptions about each other.

## The myth of the Celtic Renaissance

Central to this mystical worldview was the 'Celtic Renaissance' – that this Celtic nation had had a great and brilliant past, which needed to be brought to life again; hence the Celtic Renaissance. But this was two untruths in two words. There never was a great Celtic world of which one could seek a rebirth. It is another nationalist racist myth, but it exercises a huge influence on the self-image of the new state.

We still speak to the schoolchildren in awe about the Nobel laureate W.B. Yeats. I think Yeats was a great poet, and his metaphors have gone into the English language and around the world. But I think he was also one of the nastiest, most ruthless, grubbing self-seekers I have ever read about, and a proto-fascist. His effect on the national myth has been disastrous. (A fact in witness: his famous Thoor Ballylee was part of the estate of his patroness Lady Gregory, put on the market at the breakup of the estates at a subsidized price to make such lands available to local small farmers and landless poor. But our Willy, the landless peasant, got in first – no shame at all.) One can be very contemptible and a great artist at the same time. Wagner was too, in surprisingly similar ways.

I think that all of these propositions are demonstrably wrong, harmful nonsense, invented since Napoleon's time by mostly ignorant people. They are of a racist nature that could easily be pushed over into fascism (as indeed they easily might have been, had not the fascist General Eoin O' Duffy been so intellectually challenged). When you assemble these pernicious nationalist myths you end up with a widely believed synthesis: that a *real* Irish person, as the fascist Altirí na hAiséirghe ['Architects of the Resurrection'] used to say, was '*saor, chriostúil, gaelach*', or free, Christian (for which, read Catholic) and Gaelic (a word which is widely understood but on examination means nothing). It follows that real Irish people are ethnically homogenous. They are Catholic and they have been here a long time. But if your forebears are Protestant and only arrived on 'our' shores almost four hundred years ago, you are not really Irish. You are foreign, a planter, a Protestant, your ancestors never spoke Irish, you are not really Irish at all, and we are entitled to kill you, either for simple genocidal reasons or to get your land.

Europe is divided horizontally into a Protestant north and a Catholic south. I know this is a gross simplification, but broadly true. There will never be peace in Ireland until everyone recognizes that this line cuts Ireland in half. There are two cultural groups. I remember when my colleague Conor Cruise O'Brien asked a fundamental and brilliant question, across the floor of the Dáil, of a rabid Irish nationalist Fianna Fáil deputy, Kevin Boland: 'Do you want to reverse the plantation of Ulster?' Yes, Conor, they *do*. And it has torn the heart out of my life in Ireland from the late sixties to just now. In conflict, people regress. How long will it take before real love and understanding break out between populations where there have been so many murders on both sides? To say that one is fighting for unity when one's actions deepen division is a mark of stupidity.

# 7. *Doubt is the Mother of Wisdom*

## POST-POLITICS

After my period in the Dáil, Senate and government I resumed university teaching. My extraordinarily kind colleagues in the Faculty of Veterinary Medicine (none of them, so far as I know, socialist atheists) elected me dean, where I immediately – though alas, briefly – plunged into the task of planning a new veterinary curriculum and participating in the design of the splendid new veterinary buildings at UCD Belfield campus. A little later, Gemma Hussey (then Minister for Education) appointed me chairman of the National Council for Educational Awards. The council was the body that approved courses and invigilated in the matter of standards in the sector of education outside the universities (what I call not just third level, but level two-and-a-half as well). This sector, which included the Institutes of Education, the regional technical colleges and various other specialist institutes, was then bigger than the university sector, and for a country on the edge of becoming the Celtic Tiger, it furnished an extremely important kind of graduate. It was exacting work, and most of the time I loved it.

On a personal note, for those of you with suspicious minds, let me make it clear that the Hussey who was Minister and the Hussey who became my second wife are sisters-in-law, but my appointment antedated my marriage by a couple of decades, and I did not know my future wife at the time.

## WE INVENT OUR EXPERTS

I think that doubt is the mother of wisdom. It is easy to put up straw men, attributing to opponents beliefs they never held, for the purpose of knocking them down. An example with which socialists have to deal is the statement that we believe that everybody is equal, when patently they are not. My difficulty is that I never met a socialist who believed that all people are equal. And so it goes on. The history of Europe through all its phases has been written by the victors – Christians – with no regard for the truth. It was always propaganda, inventing self-serving myths without shame.

The nuns in the Loreto convent told us about the Crusades against the Albigensian heretics and how wicked they were (not particularly relevant at the age of eight, but there it was). Modern scholarship, using the distorted mirror of the Inquisition's own documents (they had destroyed all the heretics' documents), has shown us in books pioneered by Ladurie[1] and his followers that the licentious, murderous, thieving and raping brutes were the Crusaders, and that the victims, the heretics, were much truer followers of the gentle and peaceful Christ. But the nuns were still telling the lie in 1938. I respect modern history, but up to, say, the mid 1900s history was really bunk; not just wrong, but self-serving myths and lies. The task of the historian was like the task of the priests – to invent and propagate the myths that justified kleptocracy (the 'rule of the thieves'), be it religious or the rule of modern empires.

Until the rise of modern medical science one and a half centuries ago, you were much better to go to a wise woman or herbalist. Doctors killed you (witness the practice of bleeding and of probing wounds with dirty hands). They were very pompous as a profession, and by the standards of those surrounding them, very rich. And they did harm. So why were they allowed to continue their activities? I think it was because what people wanted even more than cures was reassurance: 'So and so is the finest doctor there is, and he is doing his best for her.' They

---

1. Emmanuel Le Roy Ladurie, French historian of Languedoc, referring to *Montaillou: Cathars and Catholics in a French Village 1294–1324* (1975).

were useful in that very frightened people could receive reassurance and pass on responsibility.

Still, eminent priests, bankers and doctors frequently talk the wildest nonsense. We apparently have a need for experts, so we invent them. But we believe them at our peril. We should never doubt a belief for which we have some evidence just because some eminent person, sometimes indeed decked out in the most expensive and bizarre garb, says it is not true. We have received in the last year a similar demonstration of clay feet. (I write as the world seems to be entering recession.) All the great pundits about the economy, bankers as well as economists, have shown themselves to be ignorant and wrong. Not worth believing. But what enormous palaces they built themselves, and what enormous remuneration (salary, stock options and pensions) they paid themselves. I feel like asking, reversing the old jibe, 'If you are so rich, why aren't you clever?' But they have turned out not to be.

## THE USES OF FAITH

So in my thinking about religion I came back to a deep distrust of what its protagonists say. The reason that religion is more than just a source of oppression and cruelty, which it has always been, is because of the recent changes in the technology of weaponry. The Islamic world is being driven by Western stupidity into the arms of fundamentalists. The fundamentalist Protestants of the US have been able to accumulate quite an extraordinary amount of power over policy and have driven their country into a series of impasses in Iraq, the rest of the Near East, Afghanistan and now Pakistan. The Zionist world's atomic bomb is in the hands of increasingly fundamentalist religious Jews, quite unlike the early settlers in Palestine. All these confrontational policies, based on a covenant with a god that the believers invented, and who gives them certainty, imperil the future of our species.

If all this is true, why do we have religion at all, and why are a very significant majority of humankind still believers?[2] I offer the answers that I find sufficient to explain this. It seems that our species in its present form is about 200,000 years old.[3] When we began to have a sense of the past, of stored experience at the level

---

2. In 2005, 87.5 per cent of the world's population expressed some form of religious belief, according to the CIA *World Factbook*.

3. *Homo sapiens* is deemed to have evolved 200,000 years ago in East Africa, according to Yuval Noah Harari's *Sapiens: A Brief History of Humankind*.

of consciousness of history, and an extended sense of the present, and the power to speculate about the future, we used this dawning sense of culture in addition to our hard-wired senses to examine a most extraordinary world and solar system around us, and to try to explain it. 'What is the stars, Fluther?'[4] What are thunder and lightning, why days and nights of varying duration through the cycle of the year, and hot and cold seasons, and tides? Even more, why the peculiar cycle of human life? It seems that humans need answers. One needs the strength and confidence that rigorous science gives to be able to utter the strongest sentence that I have ever encountered: 'I don't know.'

Faced with our growing awareness of our extraordinary and awe-inspiring environment, we had to invent explanations. Initially, it seems that our explanations accounted for all movement and change by virtue of a spirit inside each volcano, inside each rivulet and forest grove. A spirit–substance duality was there at the very beginning. Much, much later (about 10,000 years ago) the final codification into what is now monotheistic male-dominated religion took place in the civilizations that were developing in the great river systems of Mesopotamia, India and China. This new dynamic single all-powerful God is very recent.

Jared Diamond argues in his wonderful book *Guns, Germs and Steel* that in Mesopotamia and Egypt something less than 10,000 years ago, with the rise of surplus food stores and kingdoms, religion took on a new role. The priesthood, in alliance with the monarchy, constituted the 'kleptocracy': the rule of thieves. While the monarch's job was to rule in society and in war, the task of the priesthood was to invent and promulgate the myth justifying the kleptocracy's appropriation of the surplus. The church emerged and grew in the shadow of the court. It seems to me that by and large, in the West, in the religions arising from Judaism, that rule is still the same. And the religions are able to maintain their grip on their supporters' minds as a result of indoctrination at a very early age.

When the world was evolving very slowly and we were less expert at killing each other, religion, while a hindrance and a source and validator of organized violence, was less threatening to human survival. And of course I acknowledge that the various religions did some good things, though much fewer than is widely believed. Remember that no good deed done in the name of a god ever lacked for praise and exaggeration by those who invented that god and earned their living by organizing his worship. I give an example. In a south Dublin parish in a well-to-do area, the wife of the local Church of Ireland clergyman told me that

---

4. From Seán O'Casey's *The Plough and the Stars*.

prior to the organization of hospitals by Christians there were no organizations charged with the responsibility of caring for the sick – a quite extraordinarily uncharitable view of humankind, as well of course as being totally untrue.

Brendan Behan was capable of brilliant one-liners, as well as great plays. Asked if he believed in God, he replied that he did, but only after dark. I recognize the comfort of certainty, and the narrative of surviving death, to people who are old and ill and frightened and threatened. Indeed, it is the one aspect of the attack on religion that troubles me. I reason like this: does religion do good? Yes. Does religion do harm? Yes. Which is greater? The latter. So people like me have no option but to organize and speak out against it. I think we must recognize that there are wide swathes of the old and frightened who will never find the courage to rework their paradigm. They need to be minded and comforted and left as they are. They are not the people who make wars.

The important targets for humanists are the young, who in general have more courage and are more capable of change.[5] The most important promoter of change would be to get religious teaching out of schools. I profoundly believe that the school should be a neutral foyer where people of all religious beliefs, and the increasing numbers who have none, should all meet, know each other as classmates and play together. At the same time, I would insist on neutrality towards religion by the state. But part of that neutrality insists that the freedom of churches and religions within any given society is very vigorously protected. The teaching of religion should be outside school, the money for religion to come from the faithful. But the freedom to organize and teach and do anything else within the law that they wish must be sacrosanct and very vigorously defended by everyone, atheist as well as believer.

## TALKING GENTLY

I am left with one final plea. I think the world is entering a huge debate on God/no God. I am not going to go over all the arguments against religious belief which have been put forward, from ancient Greece on. They have recently, in their present evolving form, been summed up in a series of bestselling books by Richard Dawkins and others, and I have no serious quarrel with their setting out. But I'm afraid I have serious difficulties with what I call their 'tone of voice'. They are patronizing, they are rude, they are condescending, and my difficulty is

---

5. The author was elected President of the Humanist Association of Ireland in 1998.

this: nobody in my village chose whether to be born Catholic or Protestant. But most of them now are à la carte Christians. Religion is great for births, marriages and deaths and other pleasing rituals. Nice music, nice stained glass, nice smells. About serious things like sex and contraception and the sanctity and irreversibility of marriage, it is totally ignored. And for the rest of the teaching it would be somewhere in between, and in quite rapid change. Speaking of the majority, the Catholics, they would not dream of describing themselves as anything else. But what sort of Catholics? The French make a wonderful distinction between believing (*croyant*) and practising (*pratiquant*). You can be both, or neither, or practising without believing, or believing without practising, and still call yourself a Catholic. When one of my kids was about nine or ten, a friend's child became very interested in what the family thought about God and my daughter said that we did not believe. The other child's immediate answer was, 'Oh, but that is rude.' So a great deal of religion is about one's position in society and one's culture.

And that is why I object to all those sincere, decent people being spoken down to and abused and told they are stupid. They are my neighbours, very many of them are my friends, and I want to talk to them and to all of the population with whom, as President of the Association of Irish Humanists, I connect on the subject of religion. I want to talk to them as equals. I want to talk gently. They did not choose their paradigm. They have been subjected, as small children, to what I call mental abuse. What they need, if it is not too pompous to say so, is love. As indeed we all do.

Please, let us conduct the debate with decency. No inventing and attributing beliefs, which opponents do not hold. No straw men. No abuse. A sincere effort on both sides to listen, and to think one's way into the head of the other, to understand what they are really saying. And, at least on the anti-religious side, a willingness to change. I hold all my opinions lightly. I have the strength to keep on reworking my paradigm to the end of my life. If you show me better, I must change, and I believe in the possibility that you may show me better. Though this may be much less easy for the religious in theory, in practice they do listen. Above all, no mockery, no put-downs, no triumphalism. If a wrong opinion is exposed, both sides gain. There are two winners, though the formulation is wrong. We are the same species, occupying the same threatened earth. Would it be too much to ask that we conduct the debate with love?

## BLESSING THE SOLDIERS

A couple of hundred thousand years ago, anyone who was not recognizable was an enemy whom you would try to kill, while they tried to kill you. And it is for me one of the most puke-making things about all the major Western religions – chronologically, Judaism, Christianity and Islam – that all of them talk peace while blessing the soldiers going to war. I think that killing 'them' because they are not 'us' is not a sin – because I don't believe that there is such a thing – but it is the wickedest thing that humans can do. If the enemies happened to be of the same religion, the priesthood indiscriminately blessed both sides: 'God defend the right'; '*Gott mit uns*'.⁶ Nobody either laughed or cried at this hypocrisy, even while the ecclesiastics were praising the Lord and the armies, while out of the corner of their mouths they continued to praise their Lord as the 'Prince of Peace'. We have all grown so used to this stunning hypocrisy as to think it is normal. How, I asked myself, can they say one thing and do the opposite without recognizing the inconsistency? I think they are not too bright. They are very good at believing the White Queen's six impossible things before their breakfast.⁷ But they are not cynical or insincere. We are a funny old species.

## THE BRUTAL STRAND IN OUR PSYCHE

When I was a kid there was still an Old Comrades' Association, which existed to recall and gloat over their activities in the world war. Clearly it was the time in their lives when they had been happiest. I recognize, of course, that back to the dawn of our species there have been people who loved war and artists of every kind to glorify it, as well as the whole mass of officialdom. Look at Armistice Day. But that part of our culture is clearly something we would be much better off without. It is said, and I think it is right, that the first casualty of war is truth – and I think that the second is decency. The testimony of the people who ran the Holocaust death camps shows very clearly how ordinary they were, but how utterly corrupted they quickly became, in quite extraordinary numbers. A

---

6. Translated: 'God [is] with us'. This slogan has appeared in a military context in Latin, Greek and Slavic; in German it was in use from the thirteenth century (by the Teutonic Knights) to the twentieth century (by the SS Wehrmacht).

7. From Lewis Carroll's novel *Through the Looking-Glass, and What Alice Found There* (1871): 'There's no use trying,' [Alice] said: 'one *can't* believe impossible things.' 'I daresay you haven't had much practice,' said the Queen. 'When I was your age, I always did it for half-an-hour a day. Why, sometimes I've believed as many as six impossible things before breakfast.'

wise population – even if, in a tiny country like Ireland, we cannot prevent war – should get rid of as much as possible of this brutal strand in our psyche. So, for me: no soldiers. No military commemorations, no brass bands, no cheerful ribbons bearing medals, no parades through cities. All of these things demean the people who carry them out, and the onlookers who think, 'How exciting!' We should stop it all.

One great intellectual step forward that should change all our thinking is a remarkable one that, as far as I understand, started with Noam Chomsky. 'Is it nature or nurture?' biologists asked. Even a great recent biologist like E.O. Wilson was on the nurture side. So were socialist intellectuals. The new individual was a *tabula rasa*. The environment decided everything. A better environment was all we needed. It is a brutal society that makes inadequate and vicious people. That left-wing bias is what makes Chomsky's achievement all the more remarkable. The computer with which he started the language revolution, and indeed the whole of cognitive psychology, was subsidized by the US army because they wanted what they hoped Chomsky would discover to improve telephone eavesdropping on people they deemed security risks. And Chomsky, who certainly at one stage of his life was a Leftist, influenced by Marxism, had the greatness of mind to reject the traditional Left viewpoint. In his studies of the learning of language by children, he concluded that the way that they built their understanding of grammar was facilitated by some hardwiring in the child's brain, a window of facility, which opened at three or four and closed again at ten or eleven. Half a century later it seems that he was right, that there are other hardwired bits of brain equipment that depend on inheritance and not experience, and that human behaviour is not solely determined by experience and reason, alas. There are certain bits of human nature which have important effects on our behaviour and which do not reach the level of consciousness. They are built in. The discovery may be just in time to enable humankind to survive – if we take notice of it, which we show little sign of doing just now.

In his remarkable (to me, anyway) 1993 book *Language and Human Nature*, Ray Jackendoff, a Chomsky disciple, extends the idea to social behaviour. The 'purpose' of language is to communicate (and store) human culture. This is a central part of the process of socialization, and Jackendoff suggested then that we had hard-wired, inherited structures in our brain to facilitate socialization. In our evolutionary history, the individual who failed to absorb the agreed paradigm of the community and failed to socialize left no genes. Marx's unsubtle and ill-educated followers, where they came to power, believed that, 'to defend the revolution' in times of temporary difficulties and setbacks, it was permissible to do the most terrible things. They learned, to all of our cost, that it is impossible to abrogate decency and loving behaviour and still retain the high moral ground. Hence Pol Pot.

Somewhere in Chekhov (I never found it again and I'm not sure that I'm not misquoting) he says, 'If there is a gun hanging on the wall in the first act, somebody will fire it in the last act'.[8] Clearly the male part of humankind has a love affair with arms and with war that may even be hard-wired, out of our evolutionary past. Anyway, it is very deep.

## THE IRISH ARMED FORCES

Why this diatribe? I live in Ireland, which has traditionally been neutral for what seem to me bad reasons. But whatever the reasons in the past, we are very lucky and we should stay the way we are. I want to articulate what I believe to be in Ireland's best interests in regard to our army. Originally they were a people's army; the guerrilla forces that fought the Black and Tans to a standstill. The record is not pristine. There were a few atrocities, which is inescapable, but not too many. And as guerrilla soldiers, if they were stupid they ended up dead. So when the army of the new state was formed in circumstances of civil war, they were mostly fairly bright and fairly decent. And they have fought nobody since.

We have a very important strategic location, so in any imaginable future war we would receive the protection of larger, more capable forces. The current argument that asks why we should get a free ride in the defence of Europe without having to pay seems to me nonsense. There is a move, and the army loves it, to join in the 'defence of Europe'. I think that for the troops of the country to fight in another land, and be remembered and be medalled and glorified for it, is degrading and corrupting for the body politic. I defend our traditional neutrality not for weak reasons out of the past, but for basic moral reasons. But I am realist enough to know that it is not possible in any thinkable future to stop soldiers playing soldiers. So the question becomes 'what kind of soldiers?' I am sure that the current army structure, with its drilling and its hierarchy, is out of date, irrelevant and harmful. In a community of 300-odd million, our tiny population is irrelevant in terms of cannon fodder. But, as we have just seen in Lebanon

---

8. In an 1889 letter to playwright Aleksandr Semenovich Lazarev, Chekhov wrote: 'One must not put a loaded rifle on the stage if no one is thinking of firing it.'

and Iraq, the main victims in modern war are the great, resolute, long-suffering ordinary civilians, against whom, in a breach with an older and more humane tradition, it now seems acceptable to make war.

Before going on, I should declare where I am coming from. I think it is impermissible to kill another human being, though I don't guarantee my behaviour in the event of an attack on myself or on someone I love. As the old Quaker joke has it: holding a four-tined fork in front of the would-be intruder, the Quaker says, 'If thou comest any further thou wilst hurt thyself.' I don't guarantee even that forbearance. I might have stuck it in him. But to take part in an army, to try to kill, in an organized way, people I have never met and who may or may not be in the right of the quarrel, just because they are 'them' and they are frightening 'us', is something I will never do. I have had the great good fortune that, living in a century of almost continuous war, I have never been called on to fight, and now at my age I would be a hindrance to any army, so it is easy to talk.

I do see one way in which we might morally and economically be able to defend a force somewhat resembling an army, but without weapons: a small, well-educated, highly trained army, trained not to kill but to cherish and restore. Armies, at their present level of complexity, have numerous and crucial non-combatant support staff. Why could we not have an army that does not degrade us by killing, but is so highly trained technologically as to play an important role in the logistics of alleviation of famine, in getting clean water available again, in restoring communications and electricity, in repairing the roads – all the things that are so conspicuously missing in Iraq and that can do an enormous amount of good? A small force of people who are experts in logistics, planning, the care of people wounded or driven mad by combat, or in information techniques and technology – these could serve European Union task forces without the moral corruption of killing people, and would end their time of service with just the kind of skills that Irish society needs when they returned home.

Hard times are coming and we need all the skills of well-educated and -trained people that we can get. The members of this force could experience all the travel opportunities and all the sexual opportunities that young men currently seek in the army. We have a tiny example from the people who have consistently behaved well and helpfully in Irish history. The Quakers have the same kind of opposition to killing that I have. But already in the First World War they were sending volunteers into the most dangerous places, as ambulance drivers and for similar tasks. We have no reason not to do it, except for tradition, and for the wish of the officer corps to experience 'real war'. It seems to me very dangerous for any democracy to allow the military to get too big for their boots and to think that they have the right to determine policy.

## WARFARE IN MODERN TIMES

Some 200,000 years ago, people fought with suitable rocks (what is called, in New York slang, 'Irish confetti'). They had no bows and arrows, no metal, only crude clubs and sharpened sticks. Now the combined military spending in the world is $1.756 trillion, which is 2.5 per cent of the world's gross domestic product.[9] This gives me a terrifying insight into human – or at least male human – priorities.

The history of the Cold War is the sad tale of humankind systematically sawing off the branch on which it is so precariously perched. The whole lives of all of the world's populations, including my life, have been influenced for ill by this confrontation. What we seem unable to get ahold of is that when in August 1945 the United States dropped one atom bomb on a crowded Japanese city and, shortly after, another one, the 'war game' changed utterly: the power to sterilize the earth became a reality and not a nightmare. There was no need to drop either of them. I call that action a war crime because the vast powers of the US navy and army were defeating the Japanese in the Pacific, the Soviet army was winning in Manchuria, and the Chinese Communist Party, having survived the Long March and regrouped, was proving a powerful foe. Japan was surrounded, and her European allies defeated. Documents later made available show that she was on the road to surrender. It remains a question as to why the US chose to kill 400,000 Japanese and destroy two cities wantonly, when the war was obviously won and their actions totally unnecessary.

In fact, the bombs were not primarily aimed at Japan. They were the first act in the resumption of the Cold War, which had been covertly going on since the October Revolution in Russia in 1917. It was suspended while Hitler was being disposed of, at much greater human and material cost to the Soviet Union, which had played much the greatest role in winning the war, than to the other victorious combatants. And immediately, that exhausted country – which was lying about the numbers of its dead in order to conceal its weakness – was forced, with

---

9. An author's note indicates that he intended to compare world military spending to world spending on education. Current data on the latter has been impossible to confirm. However, figures cited by Malala Yousafzai at the 2015 United Nations Education Summit in Oslo are indicative of relative scales of spending: the $39 billion required to provide free education worldwide for one year is equalled in eight days' worth of international military spending.

a much smaller and less developed economy, to try to match US expenditure on the new weapons of mass destruction. The competition was intensified by the even more powerful hydrogen bomb. The brilliant physicists of the Soviet Union responded quickly, but the arms race diverted essential investment by the Soviet Union into armaments – at the cost of starving the society of the funds needed to repair war damage and make life in all its aspects better for the population.

And then, in 1957, Sputnik 1 raised the ante. The satellite itself was a useless toy, a piece of propaganda hoisted into near orbit by a military rocket. But the space race was on. Who needed to go to the moon in the late 1950s? It was a way of threatening the enemy. It was a way of saying, 'Ya boo, I'm stronger than you are.' But the cost of the arms race, even for a country as rich as the United States, meant that much more important things in human terms could not be funded.

Set against the decent and proper needs and aspirations of ordinary people everywhere, this was a piece of breathtaking stupidity. I come back to that word, stupidity. There is a bitter old joke about the bald-headed generals who put their heads together and made an arse of it. But in every way that we know about since the Crimea in 1853, acts of murderous stupidity characterize the decisions on both sides. For instance, the Charge of the Light Brigade at Balaklava is still remembered as something admirable. Trench warfare in the First World War, the Maginot Line in the Second World War, where the Germans simply walked around the end, the war in Vietnam … all hugely expensive in human life, all stupid and all counterproductive.

The money spent by both sides over the last sixty years on arming and building military forces has been much more than would have sufficed to solve all the earth's real problems: starvation and endemic disease (we still have no good malaria vaccine – after all, it kills mostly blacks and very few people from the developed world, so it is not important). Ours is an energy-inefficient world that is causing global warming and destroying our environment and many species of animals and plants, and an inefficient way of producing our foodstuffs that has, at immense cost, diminished the quality of our food and gravely injured the earth's ecosystem.

All of this has wider implications and threats to humanity's survival. I'm not going to offer numbers. In my experience, once the number of noughts goes up, the number of readers goes down. But I can make some observations about the cost of world military expenditure, and what that money could do in reversing global warming, curing epidemic diseases, rescuing Africa and other areas of declining subsistence farming, and at its widest, securing our future. Arms are made to destroy life (even up to the neutron bomb, which does it without harming property). I fear that in wasted resources and research time they may succeed even if they are not used. Nationalism leads to confrontation, to a new form of the species; the old 'us and them'. But this time around, the units – nations – are bigger, stronger, more destructive and have nuclear weaponry. But nations stand in the way of 'us' coming to mean all humankind, without division. There are other challenges, better ones, worthy of our human combativeness.

## THE STUPIDITY OF WAR

Why are there so many stupid people in positions of extreme power? I think there is an answer. I think that, in part, it is this. Armies, since long before the techno-logical and information technology revolutions (which have changed the nature of war) remain unreformed. The sort of mind-numbing repetitious drilling and barrack-square bullying that has been traditional over much of the world are designed to bring out the worst in people, to reduce the other ranks to automata, to produce both brutalization and mental castration – to produce, in fact, exactly the sort of people who are antisocial thugs. Useful one hundred and fifty years ago, and now obsolete. We don't need them in our society.

Among the officers there is a hierarchical structure where (saving your pres-ence, ma'am) success and promotion depends on licking the arse above and trampling on the face below. Those who come out on top of the bundle are those who are most successful at the two activities I have named, but in other ways inadequate. Stupid, on the basis of military history, and on similar evidence, ignorant – but living in such a cocoon of *esprit de corps* that they are incapable of doubt, or of learning from their mistakes. When they get the opportunity, the brutalized lower ranks commit atrocities that are of the most enormous advan-tage to their opponents (take Abu Ghraib). If you think that it is just the violent and brutal Americans, perhaps, dear reader, you would read up on the activities of the British army in Kenya just before independence. Generals, for the most part, are dangerous imbeciles with huge budgets and, recently, the technology to kill us all.

When I look at the history of armies and wars, I see the wildly irrational behaviour of ordinary soldiers, and the completely bizarre, off-the-wall behaviour of the officer corps and especially the most senior generals. Consider the record in the twentieth century. In the First World War the general staff were so stupid that they went on for years with the same assumptions, in the face of almost unthink-able losses and to absolutely no effect or result. Sassoon says it best:

If I were fierce, and bald, and short of breath,
I'd live with scarlet Majors at the Base,
And speed glum heroes up the line of death.
You'd see me with my puffy petulant face,
Guzzling and gulping in the best hotel,
Reading the Roll of Honour. 'Poor young chap,'
I'd say – 'I used to know his father well;
Yes, we've lost heavily in this last scrap.'
And when the war is done and youth stone dead,
I'd toddle safely home and die – in bed.[10]

In Ireland in 1916, when the generals were shit-scared of what was happening on the Western front, the Irish stabbed them in the back at Easter. But the rebels had little public support until the protracted series of executions, which after the event turned the vast majority of the population to support the Rising. The imbecilic overreaction of the generals was the greatest recruiting aid to the Republican side in the Rising. But one of the hallmarks of stupidity is the inability to learn from past experience.

Wild self-serving theorizing about the effectiveness of air power in the 1920s and 1930s led to the war crimes of 'Bomber' Harris and his RAF against the German civilian population in the Second World War. The effect was not to break German morale, as theory required, but to stiffen it. But again, nothing was learned. The war crimes of the Israeli air force in Lebanon in July 2006 produced not panic among their opponents but the first bloody nose that the invincible Israeli army got, when the unfazed Hezbollah climbed out of their bunkers after some of the most intensive bombing in history and beat the Israeli infantry face-to-face. It was Israeli atrocities against the Palestinian and Lebanese people that produced not victory and peace and security, but a situation where Israel is weaker and less secure, regardless of her American-supplied technology, than she has been since the establishment of the State of Israel nearly sixty years ago. Stupid. Stupid.

As I write, the United States – still with the greatest army in the world, spending (check figure)[11] on armaments – is busy, with all that wonderful tech-

---

10. 'Base Details', written by Siegfried Sassoon at Rouen in March 1917. Copyright Siegfried Sassoon by kind permission of the Estate of George Sassoon.

11. Author's note to self, in 2008. The total US military budget for 2009 was set at $680 billion, while the Stockholm International Peace Institute (SIPRI), which measures military spending for most of the world's armed countries, calculated that in 2012 the US was responsible for 39

nology, giving a victory to Osama bin Laden by alienating previously friendly or neutral populations. I won't quote all the examples; one will do. Pakistan: a US client state with a huge population and a large army, armed with an atom bomb as a result of US assistance, is being driven into the arms of Islamic fundamentalists by the US bombing and rocketing of villages inside the so-called tribal areas, indiscriminately killing women and children as well as their Taliban targets. You don't need military intelligence to tell you that this is counterproductive and surprisingly stupid. But it is happening.

Look at the first Iraq war: a pushover. And the assumption was that a second one, justified by the lie that it was to root out the weapons of mass destruction, would be another. But the Iraqis chose not to fight the same war. They were thinking as people in extremis do, and inventing a new kind of war where the unequal technology of the US was not the deciding factor. Even after the nature of the Iraqi struggle began to emerge, the imbecile glove puppet George W. Bush, instructed by Rumsfeld and the senior soldiers, proceeded to invade Iraq and, after calling the US invasion a 'Crusade' in his sensitive subtle way, declared, 'Mission accomplished'. We are more than three years older, and it isn't accomplished. And Afghanistan is getting worse. Stupid. Stupid.

All over the Islamic world live the successors to the people who invented civilization in Mesopotamia: over one billion people (one-sixth of humankind)[12] who have been brutally ill-used and lied to by Western imperialists; who are the possessors of a vast and proud culture; who crave, as do all humans, respect and dignity. And the generals are planning for war between Islam and the West, which will certainly leave the Earth uninhabitable. Not intelligent.

---

per cent of global military expenditure; four times as much as China.

12. Islam is currently the fastest-growing religion worldwide. Figures for 2010 show adherents of Islam to number 1.6 billion (over 22 per cent of world population).

# On Zionism

Palestine/Israel, because of its location, has always been fought over – and occupied by those to the east and west: the Mesopotamian and Egyptian Empires; the Greeks under Alexander; Romans; Muslims; Western Europeans, for the two hundred years of the Crusades; Muslims again, under the enlightened leadership of Constantinople as part of the Ottoman Empire; and on its collapse, the British. Now it is yet again the arena where the world's future is under threat, in the conflict between Zionists and Palestinians, behind whom are marshalled the United States and Islam respectively. In the time of nuclear weapons, which both sides possess, if it comes to war humankind has no future.

Why does an Irish catholic (small C) atheist humanist want to write about the most intractable problem in the world? In fact, I have a lot of reasons. Though I have never been able to find the details and the relevant people are all long dead, the story of my father's family's opposition to the Limerick pogrom was told with pride in my childish hearing: that when the Redemptorist mission, set free by a supine or concurring hierarchy, smashed up and drove out the Jewish community, my family took in and minded a Jewish woman for a period of months until her people could reorganize elsewhere.[13] My mother's informed and militant anti-fascism from the time of the Spanish Civil War made her aware, as any literate person should have been, of the rise of Nazi anti-Semitism long before the outbreak of war. I recall welcoming the establishment of the State of Israel. I was often a participant in pro-Israel youth activities at the sports ground in Kimmage. I was even given a tree in Israel by a lady from WIZO[14] in recognition of my support.

---

13. A two-year economic boycott against the Jewish community of Limerick was accompanied by sporadic outbreaks of violence, notably in the spring of 1904. The main agitator was one Fr Creagh of the Redemptorists, who used his pulpit to vilify Jews and incite the local Christians.

14. The Women's International Zionist Organization. Founded in London in July 1920, it focuses on social provision for women and children. Upon the establishment of the State of Israel, its headquarters were relocated there.

At sixteen I had, very briefly, a Jewish girlfriend. The gang who were in my house contained the actor Donal Donnelly[15] (*The Knack* – remember?) and a Jewish friend called Ronnie Barron. In his house, about 1950, I met Laura Wine, my future wife. Although neither of us is religious, we brought up our kids to be not just aware of, but proud of, Jewish tradition and culture. And I studied Jewish history, including a close reading of the *Old Testament*.

Many years later, my knowledge of the Dublin Jewish community gave rise to an unconscious joke. A Christian friend who was very close to the Jewish community asked me, 'Do you know so-and-so?' 'Yes, I was at school with one of the kids.' 'And so-and-so?' 'Yes, they bought one of my father's pictures.' 'And so-and-so?' 'Yes, we met at the sports ground.' After a pause, he said, 'You seem to know half the Jews in Dublin by their Christian names.' He was not an anti-Semite; just unthinking.

The Holocaust did take place. It is one of the great crimes of history – though not, alas, unique. And it came not just out of Nazi racist ideology, but out of millennia of European Christian anti-Semitism. The Passion Play at Oberammergau continues to this day[16] and almost nobody has shouted 'Stop!'

On the wall of my bedroom/workroom is a photograph of the Holocaust memorial in Jerusalem by a much-admired friend, Godfrey Graham. I have had it on a wall, where I can see it, through two moves. It is an image that lives with me, as does the image of 'Guernica' by Picasso. It is for all these reasons that I am still shocked by the current behaviour of so many Israeli Zionists. (Note the distinction: I am not saying 'the Jews'. I am not saying 'the diaspora'. I am saying 'Israeli Zionists'.) And it was against this background that I was especially outraged, though alas not especially surprised, by Gaza.

## A REMARKABLE CULTURE

Half my children's genes are Jewish – and already we are deep into confusion. The Jews are not a 'race'. Emphatically not. I am quite certain that there are not Jewish genes. Genes have no religion. And when my mother gave up the

---

15. Donal Donnelly (1931–2012), an English-born Irish theatre and film actor. *The Knack and How to Get It* (1965) was a successful British comedy film.

16. The Oberammergau Passion Play was instituted in 1634, when the villagers vowed that if they were spared from the bubonic plague they would perform the story of the life and death of Jesus in perpetuity. The play runs for five months in every year ending in a zero. It has been regularly condemned for its anti-Semitism; some revisions have been accepted on that basis.

Catholicism in which she had been reared, did her genes change religion? We are getting into Lewis Carroll territory. Jews are also not a religion, because many Jews are agnostics or atheists, but are still Jews. It was no use telling the Gestapo, 'But officer, I don't believe all that stuff.' They gassed you just the same. So: not a race, not a religion and certainly not a nation. The very idea of a Jewish national home is only just over one hundred years old. What, then?

Clearly, the intriguing thing for me is a *culture*, of which religion is only part. It is a remarkable and beautiful culture, and until recently the finest morally and in the religious and philosophical aspects of its belief system. In London, I had sat at the feet of much the greatest man I ever knew, J.D. Bernal, whose great book *Science in History* explains the extraordinary and wonderful role of Jewish thought and belief in Europe for 2000 years, and why it was the source of so much revolutionary thought.

I would claim, without understanding or knowing much about Chinese culture, that the paradigm invented by Jewish scholars 1000 years BC is the best so far. This is an enormous claim, unless you believe, as I find impossible, that the Yahweh of the Jews was a superior class of a god to the other major gods of human history. I believe that society invents the gods it needs and not vice versa.

So what is my explanation of the appearance of the Old Testament just there and then? I look to archaeology and history. Kleptocracy, the rule of the thieves, was ever the pattern – except for the Jews. Why were they different? Not, I believe, because God chose them. The answer is time and location. In northwest Iraq, they learned about iron between 1200 and 1000 BC. Squeezed as they were between the powers of Mesopotamia and Egypt and anxious to remain free of both on the periphery, with iron tools the Jews were able to clear and cultivate land away from the great bread baskets on the alluvial planes. They could develop with the new Iron Age technology the vision of living independently and free. They had the advantage of writing, invented by their close neighbours the Phoenicians. It was not in Israel/Palestine, but over 2000 km to the north, at Harran,[17] that Abraham was promised that if he kept the covenant that Yahweh (Jehovah) had given him, he would become the sire of a great nation. Their friendly god provided them with a suitable ideology – characterized predictably, given the time and place.

It was the first religion to oppose kings and theft, and to advocate liberty and a primitive democracy, before anybody. In opposition to the arbitrary acts of the emperors, they were the first to advocate the rule of law. Most crucially and

---

17. Now within Turkey's borders, close to Syria and northwestern Iraq.

most admirably, it was built around that most precious virtue in any society, righteousness (*hesed* in Hebrew). People who doubt this should read *The Prophets*.[18] Of course they believed in one God, their God, who had a special covenant with them ('the chosen people' is a racist idea) and who was jealous and angry. But what do you expect, in the circumstances? It was the best religion around. Those same principles go right through to the French Revolution and have inspired every movement against autocracy in Western history. Wonderful. How could I not welcome their reincarnation after 2000 years of diaspora?

You can imagine that this new revolutionary paradigm was not popular in the great cities. Pressurized by their neighbours, they set off on their travels (God told them that if they wanted to prosper they would have to move on) out of Iraq and into Egypt for a while, where they found a Pharaoh who wanted to enslave them. On again into Palestine, wedged in the Nile Delta, a land of contending small Iron Age peoples preyed upon by Assyria and Egypt. With a vision, a passion to realize it and great social cohesion, they carved out a fluctuating kingdom. Significantly, the first period was known as 'the days of the judges'; the ensuing period of monarchy only lasted through three kings: Saul, David and Solomon (though I think 'king' is a mistranslation for the group leader). This came about to face the threat of the successful Philistines, competing for the same land. The rise of Rome and its conquest of Palestine ended all that. They did not fit easily into the authoritarian, centralized Roman system. Rome decided on military subjugation in the summer of 134 AD. The destruction of Jewish independence came in a stirring and symbolic way. At the fortress of Masada, a heroic garrison preferred death to surrender and threw itself over the cliff. For surviving Jews it was a case of submit or move on. The diaspora began.

## ZIONISM IS VERY YOUNG

Zionism is very young. The first Zionist Congress was held in August 1897. The central figure of early Zionism was Chaim Weizmann, a distinguished chemist. When the British Foreign Secretary Chamberlain said to Weizmann, 'I have just the place for a Jewish national home,' he meant Uganda, and the Zionists were deeply divided on whether or not to accept it.[19] British motives were not pure.

---

18. The books of the *Old Testament* known as 'the Major Prophets' are: Isaiah, Jeremiah, Lamentations, Ezekiel and Daniel.

19. 'Theodor Herzl met Joseph Chamberlain who was British colonial secretary between 1895 and 1906. He was offered Uganda as a homeland for the Jewish people in 1903. In 1906 Arthur James

They knew the Turkish-based Ottoman Empire was collapsing – they helped it to, in World War I – and they promised Palestine to both Arabs and Jews. And in the Sykes–Picot Agreement of 1917 they parcelled the region out between the British and French Empires. It was about the route to India, and the recently discovered oil.

So the State of Israel is built on a series of myths: that the Jews are a race; that they came from what is now Israel/Palestine; that all Jews are descendants of the diaspora; that Jews have cherished for 2000 years the dream of establishing a national Jewish home in Palestine/Israel; that there was really no such thing as a Palestinian people, only 'Arabs' who were really just as well off and just as happy anywhere in the Arab lands, so it was okay to ethnically cleanse them and refuse them the right to return (okay for Zionists after twenty centuries, but not okay for Palestinians after half a century); that by the Balfour Declaration of 1917, promising a national home in Palestine, Israel's legitimacy was established when it was not Britain's to promise to anybody; and finally, that present-day Israel is a modern democratic state that is the legitimate descendant of the state voted into existence by the United Nations in the autumn of 1947. All these things are self-serving nationalist myths and are untrue.

In my view what has happened is this: to a people already traumatized by 2000 years of persecution was added the almost unimaginable Christian crime of the Holocaust. I don't think many non-Jews – unless they have very close relationships, such as, in my case, a Jewish wife – realize fully just how terrible that hurt was, or the depth of feeling and of insecurity that it produced. At the war's end, the truth, known to the intelligence services of the Allies for years, became public. To the Jews the dream of a national home became extremely attractive, and the countries of Europe newly organized in the United Nations would have given the Zionists almost anything they asked, in their shame and sympathy. In some cases the aim was the covertly anti-Semitic one of solving the 'Jewish problem'. (There is no Jewish problem, only a Christian problem.) In their awful pain and terror of being wiped out, both of which feelings are totally understandable in the circumstances, Zionism and the defence of Israel became dominant

---

Balfour met Chaim Weizmann and tried to convince him that it was wrong to reject the offer. It was Weizmann who persuaded Balfour that Zion and only Zion was a suitable homeland for the Jews. However, there was not unanimity on this and in many countries the Zionist aspirations were denounced by the Jewish leadership. Nonetheless, in 1917 the Balfour Declaration was issued in a letter to Lord Rothschild, a member of the House of Lords.' From Abba Eban's *My People: The Story of the Jews.*

priorities in all the Jewish communities of the world. It was, in my view, a terrible and tragic mistake. And in committing it, the Zionists jettisoned all the great teachings that had made the Jews unique and wonderful for almost 3000 years.

I believed the slogan 'A land without people for a people without land'. I believed David Ben-Gurion when he said that the Jewish immigrants (who then were mostly post-religious socialists) would build a state in peace and harmony and respect with their Palestinian neighbours, respecting the ballot for the declaration statements.[20] So when after the war the United Nations approved the setting up of the state of Israel, I was right there behind, cheering. The early settlers were mainly secular, Left-leaning and active co-operators who established a magnificent system of kibbutz. But that movement has lost direction and momentum. The fundamentalist rabbis have gained more and more power. The balance of political power has shifted more and more to the fundamentalist Right. I now recognize that the rot and duplicity were there right from the start, though it took me a long time to see it.

Alas, as the evidence became overwhelming, slowly over the years a totally different story emerged. Ben-Gurion's words were the most brash, brazen, barefaced lies. The 1948 massacre at Deir Yassin, the ruins of which have been totally destroyed and covered over, was not an isolated action by a fringe of fanatical fundamentalist Zionists, but a deliberate policy to terrorize and then drive out the indigenous population, which was what was done.[21]

It took me a long time to accept that the atrocity at Deir Yassin had actually taken place, or that Ben-Gurion practised ethnic cleansing and the use of civilian refugees as shields for military activities. Israeli sources convinced me. All my sources in what follows are Zionists; Israeli Jewish writers have spilled the beans. The policy of expulsion of Palestinians is now clearly documented.

We now know that David Ben-Gurion ordered the ethnic cleansing of the Palestinian city of Lydda. How? Because Ben-Gurion's chief of staff has written it.

---

20. According to Eban, the General Assembly of the United Nations established UNSCOP, the Special Committee on Palestine, which decided to link its investigation with a study of displaced persons. At a pre-tour meeting Ben-Gurion said: 'A Jewish–Arab partnership, based on equality and mutual assistance, will help to bring about the regeneration of the entire Middle East. We Jews understand and deeply sympathise with the urge of the Arab people for unity, independence and progress …'

21. Over one hundred men, women and children were killed during and after the invasion of this Palestinian Arab village by heavily armed Zionists. The village had signed a non-aggression pact and had a mutually supportive relationship with a nearby Orthodox village.

We know that the new state used the Palestinian population as human shields, because the same senior soldier has told us. While Ben-Gurion was uttering pleasantries at friendly Europeans about the two populations living together in harmony, he was instructing the relevant general to panic and drive out the Palestinian population of Lod (Lydda):

> We walked outside, Ben-Gurion [the Israeli prime minister, appointed two months earlier] accompanying us. Haganah commander Yigal Allon repeated his question: 'What is to be done with the population?' B.G. waved his hand in a gesture which said 'Drive them out!'
>
> Allon and I held a consultation. I agreed that it was essential to drive the inhabitants out. We took them on foot towards the Beit Horon road, assuming that the [Arab] Legion would be obliged to look after them, thereby shouldering logistic difficulties which would burden its fighting capacity, making things easier for us …The population of Lod did not leave willingly. There was no way of avoiding the use of force and warning shots in order to make the inhabitants march the 10 to 15 miles to the point where they met up with the Legion.[22]

We know that in the British–French–Israeli war against Nasser's Egypt, the Israelis murdered their war prisoners. Why? Because the soldier who did it has told us. A general rule of life that I have found useful is this: as well as looking at a particular action, look very carefully at the response – not just of the public at large, but of those in close and immediate positions of responsibility. What I find so revealing and terrifying is that, for example, that selfsame officer who murdered his prisoners in 1956 (and to his credit, said so) went on to have an extremely successful – unblemished, you might say – career in the Israeli defence forces.

We know that the whole Zionist myth about early origins is baseless. Why? Because a recent important book, not by an anti-Zionist, but by a couple of religious Israeli-Jewish archaeologists who choose to live and work there, Israel Finkelstein and Neil Asher Silberman,[23] has told us so.

---

22. Robert Fisk's *The Great War for Civilisation* cites a portion of Yitzhak Rabin's *Memoirs*, which was censored in the official edition but had already been published in the *New York Times* (23 October 1979). Reports estimate that 50,000–70,000 Palestinians were expelled from Lydda and the nearby town of Ramleh in July 1948. Up to 350 inhabitants of Lydda are thought to have died during what some call 'the Lydda death march' to the Arab lines (Donald Neff, *Expulsion of the Palestinians – Lydda and Ramleh in 1948*).

23. *The Bible Unearthed: Archaeology's New Vision of Ancient Israel and its Sacred Texts* by Israel Finkelstein and Neil Asher Silberman of the Institute of Archaeology in Tel Aviv.

The greatest betrayal of all was one of the earliest. Half a century ago, Israel entered into a top-secret conspiracy with Britain and France to topple Nasser and reclaim the Suez Canal, which Nasser had recently nationalized. That action was perfectly legal, and compensation was paid at the price of Suez shares then being quoted in the stock market. The conspiracy with the old imperial powers Britain and France, who had carved up the collapsing Ottoman Empire in the infamous Sykes–Picot Agreement, was a direct aggression against adjacent Arab nationalism, whereas in Egypt, Syria and Iraq government was in the hands of secular Arabs who had overthrown the complacent puppets left in power by the departing imperialists. In November 1957 the conspiracy that cost British premier Anthony Eden his health and his job ensured that near-Eastern Muslim nations (Iran as well as the Arab ones) would never trust Israel again. At a stroke, they made a peaceful settlement between Israel and its neighbours impossible.

Shortly before I write this, the Israeli lobby in the United States succeeded in denying President Obama's experienced and not especially liberal nominee for the chairmanship of the National Intelligence Council. With his huge Middle East experience, Charles Freeman would easily have seen through the propaganda of the Zionist myth-making machine, even though many US Zionists take it for truth. The lobby in the US likes to pretend that it hardly exists and has little influence on overall national policy, which is itself another nationalist myth. The good news is that as he went he issued a statement, which is worth reading into the record:

> Mr. Freeman blamed pro-Israeli groups for the controversy (his withdrawal from consideration as Chairman of the National Intelligence Council), saying 'The tactics of the Israeli lobby plumb the depths of dishonor and indecency and include character assassination, selective misquotation, the wilful distortion of the record, the fabrication of falsehoods and utter disregard for the truth'.[24]

Along the way some extraordinary shabby manoeuvres have been invented. For example, for trade purposes the European Union gave a trading status to the Israeli State that was favourable to the export of fruit and vegetables. This was something that the stateless West Bank Palestinian growers could not avail of. So they were forced to sell their produce at very low prices, which was then sold on into Europe as Israeli produce, commanding the very high Common Agricultural Policy prices.

---

24. *The New York Times*, 10 March 2009.

## ACCUSATIONS OF ANTI-SEMITISM

I said earlier how much I admired the Jewish tradition, which arose from their precarious position between two great empires, for its anti-monarchy, the rule of law, its democratic and social structures, and above all, the concept of righteousness. I am anti-Zionist because I believe that Zionism has betrayed every one of those great and enduring principles. I am anti-Zionist because I love Judaism. And finally, in pursuit of my axiom that nothing is anybody's fault, though I have criticized Zionist beliefs and actions, I feel that Zionists have been driven mad by the assault on their reason of more than a thousand years of Christian anti-Semitism, culminating in the almost unimaginable obscenity of the Holocaust. I hate what Zionists say and do. I think it is against their own interests; and I understand the source of their actions. So I do not hate them, but pity them very much. And I fear for them.

For somebody with my kind of mental software, who has to doubt and re-examine and change if necessary all my beliefs, I have of course to ask myself continuously, 'Is my sharp hostility to Zionism based on solid evidence, or is it an overreaction to a betrayed love?' The response from the US Israeli lobby to an article of mine quoted in *The Jewish Chronicle* gave me reassurance. *The Dubliner* magazine was mostly a current guide to what is going on in town – arts, food, sport, theatre and music. It was owned by a man I had never met but on hearsay respected, Trevor White. A regular contributor, on a quite different level, was a man whom I admire very much, [A.C. Grayling],[25] who wrote about the great issues of the day in a way that I found riveting. And then I met Trevor, and he asked me if, in my way with different preoccupations and knowledge, I would do a monthly column. I was intrigued, and agreed. In November 2005 I got around to Israel. I hate all nationalist mythologies, the Zionist one no less than the Irish. I wrote an article which, since it caused such a ruckus,[26] is worth reproducing in full.[27] Hindsight is always clearer and wiser than what one thinks at the time. But on re-reading it now, I don't see that there is much that I would want to change.

When it was published there was a dramatic and – to me – revealing response.

---

25. British atheist philosopher and vice-president of the British Humanist Association; an informed guess where there had been a gap.

26. In his editorial the following month, Trevor White detailed the origin of the ruckus and its fallout: 'We started to receive abusive and often vulgar emails from people all over the world. Within the next seven days we received over two thousand such letters.'

27. 'The Zionist State Has No Right to Exist', in *The Dubliner* magazine. See Appendix D for the full text.

Firstly, *The Jewish Chronicle* in London reproduced it, with comments, and then the US Zionist lobby, with their dial-a-comment mechanism, got switched on and the *Jewish Chronicle* website got several thousand comments, pretty well universally hostile to me. Of those I read, I was struck by three aspects of them: they were extraordinarily similar, one to another, and read as if the people responding had not read what I wrote; they made no effort to answer the arguments that I made; and they almost all accused me, often abusively, of anti-Semitism.[28] (That was the brick in her handbag that Golda Meir had tried on me all those years before.)[29]

There is an old saying in politics, invoked when the dialogue becomes abusive, 'Mud thrown is ground lost.' And that is what I felt when the splendidly organized and disciplined Zionist lobby mounted its assault. Had they tried to answer my arguments and prove them wrong, in a relentless way, in the best traditions of rabbinical debate and Jewish exegesis, I might very well have been shaken and have undertaken a detailed re-examination of the whole question. I am a scientist and a humanist. If you show me better, I must change. But that was not what happened.

At a certain level, because of my feelings towards Jews, I would like to be proved wrong. But when the response is abuse and not argument, then I am strengthened and not shaken in my belief. In rugby, at a certain point, you 'forget about the ball and play the man'. In political debate, which often degenerates into sub-serious level, character assassination replaces reasoned discussion. When the Dublin Fine Gael Zionist deputy Alan Shatter compared me on TV to the President of Iran, who calls for Israel's destruction, I did not think he did me much harm among the un-committed. Other Zionists cheered, and the great mass of the public disbelieved him. And those who knew me believed that he had both disgraced and made a fool of himself.

I am not a believer in any religion, but among religions Judaism is one of the best (though not without its faults). But the faults are serious. The concept of a special covenant between God and a particular group of people is obviously racist.

---

28. In the 29 January 2006 edition of *The Dubliner*, Rabbi Dr David J Goldberg OBE published his response. His criticism of Keating's arguments, 'errors and misconceptions' was robust; however, he adamantly defended both Keating and White against these accusations, writing: 'I am as certain as can be that neither Justin Keating, who wrote two contentious pieces about Israel, nor your editor, who published them, are anti-Semitic. Hurling the charge of anti-Semitism is the first resort of those stuck for a better argument.'

29. As recalled by the author's family: at a Socialist International meeting (probably in London and pre-1976), he criticized Israel's policy towards Palestine during his address. When Harold Wilson introduced him to Golda Meir afterwards, she accused Keating of being anti-Semitic. He responded that if he were, he would have been hostile towards his own wife and children.

The tragic irony is that it is precisely the Jewish 'race' that has suffered the most from the systematic murderous racism of the Nazis. It is because I love many libertarian Jewish beliefs, and because I admire and love many Jewish people that I am so shocked by the excesses of the Zionist. I am anti-Zionist because I am pro-Jewish, as the Zionists' actions make a travesty of all the good things in their professed beliefs. When finally (at seventy-nine, I'm not comfortable with computers) I got around to googling myself, I found various Zionist additions – not argumentative, but abusive and wildly inaccurate; indeed, contemptuous of accuracy. They can stay where they are and I won't comment. I consider them a badge of honour.

## A NUCLEAR MASADA?

Much more important than our little local spats is the ongoing Israeli situation. I write after the election of 2009 and therefore after Gaza.[30] How can any Palestinian find common ground with Avigdor Lieberman? How can any PLO negotiator make any deal with Israel that will not result in their being eaten by Hamas in any election? How can any Israeli government deliver a return to the pre-1967 boundaries, which were themselves extraordinarily favourable to Israel? How can any Israeli government agree to the return of the refugees to their own land? The deadlock will fester for a long time. But the situation is not static. How can any imaginable Israeli government share Jerusalem? How can any Palestinian entity make peace without a share of Jerusalem?

What is frightening is that it is not a deadlock that will fester forever. The oil is running out. The US-friendly governments of Saudi Arabia and Egypt are far from secure. And in the end ruthless oil companies and ruthless US government (*pace* Barack Obama) will betray their client state. But that client state has an atom bomb that the US gave them in secret. And a very central part of the nationalist narrative is Masada, a story of death before being overcome, where the besieged zealots jumped off the cliff rather than surrender to the Romans. How do you feel about a nuclear Masada by a betrayed and beleaguered population? If in a time of oil shortage the US is really faced with the choice between 'friends of Israel' and 'friends of Islam', she will choose oil, and desert a few million Jews. And then the siege mentality will triumph and her bomb becomes usable. But

---

30. The Gaza War of 2008–9 was, at the time, the deadliest conflict on that ground since the Six-Day War of 1967. Since the writing of these notebooks, its death toll has been surpassed by that of the 2014 Gaza War.

the Iranians have it now too. (If you were an Iranian, contemplating a bellicose, duplicitous, atom bomb-armed Israel – a close ally of the Americans, who keep threatening you – would you not feel justified in having an atom bomb also?) But that way lies catastrophe. That way lies another *Shoah*.[31]

And though my opinions are not important, tiny Israel is right at the heart of the most important current world conflict, and whatever agreements between unequal powers the current Palestinian leaders may make, the wrong is too great to bind the future. There may be a place for Jews in the Near East, but I say with regret that the State of Israel, as it at present exists, will never be able to find peace. Zionist propagandists, please note: 'as it at present exists'.


## DEMOCRACY IS INDIVISIBLE

All of this is deeply tragic. For someone who cherishes Jewish tradition as one of the jewels of human civilization, it appears an immense and counterproductive betrayal. But democracy is indivisible. There is no democracy for Palestinians: either those in Israel or Gaza or the West Bank or among the refugees. There is no even-handed trustworthy rule of law for Palestinians and, most tragic of all, the Zionists have abandoned and betrayed the principle of righteousness. After ethnic cleansing, by a variety of legal subterfuges already well developed in the great empires, land was misappropriated and in place of the mutually respectful co-operation between Jews and Palestinians promised by Ben-Gurion, we have seen a half-century of the most vicious state terrorism against the Palestinians, and efforts to destroy all of the Palestinian social structures not subservient to the Zionist government. The great Jewish intellectual Max Nordau, who was originally a committed Zionist, on learning that there were already people in Palestine, remarked, 'Then it is an injustice.' So it was, and so it remains.

I try to avoid the mistake, which I find besets some commentators, of coming to believe that their wishes or opinions or judgements have the faintest miniscule weight in the scale pans of global decision. I cherish, however, a hope that the wonderful concept of righteousness will rise up again in world Judaism.

---

31. A Hebrew word meaning 'calamity' or 'destruction'; noted since the Middle Ages but now synonymous with the Holocaust.

# 8. *Globalization and Democracy*

## GLOBALIZATION

There is a growing worldwide movement against 'globalization', and it represents the Left, and more especially the passionate young who have commitment and love to demonstrate, as they showed in Seattle in 1999 with a series of policy questions – which I think they are handling wrongly. Talking about it presents me with the opportunity to discuss the problem itself as it exists now, and to try to draw on a lifetime of activism to write down some conclusions about what the broad Left should do.

Firstly, it is well to know what the thing itself is before you try to put an end to it. Tracing its history is no harm. When after the establishment of city states – of civilization, in fact – in Mesopotamia, the indigenous peoples of the Mediterranean coast learned to build good boats, capable of carrying heavy cargo over long distances, and later, when they learned to work iron so that not only swords but also ploughs became cheap, they started to push out their boundaries by land to harder earth than the Fertile Crescent (and, in the long run much more importantly, by sea). Globalization began. The Greeks, establishing colonies from the coast of Turkey to Sicily to the western Mediterranean, were pushing out the limits of the known world and increasing their might. The latter was the motive.

When Joseph Needham brought to the attention of Western scholarship the extraordinary technical advances of the huge Chinese merchant ships that in the early fifteenth century sailed around Cape Horn into the Atlantic, one fact really jumped off the page. It was an act of imperial policy, formulated in Peking, which brought this amazing adventure to an end. They were undefeated technically or militarily, but they decided it was prudent simply to stop. That bit of globalization ended there and then. In parenthesis, the Chinese did a similar extraordinary thing in the second half of the twentieth century, when they drastically limited family size over the whole country. Perhaps it required a centralized state to effect bureaucracy. And it caused a rupture of thousands of years of tradition and terrible individual pain. But, to my mind immensely laudably, they did it.[1] It is estimated that, as a consequence, the number of Chinese who do not now exist equals the total number of Europeans who do now exist. And that is an enormous contribution to the wellbeing not just of the Chinese themselves but of all of us on this overcrowded planet. Less can be more; small is beautiful; smaller is more beautiful. The relevance of this digression to globalization is that it is not obligatory, or inevitable, or necessary – at least not in the sense that the present acceleration of an age-old process exists – to establish free market capitalism on those parts of the globe where it does not currently exist for the benefit of the United States and its hangers-on.

One must recognize that with the development of enormous ships, telegraphs, intercontinental aircraft and above all, the recent and increasing triumphs of information technology, the age-old process is accelerating. Two questions which permit short answers arise. Can we stop it? The answer is no. Should we try to stop it? Likewise the answer is no. It is the wrong question. The task of political activism is not to reverse it, but to raise and answer the question: what *kind* of globalization do we want, and what power do we have? How can the broad world majority of people of goodwill who oppose it activate their strength? What should their policy be, to draw its fangs and to make it a movement benefiting not only the strong North (the reality for the last half-century) but also, and more so, to benefit the weak South and make it strong enough to defend itself? The old jibe

---

1. China's 'One-Child Policy' was implemented in September 1980 as a temporary measure to curb the social, economic and environmental effects of a soaring population. It allowed many exceptions, but was controversial outside China for human rights reasons, among others. As of 2016, this law is no longer in effect; the country instead has a two-child policy.

about the New England missionaries in Hawaii is true – 'They came to do good and they done right well' – but it need not always be so. There is now a very brilliant group of economists of great academic eminence who have analysed precisely the ways in which the developed world exploits the weaker South, and this gives us the basis of a precisely targeted and therefore effective countermovement.

I had the great good fortune, when I did some science in Stockholm in 1959, to meet Ava Myrdal, who was part of the Social Democratic government. That aroused my interest in her extraordinary husband (one of my Jewish heroes) Gunnar Myrdal, and I read his work. Before anyone else, I think, he pointed out in terms I've found utterly convincing that the people who benefited from aid were the First World donors. I believe, though the volumes of money being transferred southwards are enormous, it is and was always meant to be the developed world that gains. So we can work to increase the quantity and improve the quality, so that the Third World becomes strong enough to defend itself against predators.

The guilty conscience of part of the population in the developed countries contributing to Third World donations is now an enormous sum of money in annual terms, although it is gravely misspent. But the funds exist, the theoretical studies exist, and the brilliant agitation campaigns of two (I am very proud to say, Irish) pop musicians all combine to present a situation where the globalization crimes of undiluted predatory unregulated capitalism can be neutralized and defeated.

For good or ill (and up to now, it has been ill), the growing together of world peoples, cultures and economics cannot be stopped. It *can* be changed. In my opinion, that should be one of the major themes of the Left movement, which is beginning to find its courage and organization again after half a century of retreat and defeat – one of the great sources of grief in my life and the lives of those who think much the same way.

## MODES OF PROTEST

The young believe that they can do anything (I did so myself), and that you have to demonstrate a lot and demand things. I am not against demonstrating, which has value, especially if it is big, in bringing issues to public attention and in educating the demonstrators in political organization. But I think one must be very careful about demands. They must be practical and attainable. I can recall lots of occasions where demands were completely unattainable and foolishly imprecise, and that wastes time and turns people off. But there are many other forms of political work, easier now that we have the Internet. One is spreading information that the media will not touch. Another route, one I like very much and which, properly used, can wield enormous power, is what I might call 'directed consumption'. We can use our spending power for or against particular products.

The 'against' option – refusal to purchase, or more broadly, to co-operate – has an Irish name: a boycott. This was the name of a land agent in the west of Ireland during the land struggles of the late nineteenth century. Captain Boycott could find no one to tend his beasts or save his harvest. But it is an old, old technique, famous already in the classical Greek play where the solidarity and level of anger of women was great enough to impose a sexual boycott.[2] So Captain Boycott had as little to do with inventing it as the Earl of Sandwich had with inventing the sandwich. The uses of various boycotts are endless; the products of a particular country or a particular business are an example. But the uses can be wider, such as the boycott of Israeli academic institutions by those in Britain, or the very successful boycott of South African goods organized by the anti-apartheid movement of which I am very proud to have been a founder in Ireland. A much more recent and potentially very powerful movement is the boycott's opposite, the special favouring of particular products, such as the fair trade movement.

I have spent time on this issue because, after a lifetime of campaigning one way and another, I am absolutely convinced that violence is counterproductive in most cases. The quality of the 'gains' obtained by violence, as in the French or Bolshevik Revolutions or the Northern Ireland 'Troubles' is so flawed as to make them often less than worthless. Subtle police forces (and aren't they all) are perfectly capable of organizing a riot. The agent provocateur is not a new invention. And there are always disturbed people who enjoy setting cars on fire and throwing rocks through windows. But all such actions are counterproductive, disgracing the cause they purport to serve.

## POLICING AND CIVIL LIBERTIES

Sir Boyle Roche, in the pre-Act of Union parliament at College Green, famously and almost certainly apocryphally enunciated that, 'It is worth sacrificing a part or even the whole of our constitution that the rest may be preserved'. That is the situation in the whole of the Western world, now that we are in the midst of the 'War on Terror'. One civil liberty after another is being abolished or

---

2. Aristophanes' *Lysistrata* (441 BCE).

abrogated. Police and army intelligence agencies are increasing their powers and their budgets, and dissent and opposition to existing governments are not looked on as the proper exercise of democratic rights, but as 'disloyal', a word infamous since the time of the late unlamented Senator Joe McCarthy.

Armies and police are the only organs in a democratic state that may legitimately use violence. That puts an extraordinary moral burden on them to behave correctly. Often, I am both glad and proud to say that they show an almost preternatural forbearance and restraint. But not always. It is my belief that any social organism will struggle to obtain not the amount of power and money that it *needs*, but as much as it can get. I think that is normal. There is a continuously shifting dynamic equilibrium between, to be specific, the police force and the other social structures on which it impinges. But the great danger for any police force is to be tempted into brutality and violence towards prisoners and others they confront. They must walk a tightrope. All over the world, we see instances of them falling off into cruel mistreatment of those they confront. This is stupid because it is counterproductive, but it is a terribly easy trap. And if the ruling political power wants it to happen, never of course by explicit public statement, but by nods and winks, then the result is inevitable. If you don't oppose their action, you validate it. In our case it led to the 'Heavy Gang' (the name says it all) within the Gardaí, who got that nod from ministers during my time in government, and I am ashamed on that account.

I think you cannot let the genie of police violence out of the bottle and then get it back in again without enormous difficulty. Ever since, worldwide, the practice has been increasing. Just as the United States has utterly disgraced itself by the torture of prisoners, sanctioned at the very highest level, so we took a much smaller but still a very serious step on the same route. The information obtained by violence against prisoners is, the experts tell us, unreliable and of low quality. I think we contributed to that evolution of a gradual erosion of people's privacy and civil rights which we see everywhere. In my view, the end does not justify the means. You cannot do wrong to do right.

At this remove, my shame is neither here nor there. But I have just been reading the Morris Tribunal report[3] and it reveals a deterioration within the Gardaí

---

3. The Morris Tribunal (2002–2007; report issued 2008) was a public inquiry into allegations of corruption and dishonest policing among the Garda Síochána of Donegal. It took place against the backdrop of the Garda Síochána Act 2005, the most extensive reform in the force's history, which created the Garda Ombudsman Commission. Several very senior officers resigned or were dismissed on charges of negligence, harrassment, dishonesty or corruption.

which is both widespread and extremely serious. I used to be very proud of the unarmed Garda Síochana, who emerged from the awful roots of the Civil War and who in the vast majority were honourable and trustworthy people. In my four years of having ministerial drivers/bodyguards, I got to know my minders very well. They were – though all very different – intelligent, honourable, decent and interesting men, whom I could and did respect (though I sometimes felt that as well as driving me they were keeping an eye on me for another part of the Gardaí). I wish I could feel that respect and admiration for the whole force now. I cannot. And I think the rot started during my time in government.

It is precisely when people feel under threat, from real or invented terrors, that we must defend civil liberties most vigorously. So we must clean up the Gardaí and restore their honour. And it would be no harm to stop the charade of allowing significant organizations to investigate themselves. Do you expect one to believe the result of an investigation of the army or police misbehaviour by the army or police themselves? Now pull the other leg.

## THE ANTI-APARTHEID MOVEMENT

Causes dear to the heart of people on the far Left and totally to their credit, before they took on board the shame of Stalinism, were: the movement against nuclear weapons, the Campaign for Nuclear Disarmament; and the battle against the white racist regime in South Africa (supported, remember, by Margaret Thatcher as late as 1987).[4] The organization in this case was the Irish Anti-Apartheid Movement, and I was a founder member of both this and the Irish Campaign for Nuclear Disarmament.

One of the people I greatly admire was a man who came from the east coast of South Africa, from the Muslim population who had settled there as merchants and traders. I refer to Kader Asmal, who joined the staff of Trinity College Dublin in 1963.[5] Kader was an academic lawyer, who had endless energy and who seemed like a brilliant organizer. I put it in that somewhat grudging way because I was never sure how much was Kader and how much was his really wonderful wife Louise. Whatever the mix, the work got done. But even before Kader came, on a much smaller and ineffective scale, the Anti-Apartheid Movement was there and

---

4. At a 1987 press conference in Vancouver, Thatcher called the African National Congress, Mandela's party, 'a typical terrorist organization'.
5. Kader Asmal was born on 8 October 1934 in KwaZulu-Natal and died on 22 June 2011 in Cape Town.

already functioning, and we followed developments in South Africa closely. One of our heroes was the great writer Nadine Gordimer, who was later – and totally deservedly, I think – awarded a Nobel Prize.

Another remarkable anti-apartheid activist that I remember from those times was Arthur Goldreich. In South Africa he had been one of the people intimately involved in the musical *King Kong*.[6] I recall him in our house in Tallaght picking up a guitar, tuning it and entertaining us all. Subsequently he went to live in Israel. Resistance to apartheid gathered the very brightest and best of South Africa, and I think, especially against an Irish background, that the preternaturally wise and forgiving leadership of Nelson Mandela has enabled a transition to a peaceful development with reconciliation, peace and even love developing amongst hitherto bitter enemies. Would Northern Ireland unionists and nationalists please note.

The whole question of apartheid became quite a significant issue in Ireland. One particular episode I am especially proud of related to the workforce in Dunnes Stores, one of Ireland's largest supermarket chains. There was an effort at a boycott of South African goods. The selfish and the greedy and the shortsighted ignored it. But these heroines, mostly women and young people, carried out their own boycott, a refusal to handle South African produce.[7] To me, to this day, they are a beacon of hope – that on an issue of principle, ordinary humans can take a stand for justice and fairness for people half a world away, whom they never met and never would meet. The Irish Rugby Football Union marched right on to ignore the boycott on South African rugby teams playing in Ireland, but the demonstrations against the boycott-breaking became quite significant.

Of course we are all retrospectively on the side of decency and justice. Nelson Mandela is one of the most admired people in the world, and rightly so. And it is decent to forget all the people who opposed what he stood for to the bitter end. It wasn't bitter, of course. It was extraordinarily sweet and loving and forgiving and peaceful – an example to the world.

Kader and Louise Asmal went back to South Africa (for Louise a first time, I think). Kader became a minister in the new multi-racial government. We see

---

6. Goldreich designed the sets and costumes for *King Kong*, the black South African musical staged in London in 1961.

7. In July 1984 21-year-old Dunnes Stores cashier Mary Manning refused to handle a customer's South African fruit, as instructed by her union, and was suspended. Ten colleagues joined her in a strike that lasted two years and nine months, until the Irish government introduced a ban on the importation of South African produce. Mandela met and thanked them while visiting Dublin in 1990.

each other when he comes to Ireland, which he loves and visits when he can. I have very little association with my old friends in the Anti-Apartheid Movement – not because I am not interested (I love that cause), but because they don't need any outside help now. Indeed, it is a matter of us learning from them. And for me there are other issues (ecological) that have a greater call on the time I have left. But I'm proud of my participation in that particular struggle against racism.

## THE ENDING OF SECRECY

There is a relatively recent phenomenon that I think will have immense importance in the future. It is that information hitherto secret now rapidly becomes available (and indeed, appears on the Internet). A number of separate strands contribute to this ending of secrecy.

One is the existence of magnificent and physically very brave investigative reporters. The one I admire most is Robert Fisk. They do us a great service. At one time I was a fairly active member of the freelance branch of the National Union of Journalists in Dublin. We used to pass resolutions demanding what I thought proper actions about issues, on the condition that they were taking place a long way away. But after the meeting broke up, reality broke out. The cuter part of the membership (or perhaps just the ones with the most pressing mortgages) spent quite a bit of time trying to decide what policy line the owners and the editor of the paper wanted to put out. Nobody needed to censor them, or persuade them to conform. They were self-censoring.

I have a journalist friend who got very cross with me when I said that I did not believe privately owned media could be depended upon to report world news in a balanced way without having a private agenda. 'What do you want?' he said. 'Do you want state-controlled media? Do you want something like Russia?' Absolutely not; their manipulation of the news was totally impermissible, as it is to this day in very many countries. But we are not faced with a pair of simple opposites: *Le Monde* or *The Times* of London. To my mind, *Le Monde* is one of the great newspapers of the world, and it is owned by a non-profit grouping in which the journalists are strongly represented. Remembering that *The Times* is owned by Rupert Murdoch, in my mind there is simply no contest. In Ireland, the very profitable *Irish Farmers Journal* was turned into a trust by its founders in an act of extraordinary altruism.

A second strand is the general movement towards Freedom of Information Acts all over the world. The documents ultimately come out. While this is great, we must not expect too much. In any sensible government, or general staff, or directors' meetings of huge corporations (some of which are richer and more powerful than small nation states) – in any of these locations of real power, when the real business is done, it is outside the formal convening of the meeting. Before the staff come, before (hopefully) the recorders are switched on, the real decisions are made. The purpose of the formally convened, legally grand meetings is to ratify them. It is not all written down. (Indeed, the really important stuff is not written down at all.)

Thirdly, there is a new player in the media scene: the Internet. Bloggers ferret things out and make them available to the public. You can find a reasonable take on almost anything if you are computer-literate and have the time. Unfortunately, that does not include everyone. It is the *Sun* rather than the *Guardian* that the majority choose. And on TV, they feel comfortable with the familiar face of a newsreader. Most people don't want to be bothered. They just want to get on with their lives, but if you really want to find out, these days you can. I think this ending of secrecy has great political implications for the future.

There is a final reason: a very prominent person gets more from a successful book than they did from a lifetime of an even substantial salary. And there is a huge human desire (witness this book) to boast a bit and to blurt out.

## DEMOCRACY BY DEGREES

Like motherhood and apple pie, everyone seems to be in favour of democracy. But unlike motherhood and apple pie, nobody seems to be quite clear what it means. There is a sort of unwritten equation: democracy is good; we are good; therefore what we have is democracy.

It was clearer what it meant in ancient Greece, where the term comes from. 'Demos' is 'the people', and the '-cracy' part means 'rule' – aristocracy, kleptocracy, etc. Who were the 'demos'? Not everybody. Not, for example, women – half the population. Not slaves. Not strangers. Just the free males born into a particular city-state. Some Greek cities never had it. Some alternated. But it was a long, long way from 'people power'. It is given a certain patina of virtue by the wonders achieved by Athens before its decline, though my *bête noire* Plato was on the side of the tyrants (their word).[8] And then for thousands of years it went underground,

---

8. The word '*tyrannos*' is of pre-Greek origin. Early uses of the term carried no pejorative connotations, but referred simply to one who had gained executive power in a *polis* by unconventional means.

though one of the great contributions of Jewish culture and religion is that it was anti-monarchist.

The Church of Rome makes no pretence, and never has, of being a democratic organization. Kings were by definition anti-democratic. Stirrings came with the Reformation. Presbyterianism is an admirably democratic Church. Tom Paine and the French encyclopaedists argued for people's rule. In 1776 the United States achieved one of the truest and best democracies ever attained. The New England village meeting was a high point. However, the rights and freedoms never extended to the indigenous peoples, who were being murdered by such simple expedients as giving germ-infected clothes to people who had no natural resistance to diseases of which we, the whites, had long evolutionary experience. And of course, once they came to be imported into slavery, it did not extend to people who were not 'free'. So it was once again partial. And in my view, its quality has declined even further. George W. Bush, for whom the congruity of words and deeds was a coincidence, prattled about democracy while he was at the core of a political dynasty that had maintained a cohort of loathsome dictators in their client states all over the world. So, George W. Bush's democracy is not mine.

The great high tide was the French Revolution, slightly later and much more profound than the American Revolution. Of course, it ended in tears. Revolutions have a way of betraying their best instincts. The French Revolution ended with the dictator emperor Napoleon. And for a century, with odd outbursts in 1848 and 1870, it was ruled by a series of more and more comic-opera leaders. Similarly, in Russia, Stalin betrayed all that was noble and beautiful (and there was a great deal) in Communism. How quickly 'Soviet man' reverted to greedy peasant or capitalist when he got the chance! And yet the high tide of revolution leaves a watermark that subsequent betrayals can never quite erase. That wonderful slogan 'Liberty, Equality, Fraternity' has echoed down the centuries as an inspiration to those who have sought a freer and more just society.

One of the greatest moments in Irish history was when Michael Davitt, in prison, decided that democratic institutions in the United Kingdom had advanced far enough to provide a better means of struggle than guns and bombs, and that violence was obsolete. But what sort of democracy was it? Pitifully inadequate, but improving. While there was a House of Commons of considerable antiquity, seats were bought and sold, rotten boroughs abounded, and, as Irish records show, elections in the early nineteenth century were an excuse for a piss-up.

The battle between the corn-growing rural landowners, who wanted dear wheat, and the new industrial bourgeoisie of Manchester and Birmingham, who wanted cheap corn, deepened democracy and weakened the traditional aristoc-racy. And then the working class came on the scene. They succeeded in widening the franchise. They succeeded in having MPs who began to be 'tribunes of the people' and not sycophantic smokescreens, pretending that a degree of democ-racy existed which in reality did not. It took the heroic and highly organized struggles of the suffragists to get votes for women, achieved only well into the last century.[9]

There is a moment in Lampedusa's wonderful novel *The Leopard* when Tancredi, the young supporter of unification, says, 'If we want things to stay as they are, then things will have to change.' Perfectly naturally for them, the posses-sors of wealth and power down the ages have fought brilliant rearguard actions, changing in order to remain the same.

## POWER LIES ELSEWHERE

Parliaments have always had two aspects: one genuinely about power, especially in crises, when the king needed money and material; the other was a beautiful, often ornate, quite expensive and pretentious charade. You, the Others, may play at parliaments, and we will give you an historic building of great prestige and excel-lent food and wine and (during the last century) city-centre parking and offices and money and expenses and kudos, but we will keep the power, thank you very much. Go on talking. The story told to children (and grown-up children) about government, parliament and parliamentary government is a ruling-class myth. Power, quite obviously, lies elsewhere.

I have been a member of the Irish Dáil and Senate, of the European Parliament and of the Council of Ministers of the European Union, so I have some direct experience whereof I speak. Well aware as I am that other parliamentarians expe-rience the whole parliamentary process quite differently, my duty here is to tell it my way.

About the Irish Senate, I can be quite brief: I believe in single-chamber parlia-ments. My belief is that it should be abolished. Note what I am *not* saying. I am *not* saying, 'The whole thing is a sham, get rid of it.' Because of the two aspects I spoke of, I passionately believe in keeping parliaments. But there are condi-tions. These are that the whole progressive movement (whatever its changing

9. The right of women to vote on the same terms as men was established in Britain as a result of the Representation of the People Act 1928. An earlier Act (1918) had granted the vote to some, but with restrictions. Equal suffrage was granted in Ireland in 1922, upon independence.

components in organizational terms) devotes itself to the struggle to extend the real power, and eliminate the bogus.

Who are the opponents in this struggle? One single phrase sums up the different constituents: unregulated free markets, which encompass the great global companies in whatever sector, the financial institutions, complacent governments and cynical general staff who have forgotten their allegiance and their oath to serve the people.

They have built a panoply of theoretician hangers-on in universities and research institutes, who in pursuit of generous funding will churn out books proving that greed is good, that humankind is fundamentally hierarchical, that everybody is better off if market regulation of all kinds is diminished, and that the poor and middle sectors of wage and salary earners are better off if a larger slice of necessary taxation is loaded onto them as income and purchase taxes, and less is put onto industry and finance. Stated baldly like this, one is tempted to quote the Duke of Wellington in saying, 'If you would believe that, you would believe anything.' And yet, until the present crisis, such has been the persuasive power of subtly biased privately owned media.

Various market economy countries profess themselves to be worried. I believe the Australians have experimented with paying a small bonus to people who vote. In national elections, polls are small. George W. Bush was elected to do the awful things he did by less than half the votes of a turnout of less than 50 per cent of the electorate; a minority of a minority. The European Parliament is scrutinizing and beginning to wield some power over the Commission, and even over the Council of Ministers (whose decisions have the power of law over the whole EU and have become much more important to us than what goes on in our national parliament). However, direct elections to the European Parliament are treated with distinct disdain by the electorate.

The public distrust is not misplaced. The institutions of the European Union are freer than those of the nation states, where the power elite have had much longer to set up their control systems, and the networking starts in select schools. But I have first-hand experience of the extent of lobbying in Brussels. I believe there are more lobbyists than Eurocrats, and they have what would be – to the ordinary wage earner – enormous budgets. They have analysed Commission personnel in great detail and know intimately who is who. And it is the Commission that does the drafting. The permanent representative from each national jurisdiction is a career public servant, largely unknown, who, via CoReper, the Committee of Permanent Representatives (an immensely powerful structure), becomes an enormously powerful person.[10] But to the ordinary consumer of media reports, this is not news. And though a great deal of information about the structure and actions of the Community's institutions is available, the person in the street has a strong feeling that they are being kept in the dark.

So how do you have democracy in circumstances where the great companies have enormous PR budgets, where the media are privately owned, where bribery of both politicians and executives with decision-making powers is widespread on every continent? It is just about possible, in a partial way, but I think it is important to recognize *how* partial it is, how much of what is called by the name of 'democracy' is in fact a smokescreen and a charade.

Reform of a very complex, rapidly developed and unwieldy institution is very difficult. It is like building a block of flats while the tenants are in residence. Difficult, but necessary. The Treaty of Lisbon, rejected by the Irish in the referendum of 2008 in foolish pique and a desire to punish the sitting government, is imperfect. Of course it is; in the circumstances, how could it not be? But it is a distinct improvement. In mitigation of the electorate's action in shooting itself in the foot, I would add that, with its eye fixed on a totally different ball, the feebleness and foolishness of the government's campaign surpassed belief. But the point I am labouring is that electorates have an instinct that the power is elsewhere, and that the democracy they experience is a bit of a sham. And in this, in my view, they are right.

## DEMOCRACY IS A SKILL

Radicals on the Left sometimes make comprehensive and detailed demands for fundamental reforms, and then sulk because an uncomprehending progressive movement will not give them what they want. I used to do it myself. But now I believe in small, attainable steps. Real gains are slow and difficult, not the least bit dramatic. One grinds away for the broad aims of liberty, equality, fraternity and – I now add – autonomy. One seeks fairness in the social system, and redistribution. One seeks fairness in regard to the Third World, which is still the victim of imperialism (and yes, I use that word; it still exists). Small gains, against the obvious enemies – but relentless.

What we have now is vastly better than the democracy of 150 years ago. And the advances were obtained by political struggle.

10. From the French *Comité des représentants permanents*, the Committee of Permanent Representatives in the European Union is made up of the head or deputy head of mission from each EU member state and sits in Brussels.

So, democracy is not just about parliaments. It should extend to all aspects of society. Like what, apart from business enterprises? Well, schools and universities would be a good start. The influence of Roman Catholicism on the major social structures is very powerful in Ireland. And the Church is not democratic. In Irish management there is a lot of what has been contemptuously called 'the bicycle position' (a racing bike, that is): you lick the arse above and trample on the face below. But social scientists have shown that the less steep the slope of management hierarchy, the better the result. The small, less unequal management grouping seems to work best. And if we look even at primate social structures among, say, the bonobo, this will be no surprise.

It is forty years since I attended, as a fraternal delegate, an annual conference of the Swedish Social Democratic party. The theme was *jämlikhet* – worker participation in management. In present-day Germany, the Works Council is a powerful organ. It has not made management impotent, nor destroyed competitiveness or quality. On the contrary, workers identify more with the enterprise. And the quality and profitability of the German motor industry (for example) is rather better than its US rival. A BMW or a Chrysler? The participation of workers ensures that the bottom line is not the only criterion of success. It diminishes the enormous disparity between the best-paid and the worst-paid that is so corrosive of morale in society. And workers who have very little personal wealth are even more anxious to avoid unemployment than management, who often have plenty of personal wealth. In locations where social morale is high and there are strong community ties, like the Scandinavian countries and Germany, worker participation has been proved to be beneficial for the whole enterprise.

I was in Denmark at the time of the Paris 'events' of 1968. Everyone remarked on how quiescent the erstwhile turbulent Danish students seemed to be. They had not lost their militancy, but the enlightened university rector Mogens Fog had pushed through many of the reforms in pursuit of which the Paris students were demonstrating. There are powerful arguments for the same sort of approach in secondary schools, in a way that was practised by the great educational reformer A.S. Neill at Summerhill School since the early 1920s.

And what about other social structures? Health, social welfare, care of the aged, the running of financial institutions? If one insisted on moving gently along an extended learning curve, one would benefit from more democratic management. (An interjection: everywhere the reader meets what appears to be a dogmatic statement, read: 'in my opinion'. It gets boring repeating it all the time.) And even – breathe it not – would the armies of the world be quite so brutal, wasteful and determined to make the junior soldiers into mindless automatons, if there was some participation by those very junior soldiers?

Democracy is a skill. It has to be won, and it has to be practised to be understood. Total equality may be impossible. And it is only one half of our evolved social paradigm; part hierarchical/authoritarian and part egalitarian and co-operative. But I am convinced: i) that the bit we have is good; ii) that we need more; iii) that we should look at what currently exists, warts and all, and; iv) that the people, the 'demos', will only get what they win by struggle. The hierarchies are not going to give it to them.

# On the Future of the Left

## THE SHADOW ON SOCIAL DEMOCRACY

The collapse of the Communist ideal in the hands of Stalin and his henchmen sullied and undermined the whole idea of socialism. It was all very fine for ex-Communists like me and all the other Social Democrats, from Trotskyists to Fabians, to say 'not us'. The idea that you could build an economy to be more equal, just as people-centred and not based on the 'free market' took a terrible blow, and for decades social democracy drifted along with charming opportunists like Bettino Craxi and Tony Blair and obscene betrayers like Ehud Barak of the Israeli Labour Party, who is happy to go into coalition with Avigdor Lieberman. I say 'charming' because without that quality, they could not have imposed themselves on an electorate. Blair has a bit less of the blood of Iraq on his hands than do Bush and Cheney. But it is still a great deal. Social democracy is not as shamed and disgraced and discredited as Stalinism, but it has lost a lot of its reputation for caring decency. Stalinism, I think, is destroyed (and a good thing too, I would add) but social democracy can be saved and rehabilitated.

The big event that has ushered in the possibility and the necessity of doing so is the collapse of the US model of the free market. When Alan Greenspan can say, 'I was wrong'[11] (and it takes immense moral stature to do it), then all the rest of the world can say, 'Thank you for saying it, and yes, you were.' All very fine and large. But politics, however awful the past, is always about the question, 'What do we do *now?*' The emphasis is on immediacy and action. What one tries to do must always be practical and possible, and must relate with such power and immediacy to the real problems of real people that they will support it. Utopia is not a practical alternative.

And now comes the hard bit: I wanted to try to identify what are the hurts and pains and doubts (and hopes) that preoccupy ordinary people in their everyday

---

11. 'Greenspan Concedes Error on Regulation': *The New York Times,* 23 October 2008.

lives. My answer is two, which are bound up together so that you cannot solve one without facing up to both.

The first issue revolves around words like equality, respect, self-esteem, dignity – and an economy well enough managed to ensure these things, in a world where more and more people are gobbling up more and more of the world's finite and rapidly depleting resources. And remember, it is all very fine for us to achieve a higher standard of living and a much higher quality of life. We can and must do those things. But it is simply not workable to say, for example, to the great mass of the people of India, soon to be the most populous country in the world, 'Sorry, friends, you came on the scene too late, you must not aspire to the sort of standard of living you see on your TV screens, which currently exists in the West.' They *can* so aspire. More and more of them do. And they won't be stopped by an increasingly feeble West.

So the two great questions that I see are: 'How do we provide much greater equality, in every aspect of life, with all the moral and social implications that that brings, to the great majority of the world's population?' And simultaneously, 'How do we manage the environmental crisis, energy, global warming, ecological degradation and all the issues that come under the "Green" umbrella?' (In passing, I believe that Ireland's Green Party is correctly recognizing the centrality of one of my two main questions. I just allow myself to wish that they were more effective and less opportunistic in the pursuit of those objectives. But I cannot find it in my heart to be very condemnatory.) In my book, the Green issue is half the broader 'progressive' issue. Greens and Social Democrats are natural allies. If the Social Democrats had been a little more at the cutting edge in analysing real problems, they would not have evolved separately from and frequently in conflict with the Greens. I think, speaking as a Social Democrat, it is our fault more than theirs. But the past is unreachable, and 'fault' is not very important. I think myself as 'Green' as any of them and I will always work with them.

The socialist pioneers advocated the brotherhood of man, love, trust, equality, justice and the recognition of the dignity of every person. They did it out of the long human tradition of trying to do as much good and as little harm as possible. They did it because in the struggle between hierarchical states, power-asserting humankind and loving co-operating humankind, they took the latter viewpoint. It was a moral stand, on what were almost intuitive grounds, about the possibilities for human goodness; noble in intention. But what we have missed until very recently are the cumulative lessons of more than a century of careful sociological research. Now we are in a position to know what is good and what is bad for human society.

A word about knowing – a humanist scientist like me does not ever 'know' in the way of a person who bases their belief on revelation and faith. On a scale of 0 to 10, a fundamentalist would claim to 'know' with certainty, at 10 on the scale. I don't know anything in that way. At the very outside 9½, perhaps, when the double blind measurements are very well designed and irreproachably carried out; no 10s. But recent evidence gives me reason to believe, with 6½, 7, 8 or 9 degrees of certainty, that a particular set of social arrangements are better than what we currently have. For those who want to have a look at this evidence, they will find in the bibliography a remarkable assembly of each in a wonderful book called *The Spirit Level* by Richard Wilkinson and Kate Pickett.


## THE FREE MARKET

The last quarter-century has seen the triumphant march of the free market. Bogus ideologists go back to Adam Smith, but they might take the elementary precaution of reading him; not just *The Wealth of Nations*, but *The Theory of Moral Sentiments*. A market untrammelled by social responsibility, answerable only to the all-justifying 'bottom line' ('my first responsibility is to my share-holders'), was utterly triumphant – even, God help us, in the ranks of New Labour. For 'New', substitute 'Ex-'. And Fukuyama could announce 'the end of history'.[12]

Let me include a relevant anecdote. When I became 'the Min', Ireland had a substantial footwear industry. Lots of cattle, lots of hide, lots of able tanners, lots of good leather, lots of good shoes and shoe factories. But they were on a small scale, they were cutting each other's throats, their designs were out of date, there was no product development, and people like the North Africans, before the Chinese and other Southeast Asians, were coming. Would they like, I asked them when I invited them to come and talk to me, to set about amalgamation, cost-cutting, hiring designers, going upmarket as far as a really good designer could take them? We would switch on the best support of the IDA, the export board, and we would find some special money for them, but on condition ... It was nice to see the Minister's office, and to see what he looked like close to, but they did not even need to go away to discuss that; they knew the answer instantly. Thank you, Minister, but no thank you. None of them survives today.

---

12. Francis Fukuyama, political scientist/economist and neoconservative. 'The End of History and the Last Man' (1992). Essay first published in 1989.

The reason for this digression is to show that people's conception of their own interest is extremely unreliable. The great polymath and mathematician von Neumann (educated in Hungary and an anti-fascist refugee; Hitler's loss and America's gain) has shown that it is in the short-term interest of fishermen who have invested in the trawlers and the shore facilities to harvest the resource (fish) until there are none left. This has happened to the greatest fishery known to the medieval world, Northern Cod in Newfoundland, and to the North Sea.

I have used the words 'short-term'. What is short-term or long-term? Harold Wilson famously said, 'A week is a long time in politics.' In my experience of Irish politics, a month is short-term, but anything over a year is long-term. There is a saying that the public memory is one hundred days. But at the other end of the spectrum is the possibly apocryphal story that when a West German journalist asked Zhou Enlai, the Mandarin-trained number two to Mao Zedong, 'What do you think about the French Revolution?', he replied, 'It is a bit soon to tell.'

As I write, the world is going through what looks like the greatest economic upheaval since 1929. The future is quite unclear. But certain lessons can be drawn and – if we are seriously trying to work towards a deep democracy – are worth articulating. Most of the pundits are pompous bloody fools, but they have conned society into giving them titles like 'Professor', or, much more importantly, into giving them cathedrals or banks, grovelling servitors, the best transportation to meet their colleagues, the best dining rooms with the best cellars ('best' in all of these contexts meaning 'most expensive', because they are so ignorant that the price list is their only guide). In the longer term, their salaries are not just obscene multiples of what ordinary people earn, but they guarantee themselves the same kind of pensions. And they have been shown in the last year or so to be not just dangerously ignorant and incompetent, but utterly cowardly in a crisis. You spend your life denouncing any control or even overview of the magic free market, and when the crisis that you made finally strikes, you come without shame or resignations or apologies with your begging bowl saying, 'Please, tax-paying citizens, save us. Bail us out. We were wrong all along. We don't believe in the unfettered market any more. Save us (and, in passing, please leave our palaces and perks and pensions intact).' At the moment our world seems willing, *faute de pire*.[13] The British are proposing a scheme that, if adopted by everyone, will stop the rot but not tackle the basic ill. Gordon Brown is the hero of Nobel laureate economist Paul Krugman.[14]

13. Translation: 'for want of better'.
14. Krugman was awarded the Nobel Memorial Prize for Economic Science in 2008. The Royal Swedish Academy of Sciences deemed him to have 'integrated the previously disparate research

So, nearly two decades since the Berlin Wall came down and Stalinism collapsed, over a quarter-century since Margaret Thatcher sank the *Belgrano* and the social market of controlled capitalism, the Left, shamed by Stalin, can begin to raise its head, can begin to think forward, can begin to say, 'Our passion for equality was not wrong. Greed is not good. The free market undermines not just honour and decency and the possibility of redistributing the world's vast wealth, it undermines in its passion for growth the future of the ecosphere and therefore the future of humankind which has evolved in that delicate ecosphere.'

## AN EMPIRE IN DECLINE

Very recently the German finance minister[15] (there is currently a coalition of CDU and SPD)[16] said that an era had ended and that US economic hegemony was over. I remember a time when if an American power person farted, his German counterpart trembled. Not any more. More and more, people around the world are ceasing to tremble. They are speaking out against an appalling record, which stretches back beyond Vietnam to the propping up of obscene dictators like the Shah of Iran or (yes, check it) Saddam Hussein. Empires in decline are characterized by stupidity. The United States keeps shooting itself in the foot (witness the bombing of Pakistan), but we are all still so polite, even when US financial institutions are being bailed out by the Chinese, and the dollar is being kept up by those same nasty yellow men because they hold so many of them. European social democracy must find the courage to become much more stridently and explicitly anti-American. Tony Blair, who was never quite sure if Britain belonged in Europe or in the mid-Atlantic as an ally of the US, is gone. There is no need to stay committed to the war in Iraq or in Afghanistan – or, in Ireland's case, to stay silent when Shannon airport is used by the US to transport prisoners to places where they can be tortured without anyone knowing. Currently we are complicit, and the Left says nothing.

Why I say this: it is a mistake to think of the United States as homogenous. It contains huge complexity, or, if you allow me, huge contradictions. Many of

---

fields of international trade and economic geography.' The previous day's *New York Times* column by Krugman claimed that Brown's bailout plan for the British banks had saved the world financial system, saying, 'This combination of clarity and decisiveness hasn't been matched by any other Western government.'

15. This notebook is dated October 2008; the German Finance Minister was Peer Steinbrück.

16. Christlich-Demokratische Union (CDU); Sozialdemokratische Partei Deutschlands (SPD).

the people I admire most in recent decades have been American. There is a black culture growing in depth and in self-confidence. There is an Hispanic culture with great historical roots in Europe as well as in South and Central America; there is a growing Islamic lobby, gaining in strength and organization as a counterbalance to the vastly powerful Zionist lobby, which is worthy of careful study by other groups with similar aspirations. There are wonderful creative people in all the arts. In individual terms, I see marvellous research in things like cognitive studies and the whole range of scientific know-how. Individually, the person I think I admire most in the world is Noam Chomsky. One could go on.

The point is that the present Bush administration[17] is in some ways an aberration. The election was doubtful in its legality. The terrible disaster of Iraq was not just a catastrophe for that country, but for America too. The rise of Barack Obama, unthinkable a few decades ago, is partly in response to an incompetent administration topped by a man who was clearly not the whole shilling. What is most striking about the US in the Near and Middle East is its sheer incompetence and stupidity. They are handing huge victories to Islamic fundamentalism – greater, I think, than Osama bin Laden could have dreamed or wished – by using aircraft indiscriminately against civilian populations. And they have now done this across natural boundaries, into the territory of a nuclear power that is an ally: Pakistan. That country is now destabilized. The US protégé Mubarak is no longer competent. His successors are trying to rule a divided country that is, with every US bomb, being delivered to the fundamentalists. The threat to all of us was not the non-existent Iraqi weapons of mass destruction, but the very much existent Pakistani weapons of mass destruction. And the mess, world-threatening as it is, was made by US foreign policy.

So the US, now rapidly declining in every aspect of human activity, from economic practice to basic science, remains, and will for a while remain, the most powerful country in the world. And her very soul (if a humanist may use that form of words) is being fought over at the moment. It is no help to the US Left (there is one, and very brave they are) for the European pseudo-Left to support what Bush gets up to. What the Left needs to say courageously to America is like this, it seems to me: 'Yes, we love you and respect you and admire you, and yes we hate you and despise you and condemn you.' There is more than one United States. The struggle within is getting sharper. We should be supporting our side, and hindering the fundamentalists in every possible way.

17. This segment was written during the second term of George W. Bush's presidency (January 2004–January 2009).

## TOWARDS A DEEP DEMOCRACY

What should socialists do now in the circumstances? The public is slow to learn, to see the new and the old, the valuable and the worthless. We should keep up a continuous criticism of what the world got up to in the period since the first oil shock – the Right, but also the Left. The people are not quick to rework their paradigm, but they are not stupid. So we must keep pounding.

The socialist movement has been shamed because it has not wholeheartedly adopted a Green agenda. Green parties worldwide have very properly gained a significant part of the voters' support. Where they are right, we must support them. But they have certain difficulties. The best and most sensitive of the bourgeoisie support them. But in the longer run, the great polluter is the uncontrolled market. In the end, Green = Left. And the efforts by the Greens to avoid this conflict must be opposed and explained to them.

We see the rise, everywhere in Europe – and this will become more intense as the depression hits – of chauvinist anti-immigrant feelings, and these are very easily turned to racism. So we have to have the courage, even when this is not popular, to oppose with all our strength the chauvinist populism of neo-fascist Europe. We have to work on the immigrants, organize them to be part of the oppressed in a world where the right to move in search of work must be defended. Likewise, we must have the courage to oppose isolationism and protectionism in trade. These originate not just in the neo-fascist Right but also in the unthinking, unlearning, unreconstructed old Left, who do recognize that globalization cannot be reversed, that nationalism has no future except a destructive one, and that the thought that small nation states can re-establish their autonomy and their choice in matters of investment is a recipe for economic disaster followed by state repression.

The Left should have the courage to take on the professions that enjoy monopoly status. It should, in my view, embrace a deep and thorough separation of Church and State, and struggle to exclude from the educational system those religious forces that often dominate it still (as in Ireland). The same is true of the religious position in healthcare. And the law is much too expensive, complex and unreformed to make it accessible equally to everyone.

Doctors in Ireland are writing themselves vastly expensive meal tickets in return for delivering a really rotten service. I have been hospitalized in France as well as Ireland; there is no comparison. In the former the level of expertise, the equipment and the quality of the treatment are much better than in Ireland. But the personal human quality of Irish nurses is much better than in France.

With the various births and illnesses in my family (and remember, I am a great-grandfather), I have found Irish nurses wonderful, trying to carry out their calling with love and care in a system that is practically unworkable. In rural Ireland local hospitals are defended fiercely, but small units with a small throughput can never be as good as big ones. What the people of the small town are failing to see is that getting to hospital is now more rapid than when it depended on the speed of a horse. Now, with mobile phones, motor ambulances on good roads and even, in extreme need, helicopters, the distance to hospital in a little country like Ireland is almost irrelevant. This is a situation where small is not beautiful, and I feel that the 'defend our local hospital' demonstrators are acting against their own interest. But I don't expect the protests to stop. And the formula of allowing private hospitals on the grounds of public hospitals is a guarantee of two levels of health service, one for the rich and one for the poor.

## THE LEFT AND THE LAND

I think, too, that the Left must face the question of the countryside. Some of this book (a small part) was written in Languedoc. This is an area that I first got to know more than forty years ago, and that I love. In the 1960s, the countryside was red. They voted Communist. In recent elections, the neo-fascist Le Pen has one of the largest slices of support in the whole of France. In discussing the Common Agricultural Policy, nobody examines the situation in which it was first dreamed up, in the years after the war. The Communists in Europe had a 'good' war. They stood where their betters ran away. They established an effective underground guerrilla structure. They fought and died. They gave hope and honour to countries that had been defeated and occupied. They gave France something to counterpose to the pathetic Vichy regime. So they came out of the war with a great deal of political support. The US was extremely frightened of Italy going red at the time of the 1948 election. 'Send some US gunboats' still worked.[18]

---

18. Truman had ordered a battleship to the eastern Mediterranean and a destroyer to the Neapolitan coast in 1946. In 1948 the CIA covertly interfered in the elections, sending ten million letters, making numerous shortwave radio broadcasts and funding publications warning Italians of the supposed consequences of a Communist victory. '"We had bags of money that we delivered to selected politicians, to defray their political expenses, their campaign expenses, for posters, for pamphlets," ex-CIA agent F. Mark Wyatt said … The practice of buying political clout was repeated in every Italian election for the next 24 years.' (*New York Times*, July 6 2006).

What all of those intent on saving Europe from Communism dreaded was the joining together of a red working class with a red peasantry. (For the record, I am very glad, though I thought the opposite at the time, that time was gained and the worker/peasant alliance never materialized.) The Communists of Western Europe did not yet believe in the Stalinist betrayal, and the result of a Communist victory at the polls would have been disastrous. So what to do? The wise old fathers of the European Union knew the answer: buy off the peasants. It worked, at the cost of enormous mountains of surplus produce, enormous claims on the European purse (ultimately paid for by the consumer) and a huge disruption of world trade in agricultural produce, to the disadvantage of the Third World and the poorest people in it. It was the 'right thing to do' in the sixties and seventies when the European Union got going and while the peasants of Europe were given decades to disappear.

All that is in the past. The question now, for all those living in the fool's paradise of European small and medium farming, is this. Do you think – in the context of the world recession, where European industry is threatened on the basis of high costs, where for working people food is still a very significant part of the total living costs – do you think that the CAP will continue in its present form, with highest subsidies for inefficient production? The Doha Round[19] is currently stalled, as I write. The rural vote is given short-term reassurance. Yes. But on the balance of forces, do you think the present situation can continue?

In Ireland we are the producers of bulk commodities, medium-quality meat and milk of less than medium quality, and we assume that we have the right to have a market for them forever. I think that the forces against this policy are too great. In the UK, agriculture is 6 per cent of the economy, as against 3 per cent half a century ago. In Ireland, when I was appointed Head of Agricultural Broadcasting there were 250,000 farm enterprises; now there are roughly 140,000. When you lose numbers and economic significance, you lose clout.

I think Irish agriculture needs a totally new agenda – green, local, upmarket, organic, combined with an integrated policy for the countryside. If you think that all this is anti-countryside or anti-farming, I can only answer that in my life I have chosen to farm. I had choice and I have exercised it. I have chosen to live in a village, or, if you include France, two villages. I don't like cities. I want to see the countryside live. I want to see villages and small communities live. But if they don't change, they won't. The Left should find the courage to say this, and to provide an integrated rural policy stretching all the way from energy to tourism.

19. The Doha Round is the current trade-negotiation round of the World Trade Organization. Its objective is to lower trade barriers around the world and thus facilitate increased global trade.

## EUROPE'S EXPANSION AND FUTURE

So what about the future in Europe for the now revalidated and rehabilitated broad Left movement? What about the European Union and the future of the whole crop of small nation states that have come into existence even in the last few decades (the former Yugoslavia and the former Soviet Union)?

I opposed entry into Europe in the first vote on the question, which in Ireland took place in 1972. It was a learning curve, and to a degree I was saved from thinking hard about my beliefs on Europe because I was certain, even when the 'Yes' lobby began to have doubts, that we would be heavily defeated. I inherited a Labour Party policy, I felt that certain aspects of our negotiations had been badly handled (fisheries, an industry in which I have always had a strong personal interest, is an example), and I knew that the cute old founding fathers of Europe had been moving the enterprise along in small steps, trying to avoid frightening the population by a resolute unwillingness to discuss long-term policy, pretending that it was just a trading bloc. In hindsight, the effort to open the debate was justified, and the failure of the institutions to do so in frank terms planted a distrust that is now having destructive effects (witness Ireland's foolish 'No' to the Lisbon Treaty).

How big is Europe, and where are its boundaries? The answer is not simple. There are lots of 'yes, but –' responses to relevant questions. Is Russia in Europe? Yes, though really it is an Asian power too. The statement that Europe ends at the Urals is true, but it is a boundary within a single state, Russia. What about Islam? Resurgent Islamic armies conquered the Christian city of Constantinople (now Istanbul) in 1453. The extent to which the Near East used to be Christian before the rise of Islam certainly was a surprise to me when I came to check it out. And the wonderful, beautiful, civilized El Andaluz was a Muslim land in southern Spain before its extinction at the hands of Ferdinand and Isabella. If Christian enclaves existed on the southern shore of the Mediterranean, which they did, similar Islamic enclaves existed on the northern shore of the Mediterranean. And the armies of Islam were stopped by Christian forces at the gates of Vienna in 1683. There are to this day major Islamic communities in Albania, but also throughout the Balkans. Five miles towards the sea from the village where I write this in the Languedoc is the Tour Sarrasin (now an excellent restaurant). In brief, the Mediterranean is not a simple boundary – Christian to the north, Muslim to the south. Europe, in the fewest possible words, is partly Muslim. And this relates to the future.

The question that Europe must answer now is: 'Do we want Turkey on the inside or the outside?' In this regard I have a relevant personal memory. At a particular moment in my time in government, Garret FitzGerald said to me, 'It is the Irish Presidency. Someone from Ireland needs to go to Turkey to sign the association agreement. Would you like to go?' At that point of my life I would go anywhere at the drop of a hat. Off I went. In Ankara, at lunch, I was sitting beside a Turkish minister (I think it was Foreign Affairs). After the small talk, he said to me, 'I'm not a politician. I used to be a university professor/diplomat/economist' – I don't remember. But I remember the next sentence: 'They made me a minister.' At an evening meal in my short stay I was sitting beside someone who I think was the Premier. I heard a remarkably similar sentence: 'I'm not a politician. I was a university professor/diplomat/economist, but they made me Prime Minister.' Who was this mysterious, all-powerful 'they' who could do all these things? It was the army. There was a façade of democratic government when the heirs to Kemal Atatürk ran the country. The important point is that in a world of Islamic resurgence Atatürk was a secular leader who kept the religious establishment at bay. Turkey is a huge country, 72 million people,[20] with a great history, the remnants of a brilliant bureaucracy (left over from the Ottoman Empire) and a great culture. I know that their democracy is far from perfect – which democracy is? But I think that even when it expresses itself as the Muslim Brotherhood Party keeping the army at bay, it is still progressing.

Crucial for the future not just of Turkey, but of the EU and the world, is our answer to the question 'Turkey: in or out?' It is on the threshold, if we support its entry, of progressing into a modern market economy state, with a strong middle class, with the developing separation of Church and State, and of the rule of law. It is on the way to becoming a modern nation state, the ideological basis Islamic rather than Christian, but struggling towards the flowering of its nationhood before accepting that diminution of national sovereignty, which is inescapable in a developing European Union. The alternative for us, 'Christian Europe', is to drive them back into the arms of the fundamentalists. I have no doubt as to which solution I want, and which is best for Europe. I want the Turks in, within a reasonable space of time, and on welcoming conditions. I think those in Europe (the French, for example) who seek to prevent Turkish membership on any reasonable kind of timescale are acting against the interests of all of us.

---

20. The Turkish Statistical Institute reckoned its total population at 72.5 million in 2009 (77.7 million in 2014).

All of this raises the question of how Europe is to be managed and run. How many members can you accommodate? When I encountered the beast first, it had six members: the core of Germany and France, Benelux (which four decades ago was already moving towards being a single entity) and the lame corrupt hangdog of the EEC, Italy, stuck on in the south. On January 1 1973, that six became nine with the addition of Denmark, the UK and Ireland. The institutions elaborated to cope with six countries were able, fairly painlessly, to accommodate three more. Fine. But now we are twenty-seven, with a few more standing in the wings.[21] The present structure simply will not do. Nor will the situation where one inward-looking petulant greedy member (guess who?) can block development.

## CONTINUOUS REVOLUTION

I am a believer in continuous revolution. Just as I expressed the belief elsewhere that each individual must, for as long as they draw breath, keep demolishing and rebuilding their paradigm, I think that a world changing at a much greater pace than ever before will find its institutions obsolescent almost before they are consolidated. So we must have continuous revolution in our institutions. Such changes do not proceed in a linear way. We have a long period of relative stagnation, and then, often in response to a crisis like the present one, things flip; change, in the face of a response to challenge, becomes possible.

This is a long lead-up to saying that I am not just pro-Europe, I am a passionate federalist. I want the central institution of the Community to be big enough, strong and coherent enough to speak for all of us in circumstances where the nation state is now seen to be pathetically impotent. (Rhetorical question – how do you think that four million people standing tall and proud on their national identity would cope with the present economic crisis?) Globalization, for good or ill, and that depends on what we make of it, is far advanced and irreversible. We need a larger entity, a federal Europe. From culture, art, pop music and cuisine to the management of research and development and the promotion of our part in world trade and for selective profitable investment, I want it. I welcome it. We need it. Alas, they are now in the centre of Europe, angry with Ireland for what I believe are good reasons. They have limitless, understated, often subtle ways of

---

21. In addition, Croatia has joined the EU since the time of writing, making a total of twenty-eight members. Several other states are formally acknowledged candidates: Albania, Iceland, Macedonia, Montenegro, Serbia and Turkey.

saving us and punishing us for our shortsighted selfishness. I hope it does not come to that. They are quite entitled to establish a two-tier Europe, with us in the slow lane. And if we want to exclude ourselves completely, or without intending it proceed with a line of policy which ends in our exclusion, *tant pis.*[22] So much the worse. They can live without us. Can we live at anything near the standard to which we have become accustomed without them?

---

22. Translated: 'too bad!'

# 9. Loves, Loss and Leavetaking

I have been really, deeply and totally in love four and a half times in my life. I reckon that is a lot and I have been extraordinarily lucky. The first and last were my first and second wives. The three in the middle were: one Swedish; one middle European, a bit Romanian and a bit German; and one Chinese. I am naming no names and gossiping no gossip, but mostly these were vastly enriching experiences. In each case I learned not just about life or sex, but about their culture. One of the great things about being in love is that it peels off layers of rejectionist indoctrination, and that one comes to quite strange cultures with an open mind, which follows on an open heart; with love, even.

The half was a love that might have been, but in practical terms it had no future. The woman I loved had a career in another country, one which was the centre of her life, which defined her and which I would not have countenanced her giving up. It was with pain, but the right decision, that we stopped. I have benefited enormously from these loves, and I believe that in the three cases, though circumstances made it impossible for us to make a life together, we retain respect and real affection. In that, again, I feel immensely lucky.

Of my first wife, Laura Wine, I can say nothing but good. I admire her very much. We have children together, to whom she was a splendid mother and who are the joy of both of our lives. We grew apart, and it was right, I think, to stop when we did. But we did it without bitterness or rancour, before we had come to hate each other, and we settled our affairs amicably without recourse to law. Since I don't believe that marriages are made in heaven, I believe that there are circumstances when it is right to stop, and my conclusion is that in that case one should stop soon, making every effort to avoid rancour and bitterness. But let no one say that the ending of a long and often wonderful marriage is easy. It is awful. And it is not something you can switch off. You must live through it and let the pain fade.

Both of us have remarried and whenever she and her new husband, a man I know and like, are in Ireland (they live in the east Mediterranean) they have dinner with my new wife and myself, which is an occasion of joy (certainly for me) and of mutual goodwill. She was a wonderful mother to our children, and I recall the good times – twenty-something years of them – with pleasure and respect.

The second love I will not write about at all, except to say that when you fall in love with someone from another country and to a degree another culture, all sorts of boundaries dissolve; one gets an insight into that culture of a more loving way, and one can learn new things which are in conflict with one's own cultural formation, which I think would otherwise be very difficult. Again, I am immensely grateful, and it was a lifebelt for me at a very difficult time. I was too close to the end of my first marriage for me to contemplate a new one (what someone has caustically defined as 'the triumph of hope over experience'). And then it was too late. But I gained immensely from our love, and I hope you feel there was something in it for you too, so thank you.

The third great love, as great as the others, was for a Chinese woman. When you love someone from a particular culture, your mind and heart espouse their culture with a particular passion. And that happened to me. I have been to China. Not just Hong Kong, but also into the People's Republic to Xiamen, which as a Treaty post used to be Amoy, the coastal city that Marco Polo pretended that he visited.[1] It was an extraordinary experience because I felt – impossible, I know – almost a sense of coming home. The people were about the same size as me.

---

1. Accounts of Marco Polo's travels exist in divergent versions and are often regarded with scepticism. In twenty-four years abroad, he visited the court of Kublai Khan in China and also the south coast, possibly including Amoy/Xiamen. On his return to Italy he was imprisoned by the Genoese, then at war with Venice; he dictated his experiences to his cellmate Rustichello di Pisa, a professional writer of romances, who emphasized the fantastic and made *The Book of Marvels of the World* (c.1300) a bestseller. Nonetheless, its detail could apparently only have derived from authentic experience.

The clothes were warm and comfortable. The food, I adored. It seems to me that, if you like dark hair and eyes, which I do, the people were very beautiful. The levels of local practical skills were extremely high. The Irish painter Patrick Scott, whom I count as a friend, has made a collection of domestic Chinese artefacts: small objects used in the process of simply getting on with domestic life.[2] They seemed to me some of the most beautiful things I have ever seen.

I wasn't about to marry for reasons of personal trauma. I think my partner's friends presumed that it was a kind of basic white European racism: a Chinese woman is good enough to sleep with, but not to marry. In the end her family got around and married her. They found an older well-to-do Chinese man in a far country, and away she went. I'm sorry. I loved her and she did me immense good by opening to me what I think is arguably the greatest culture in the world.

And then: a pause. In my late fifties and early sixties, suffering from Paget's disease – which I then believed to be relentlessly progressive and without treatment – I felt myself to be no partner for any woman. There is a sentimental ballad that people used to sing in pubs when I was a kid, in the pre-television era when people did sing and recite in pubs: 'At seventeen he fell in love quite madly with eyes of tender blue'. The relevant bit says:

'When he reckoned he was past love, it was then he met his last love
And he loved her as he'd never loved before.'

Thus the old song. And another one from my singing pub teens says, 'Going to a wedding is the making of another'. About 1992 I was invited to the wedding of the daughter of old friends, Brian Hussey and Sue Minet. Brian then farmed near me. At a certain point I rented land from him for my overflow heifers. When interest rates climbed to 20 per cent, my over-borrowed farm had difficulty in paying the rent, which I am very ashamed of. But I think I am forgiven. One of the daughters of the house was getting married and I was happy to go to the wedding, without a partner. Brian's twin brother Derry is married to a lady I have a lot of time for – Gemma Hussey, who was a minister in a subsequent coalition government after I had withdrawn from the scene. In the Fine Gael party interest, be it said, but she was of a modern, Social Democrat-leaning Fine Gael, and when I was in the Senate I knew her as a militant feminist. While I could still dance, I loved to. Gemma knew this. When they struck up an old-time waltz she said, 'Dance with me,' which I was delighted to do. We went through a little

---

2. Born in Kilbrittain, Cork on 24 January 1921; died in Dublin on 14 February 2014.

fiddly bit called the valetta successfully, and I enjoyed myself. And then I thought it would be nice to dance with Brian's sister Barbara. I asked. She accepted. We did – and much more.

Up to her retirement Barbara ran a Dublin law firm, which she had established. It made no money, but it fought a brave and brilliant battle for civil rights. A pioneer of the free legal aid scheme, she became a specialist in separation law and, when it came along, in divorce. She instructed Mary Robinson, who subsequently became President of Ireland, in a case concerning information about abortion that ended in the European Court in Strasbourg. She was one of the small number of self-sacrificing people, inspired with a passion for fairness and equality for everybody, who were able to (partially) save the legal profession from accusations of greedy cynicism and of providing at a high price recourse to legal defence only to those who could afford it.

Both Barbara and I were a bit cautious. We had both, I think, had some hurt. Certainly at my age I was very cautious of total commitment, which in my book is the only proper sort. We circled each other carefully for a while. But then we took the risk. At the end of 1992 I moved in with her. We have been together now for seventeen years. For me they have been years of unalloyed wonder and delight.

People make speeches at weddings. As an old politician, broadcaster and teacher, I make speeches given the opportunity unless the people get up and walk away – which, mostly, they are too polite to do. When she and I were married, I speechified, no doubt mostly trivial, but I said that while Christians record time as BC and AD, I record time as BB and AB: Before Barbara and After Barbara. Hand on heart, I can say that I never experienced and never expected to experience the joy and happiness that I have found with her these last dozen years.

My first wife, Laura, when she was told that Barbara and I were an item, responded by saying, 'Oh, I'm delighted. I think that's wonderful. At least, I think it is wonderful for Justin. But I'm not so sure about for Barbara.' That is exactly how I feel. Neither of us is easy. As I age and the Paget's disease takes hold I am a bloody nuisance. None of me works properly. And there is a litany of medicines, hearing aids, false teeth, etc. each morning, and help with putting my socks on. The degree of sweetness, patience, sensitivity not to humiliate me, and simple love that I have received surpasses anything I would have believed possible. And I find the contradiction. Here I am giving out about almost everything. Opinionated, with a short fuse, contrary, crotchety, critical of everything and everybody – and yet in our home I enjoy the most calm and serene happy time I have ever known.

In my own life I have moved (I nearly said 'progressed', but that is a matter of viewpoint – in my view, it was progress) from the guilty groping of my ignorant teens. But it was slow progress. And now in my old age I am impotent. But I have news for those who dread this consequence of old age: don't. What the police reports call 'penetrative sex' is not necessary for a happy and fulfilling sexual relationship. As usual, the important principle is to think your way into the other person's head. If you set out not to pursue but to give pleasure you will promote a reciprocal response. The joy of sex is not ended by the physical diminution of old age.

Many of the very best and sweetest things in my life have come from women, the last not least. If we are going to avoid destroying our world, we have a huge need to encompass women's wisdom, not simply as surrogate men – in fact, absolutely *not* as surrogate men – but as the exponents of their wisdom. Better about problem-solving. Better about avoiding direct physical confrontation. Gatherers more than hunters, to whom cherishing the earth comes more easily than it does to exploitative, combative males. Please, *mná na hÉireann* and women of the world: help us men, who have not managed so well. And forgive us.

## THAT IS THE END

This is perhaps the moment for a personal digression. I am by training a scientist. I saw an interesting piece of research somewhere recently indicating that religious believers clung to life much more passionately than atheists, who are going nowhere. I had a flirtation with death in the very late 1970s, when my Paget's disease was very strongly active and the biochemical tests (levels of alkaline phosphatase, etc.) were terrifying. I went off and read the medical books. The prospect was of death, fairly soon, in a very unpleasant and possibly very painful way. So I had a hard look at my atheism. Was this the end? No amount of fear – and anger that I was going with half my life unlived – could make me believe something so inherently improbable. It died down. I survived.

I am a relentless humanist, though I do not think God important enough to define myself by denying his existence. I don't use the word 'atheist' much. But I need and use poetry as much as anyone I know. With a little liquid lubrication I can recall hundreds of songs. A very treasured possession is a copy of *The Golden Treasury of Scottish Poetry*, autographed by both Hugh MacDiarmid (a great poet who carried out an interesting tightrope act, not unknown in Ireland a little later, between Communism and nationalism) and Hamish Henderson. And since my undergraduate days I have been both a friend and great admirer of John Montague. He has suffered, I think, from comparison with Seamus Heaney. Both are from the North and lived in 'interesting times'. Montague is less charming and less academic than Heaney, but he has a bite and a cold eye that I admire very much. I read him often.

And I love Gothic cathedrals and stained glass. Those flying buttresses, testing the very limits of what stone would stand, were made by unknown artisans. They did not have the benefit of an analysis of the physical properties of their building materials, or engineering calculations of loads and stresses. They did this, those semi-literate artisans, out of their genius and the analysis of a few celebrated mistakes. And the men who made stained glass knew nothing of the physics and chemistry of glass, or of the pigments they used to such breathtaking effect. Unlettered artisans – and geniuses. What I see is not homage to God, but homage to man.

At eighty, death faces me now. I can't have much longer to go. But my last years have been and are wonderful. I experience around me – among people who are, in the local phrase, 'in the whole of their health' – a dread of old age. And I can only say to them: don't dread it. Embrace it. Dodge and weave and get cute to retain as much of your strength as possible, but don't fight ageing head-on. The willow bends before the gale. The oak tries to stand straight. The willow wins. I accept waning strength and set it against the other bonuses. Nobody ever told me that love in all its aspects would persist so intensely as I head for eighty. Nobody ever told me that the joy in family – now three generations of them – would be so enormous.

I will die. It is a condition of life. Probably quite soon, though I live carefully and perhaps the dramatic explosion in medical knowledge will keep ahead of my decline. But whichever way: I, like everyone else, will inevitably die. And for me, that is the end. The consciousness which flickered to light on the top of Killakee mountain all those decades ago will end. The screen will go blank. The stored information and conclusions in my brain (the paradigm) will simply dissolve as the neurones and synapses decay. And there is no supercomputer somewhere, recording all I've done and said, which can review it and pass judgement on my life. That is the end.

I don't want to be buried in a coffin in sacred ground (whatever *that* is). I don't want to be cremated, because from my ecological viewpoint that consumes too many calories in fuel. What I want is to go into my nature heath in East Kildare, in a biodegradable bag, so that I may add a little to the fertility of what I hope is a properly farmed and thus already fertile area. I will be recycled. While I don't believe in reincarnation, I will be happy to add a few useful molecules to a beautiful environment. Please, old people as old as I am, don't 'rage, rage against the dying of the light',[3] because raging won't change anything. Accept. But on the way, without the guilt that religions impose to help control and dominate us, enjoy. Life is sweet.

---

3. 'Do Not Go Gentle into that Good Night' by Dylan Thomas. First published in 1951. *The Collected Poems of Dylan Thomas: The Centenary Edition* [to commemorate his birth], (Hachette, 2014).

Headstone. *Courtesy of Eilis Quinlan.*

# *Epilogue*

Justin Keating died on 31 December 2009 at Bishopland, Ballymore Eustace, County Kildare. It was late afternoon when his heart stopped. The sun was setting on the last day of the year.

On 5 January 2010, two days before what would have been his eightieth birthday, there was a large gathering at Bishopland for a humanist celebration of his life. It included tributes from his friends and family, his widow, children and grandchildren. It was a glorious bright winter's day, with a blue sky and deep snow on the ground.

After the memorial, Justin was buried in an eco-friendly cardboard coffin at Eadestown Cemetery, Naas, Co. Kildare. His old friend and comrade, Ruairí Quinn, delivered a funeral oration and farewell. The day ended with food and drink and lively recollections, as he would have wished.

Justin's grave is marked by a simple granite headstone from the local quarry at Ballyknockan. It carries the following inscription:

Justin Keating
Born January 7th, 1930
Died at sunset on
The blue moon of
December 31st, 2009

Much Loved

'Nothing is written in stone'

### Ballycotton Cliff

*Before reading her father's poem at his funeral, Carla recalled a happy occasion in September 2001 when she and her family stayed with Justin and Barbara at a rented house in Ballycotton. Later during that holiday, Justin composed his poem.*

I'm a gatherer again, the hunter-gatherer's child.
A pert eleven-year-old, large-eyed, excited,
Pleased to copy my mother and be part of the grown-ups' action,
Picking blackberries. Not play (that's for children) but useful work.
Bitter-sweet and aromatic, their taste carries me back through the dashing
    decades,
Back sixty years.

'Leave a few for the fairies,' my mother said. 'Of course, I don't believe in fairies,
But that's what the old people always told you, and the idea is right.'
And then with the mock-solemn face she used to signal something important,
She added, 'Never over-exploit the resource.' Big words for someone my age.
But I was so happy I never forgot them.

Taste. Why have I not trained it more? It's like a muscle that grows with use.
Wine makers and tea blenders are not special people but they just work at it.
But I rushed through my life never pausing to focus my taste, missing so much.
Even unfocused, today's berry taste contains the world.

'Why are there blackberries, mammy?'
'The birds eat them, and they digest the nice soft bits, but the hard seeds pass
    right through.
They shit them in some new place packed in a nice gob of manure
And if the seeds find a lucky spot they grow,
And later on the new plants produce new blackberries.
It's the clever way, using the birds by giving them something they want,
That brambles invented to spread themselves.'

Today I'm a gatherer once more, taking care not to destroy the resource.
I'll probably never pick blackberries on this cliff again.
I'll leave some for the birds,
For more brambles next year,
For more fruit for the gatherers who come after me.

# APPENDICES

# *Appendix A*

## The Greening of Humanism:
## On the need for a greater ecological awareness

### Justin Keating

We can destroy the earth, or we can save the earth. It depends on our actions. As never before, the survival of humankind is threatened. The source of the threat is human action.

Patriarchal religion, where each separate population invented a god and imposed belief in him on others by force, caused immense suffering through wars and immense cruel oppression of women, but otherwise you could argue that it didn't do much harm! But this is no longer true.

Our survival is at stake due to an unrestrained and profligate use of the earth's resources. Of course this is not the sole cause of our peril, but the state of mind enshrined in the Book of Genesis is a validation for all those who believe in the cult of more growth and more consumption, encourages a more exploitative approach to nature.

It is worth quoting to remind ourselves what a wicked book the Bible is. This is Genesis 1:28. God's injunction is: 'Be fruitful and multiply, fill the Earth and subdue it, have domination over the fish of the sea; over the birds of the air and every other living thing that moves on the Earth'.

And who was to do the subduing, and who was to exercise the domination? Not humankind, but mankind. Since Eve is the source of sin and pain in the world, without whose machinations we would all still be living in Paradise, it is necessary in order to prevent her from wreaking further harm on mankind to subdue and dominate her too.

I wish I were exaggerating, but for two and a bit millennia Jews, Christians and

Muslims have lived by this teaching. In that period scientific advances in agriculture and medicine have given us a world not peopled by the pair in the Garden of Eden, but by something between six and seven billion and growing. We are deforming the Earth. We are too great a burden for Gaia to bear.

While this is happening, the only source of salvation, the application of reason undistorted by revelation is under attack. The humanist worldview, we are told, has no spiritual dimension. But it depends as usual on the meaning you attach to the word, in this case to the word 'spiritual'. If you are emphasizing the dualist split between the spiritual and the material, between the soul and the body, for me, that is meaningless nonsense. If you simply mean, as seems commoner nowadays, the sense of awe and wonder and reverence with which we all feel inspired, then I think it is something which every human seeks and needs. But then I am convinced that humanists, from the nature of their system of belief, have a greater reverence of a truly valid kind than any religion can provide.

So what do I revere, more beautiful and inspiring than any stained glass, or choirs, or organ music or ornate vestments? My answer is in one word – I revere nature.

In our evolution we developed a mind which was aware of past and future, of beauty and its opposite, but without much understanding. So we invented an explanation of a mythical kind for what we experienced.

Much later, in the great river valleys – Tigris/Euphrates, Nile and the fertility-giving watercourses of China and India – settled agriculture arose, and with it surpluses of food and the development of class society. The richest found ways to appropriate that surplus. The really remarkable question is why the rest of humankind accepted this injustice. According to what I consider a brilliant analysis by Jared Diamond, the old myths were hijacked, and monotheistic patriarchal religion was invented to justify the theft by the wealthy. The new societies were ruled by a new group for which Diamond coined a new name. Since they stole the surplus he called their society a kleptocracy – the rule of the thieves – kings, aristocracies and (people who lived in equal splendour) the priests. With only a few exceptions they were able to divert our sense of awe and beauty onto their gods.

The basic feeling, the need for beauty, the delight and awe inspired by our surroundings could not be eliminated. 'If you have two loaves of bread, exchange one for a flower.'

It was for reasons like these that I was so touched by Dick Spicer's article in the March–April issue of *Humanism Ireland* in which he expressed his delight with his relationship with the birds around us. In that sense we all do need a spiritual dimension in our lives. For Dick it is birds, for me mammals, which was the inspiration for my professional life as a mammalian anatomist. But the complexity of our universe is such that there is a very large number of areas of inspiration. Nobody ever expressed that delight and excitement better than Carl Sagan in books like *Cosmos*. He was a cosmologist, and also one of the world's most passionate and eloquent humanists. But it can be something as local and intimate as growing prize leeks or keeping homing pigeons.

So my fundamental thought is this. The two great causes of my life, Humanism and Ecology, are in my experience two aspects of the worldview I seek, though without too much hope of imminent victory, but at least believing that we can ensure survival for our species, a world where we combine humanist ethos with a profound love of the earth. It is the opposite of the Book of Genesis. I seek not domination or subjection, but to live on earth in symbiotic harmony with my surroundings – all of my surroundings – of which the human part is obviously the most important.

More than forty years ago I wrote: 'We hold this earth in trust for future generations, and they will judge us by the state it is in when we pass it on.' Since then all the measurements of the pressure on our natural surroundings (population, carbon dioxide emissions, fish catches, the number of motorcars etc, etc) have all increased markedly. So the problem is greater. In fact, in a sense it is new. Now there is doubt about the very existence of those 'future generations'. We can destroy the earth, or we can save the earth. It depends on our actions.

The most dangerous belief is that God made the earth for us humans to exploit and subdue and dominate, and that if we obey him he will ensure our survival. The conviction that I want to enjoin on people is that while there is a very heartening movement of ecological awareness, organisation and action everywhere, the very best roadmap for survival is the combination of green and humanist beliefs.

*This is an amended version of a talk given by Justin at the 2008 All-Ireland Humanist Summer School in Carlingford*
*Humanism Ireland* • No 114 • January–February 2009

# Appendix B

## Oil and Gas Licensing Terms

In 1975 Justin Keating introduced new licensing terms for oil and gas exploration and exploitation off the Irish coastline. He had visited Norway to investigate and greatly admired the Norwegian government's foresight in copperfastening its population's future. Ireland's continental shelf had not yet been designated for exploration, though Marathon had announced its discovery of a 'small commercial gas field' near Kinsale two years earlier.

The new terms:

- Allowed for state holdings in a commercial field of up to 50 per cent
- Claimed royalties on a sliding scale of 8–16 per cent (on sales, not profits)
- Set a 50 per cent tax on profits accruing from any oil or gas development
- Required license holders to land in Ireland any petroleum found, and to provide training[1]

Keating's successor Des O'Malley showed no enthusiasm towards a state company. In 1987, Fianna Fáil energy minister Ray Burke relinquished the state's right to any share of a discovery, abolishing royalties and introducing tax write-offs; this without going to a Dáil vote.

In 2008 documentary film-maker Rístéard Ó Domhnaill engaged Justin Keating in what was to be his last recorded interview. The resulting film, *The Pipe* (2010), won several prestigious awards; it tells the story of the community of Rossport, Co. Mayo, in their struggle against combined pressure from Shell Oil and the Irish State.

---

1. From *Optimising Ireland's Oil and Gas Resources* (SIPTU).

## BULA AND TARA MINES

Tara Mines, at Navan, Co. Meath, is the largest zinc mine in Europe and the fifth-largest in the world. Keating's 'consistent aim was to create an Irish multinational with significant state involvement which could compete with the global mining industry'.[2] A mining lease was granted to Tara Exploration and Development Company Ltd. whereby the state retained a 25 per cent shareholding and received 4.5 per cent royalties on taxable profits. In July 1973 Keating concluded a deal with Bula Limited whereby the state received a 25 per cent stake for no financial consideration and an additional 24 per cent for £9.54 million, a price determined by experts appointed by the Institute of Arbitrators in London: in effect, a 49 per cent stake for the price of 24 per cent.

Keating came under frequent attack for his department's decisions, notably from Des O'Malley and Noël Browne, and later won a libel case against the *Sunday Tribune*, which had accused him of dishonesty in his handling of the mines affair.

These policies too were reversed. The mines were acquired by foreign investors at a very low cost in 2002, after Bula Ltd had gone into receivership, and continue to be extremely profitable.

---

2. *Dictionary of Irish Biography.*

# *Appendix C*

## Barron is Right about 1974 Bombs

In 1981, when the general election came around, I ran for neither the Dáil nor the Senate, though I had been a member of one or other of them for the previous twelve years. Amid the larger excitement of the election, with the appearance of new faces, I was able to slip away quietly, without any announcement or farewells, *writes Justin Keating.*

Though I had lots of strong opinions about the government of which I had been a member from 1973 to 1977, I forbore to publish them and did not respond to media enquiries.

Now, twenty-odd years later, and with all my anger leached away, I want to break silence and comment on the Barron Report into the Dublin and Monaghan bombings of 1974, which left 34 people dead. I ignored the media requests for a response until I had read the report carefully, and this I have now done. My reactions are different from those of other ministers of that Cosgrave-led government who have made public comment, and since I demur I feel a duty to put my beliefs into circulation.

A few peripheral comments first. There seems to me to be an effort to rubbish the Barron Report, and to criticise adversely the retired Supreme Court Judge, Henry Barron, who was its author. I know him very slightly in a personal sense, but over many years I have heard quite a lot about him. I believe that we are extremely lucky that a person of his calibre was available to succeed the late Mr Justice Liam Hamilton. Mr Justice Barron is nobody's man, except his own. He has the reputation of being absolutely straight and upright, and of being the possessor of a very powerful legal mind. If I have heard criticism over the years it is that he was meticulous about the small print of a case to the point of nit-picking – surely a virtue in this inquiry.

I think his report is splendid, I accept his findings and my only regret is that unco-operative outside forces, including those in the UK, prevented him from going further.

As a judge, working in a very sensitive area, he can only categorise something as fact if the evidence is strong enough to stand up in a court of law. He makes meticulous distinctions between fact on the one hand and probabilities or possibilities on the other hand. Very properly in my view.

But life is not like a court of law. We do not live and decide and act only on the basis of what we can prove to be true, but on the basis of what we have strong reasons to believe to be true. When I come, in a moment, to comment on some of Mr Justice Barron's conclusions, I will offer beliefs and opinions which I cannot prove to be true in the law-court sense, but which I nonetheless hold that I have good grounds for believing.

Taking Mr Justice Barron's conclusions in order (pages 268 to 288 of the report) I offer the following comments and responses.

– That the Garda investigation was inadequate. Yes, I believe that.

– That they failed to involve the appropriate official, the Attorney General, in their decision on prosecution. True also.

– That the government of the day (of which I was a member) showed little interest in the bombings. With great regret, I have to say that this corresponds to my recollection. But as Minister for Industry and Commerce, known to disagree with Dr Conor Cruise O'Brien about Northern Ireland, I was often excluded or bypassed on such matters.

– 'That members of the security forces in Northern Ireland could have been involved is neither fanciful nor absurd, given the number of instances in which similar activity has been proved.' This is well said. I go further. On careful reading of the whole report and the script of the unrefuted 'Hidden Hand' documentary, and on other information (not evidence) from the time, I believe that Northern Ireland security forces were involved. The question that immediately arises is 'up to what level?'

The bumbling, ineffective but decent Northern Ireland Secretary, Merlyn Rees, in my opinion, would certainly not be an accessory to murder. And security people do not if they can help it either furnish information to an inquiry from another state, or indeed put in writing such decisions. And indeed often do not tell their political bosses.

In the last sentence of his conclusions, Mr Justice Barron states: 'Unless further information comes to hand, such involvement [by British security – JK] must remain a suspicion. It is not proven.' This is fair and judicial. But the commission was severely handicapped by failure to co-operate on various sides and by the loss (deliberate destruction?) of significant documents. What Mr Justice Barron calls a suspicion I believe to be true.

In general I think that Mr Justice Barron got it right, and I congratulate him on difficult work well done. I accept his findings. Though as Minister for Industry and Commerce I was far from the immediate problem, and believe that some of the details were concealed from me, on the basis of collective cabinet responsibility I apologize with a whole heart to all those who, in May 1974 and since, were let down by the government – families, loved ones and the whole population.

*Justin Keating is a former Labour Party Minister for Industry and Commerce*
[Reproduced from] *The Irish Times*, 29 December 2003.

# Appendix D

## The Zionist State Has No Right to Exist

## Justin Keating on Israel

I have a tree in Israel, and I once had a certificate to prove it. In about 1950 a lady from a Zionist organisation planted it for my support of the Zionist Youth Movement in Ireland. But it is all so long ago that it has probably been cut down by now, and I have lost the certificate. At the time, like many young Europeans with left-wing views, as the full horrors of Nazi genocide became known, I supported the new state. But now I have totally changed my mind.

I have reached the conclusion that the Zionists have absolutely no right to what they call Israel, that they have built their state not beside but on top of the Palestinian people, and that there can be no peace as long as contemporary Israel retains its present form. I hasten to make clear that none of this gives me any pleasure, but in the great scheme of things my personal wishes do not weigh heavily in the scale pans of history. I wish I did not think what I do; I hope I am wrong. My conclusions are based on the answers to five questions.

Did the Jews of the Old Testament come from what is now Israel? The answer is no.

Are the Jews of the world today simply the descendants of the people of the diaspora two thousand years ago? The answer is only in part.

Does the right of return apply to people who occupied some land two thousand years ago for a historically brief period, to the detriment of those who have been there since? Obviously no. Imagine a world where every people claimed that right.

Did the Balfour Declaration give the Zionists the right to establish a state in Israel? The answer is no. At the time the British government had no right to give.

Did the United Nations Resolution of November 1947 give Zionists the right to establish the present state of Israel? The answer is no, and they have continuously and relentlessly violated that resolution for more than half a century, so that any tatters that now remain are void, by their action.

I want briefly to look at each point separately. Some of what I say is taken from a book called *My People* by Abba Eban, who was Israeli Foreign Minister. He says the Hebrew tribes came out of Mesopotamia. They moved from Ur in southwest Mesopotamia to Harran, in northwest Mesopotamia. It was here that Abraham was told, by the God that the Jews had invented, to leave his land and kinsmen for a new country. Obedient to the divine voice, he moved into western Palestine, the land of the Canaanites. The above is loosely but accurately quoted from Eban. It follows that the Jews came from far away, that they claimed the land of Canaan because their God gave it to them, and there were Canaanites there already. Israel's Declaration of Independence in 1948 states, 'The Land of Israel was the birthplace of the Jewish people.' This was a self-serving and untruthful Zionist myth.

My second point is that the assumption that the Jews of the world (all of whom claim the right of return) are descendants of the Diaspora takes no account of the Kingdom of the Khazars, about whom Arthur Koestler wrote a book arguing that he and other Ashkenazi Jews were their descendents. Also, it assumes that no Jewish girl ever got pregnant (over 2000 years) by a non-Jew, and brought the child home to her parents, and it also forgets that the converted wives or husbands who were born non-Jewish can, on conversion, claim the right of return.

Point three: at the time of the Balfour Declaration, the Ottoman Empire, which was the ruling power in Palestine, was falling apart, but the British government had no rights in the area. The Declaration was made to a private person, the head of the Rothschild family, and while Balfour was promising the Jews a nation home in Palestine, T.E. Lawrence was promising the same thing to Palestinian Arabs. In law and in equity it has no validity.

Finally, when the United Nations passed its historic resolution (with Britain abstaining) it was a plan for partition. What was new and crucial was that it recognized Jewish sovereignty. The flight of the ignorant Palestinian peasants was founded on such atrocities as the massacre at Deir Yassin where Zionist terrorists filled the well with slaughtered peasants, and went to adjoining villages saying, 'Look what happened over there.' In addition, there were bogus broadcasts purporting to come from Palestinian leaders, advising flight. The Jewish–Arab partnership, pleaded for so eloquently by David Ben-Gurion – 'based on equality and mutual assistance', to quote his words – was from the beginning a lie which Zionist fundamentalists did not believe.

Those same fundamentalists, who are in the ascendant now, can only say, 'We are here because our God gave it to us.' That is too weak for me, I'm afraid.

All of this is a huge tragedy for ordinary Zionist people, who have been led up a blind alley by fanatics. But it is more. Jews have made an immense contribution to civilization, developing as they were between the great empires of Mesopotamia and the Nile, with both of which they had intimate contact, and by which they wanted to avoid being swallowed. They developed a religion and an ethos based on independence, liberty and democracy to which we all owe a debt. That religion is based on the twin concepts of Law and Righteousness, which inspired over the millennia extraordinary contributions to culture and morality. All admirable. In Israel/Palestine, where are they now?

Zionists have betrayed all of this, and that is a tragedy not just for Jews, but for all of us.

*The Dubliner,* November 2005

# Bibliography

Akenson, Donald Harman, *Conor: A Biography of Conor Cruise O'Brien* (Ithaca, NY: Cornell University Press, 1994).

Barron, Henry, *The Barron Report: An Independent Commission of Inquiry into the Dublin and Monaghan Bombings* (Dublin: Government Publications, 2003).
Bernal, John Desmond, *Science in History* (London: Watts, 1954; Boston: MIT, 1971).
Browne, Noël, *Against the Tide* (Dublin: Gill & Macmillan, 1986).

Carson, Rachel, *Silent Spring* (London: Hamilton, 1963).
Chomsky, Noam, *Hegemony or Survival: America's Quest for Global Dominance* (London: Hamish Hamilton, 2003).
Connor, Elizabeth [Una Troy], *Dead Star's Light* (London: Methuen, 1938).
Connor, Elizabeth [Una Troy], *Mount Prospect* (London: Methuen, 1936).
Cooney, John, *John Charles McQuaid: Ruler of Catholic Ireland* (Dublin: O'Brien Press, 1999).
Cruise O'Brien, Conor, *Memoir: My Life and Themes* (Dublin: Poolbeg, 1999).
Cruise O'Brien, Conor, *The Siege: The Saga of Israel and Zionism* (New York: Simon & Schuster, 1986).
Cruise O'Brien, Conor, *States of Ireland* (London: Hutchinson, 1972).

Deeny, James, *To Cure and to Care: Memoirs of a Chief Medical Officer* (Dublin: Glendale, 1989).
Diamond, Jared, *Guns, Germs and Steel: A Short History of Everybody for the Last 13,000 Years* (London: Vintage, 1998).
Dick-Read, Grantly, *Childbirth Without Fear: The Principles and Practice of Natural Childbirth* (London: Heinemann, 1954).
Donnelly, W.J.C., Monaghan, M.L. (eds), *A Veterinary School to Flourish: The Veterinary College of Ireland 1900–2000* (Dublin: UCD Veterinary Faculty, 2001).

Eban, Abba, *My People: The Story of the Jews* (Springfield, NJ: Behrman House, 1968).

Finkelstein, Israel and Silberman, Neil Asher, *The Bible Unearthed: Archaeology's New Vision of Ancient Israel and the Origin of Its Sacred Texts* (New York: Touchstone, 2002).

Fisk, Robert, *Pity the Nation: Lebanon at War* (Oxford: Oxford University Press, 1991).

Fisk, Robert, *The Great War for Civilization: The Conquest of the Middle East* (London: Harper Perennial, 2006).

FitzGerald, Garret, *All in a Life: An Autobiography* (Dublin: Gill & Macmillan, 1991).

FitzGerald, Garret, *Reflections on the Irish State* (Dublin: Irish Academic Press, 2002).

Foster, R.F., *Vivid Faces: The Revolutionary Generation in Ireland 1890–1923* (London: Penguin Books, 2015).

Garrett, Laurie. *The Coming Plague: Newly Emerging Diseases in a World Out of Balance* (London: Penguin Books, 1995).

Gimbutas, Marija, *The Civilization of the Goddess: The World of Old Europe*, ed. Joan Marler (San Francisco: Harper, 1991).

Halligan, Brendan, *Justin Keating: A Tribute* (Dublin: Scáthán Press, 2009).

Hitchens, Christopher, *The Missionary Position: Mother Teresa in Theory and Practice* (London: Verso, 1995).

Hobbs, Eddie, Dominic Sherlock and Dr Amanda Slevin, eds., *Own Our Oil: The Fight for Irish Economic Freedom* (Dublin: Liberties Press, 2014).

Hobsbawm, Eric J., *Nations and Nationalism Since 1780* (Cambridge: Cambridge University Press, 1992).

Hobsbawm, Eric J., *The Age of Revolution: Europe 1789–1848* (London: Abacus, 1962).

Hobsbawm, Eric J., *The Age of Capital: 1848–1875* (London: Weidenfeld & Nicholson, 1975).

Hobsbawm, Eric J., *The Age of Empire: 1875–1914* (London: Vintage, 1989).

Hobsbawm, Eric J., *The Age of Extremes: The Short Twentieth Century, 1914–1991* (London: Abacus, 1995).

Hobson, John A., *Imperialism: A Study* (London: Cosimo, 1902).

Huberman, Leo, *Man's Worldly Goods: The Story of the Wealth of Nations* (London: Gollancz, 1937).

Jackendoff, Ray, *Patterns in the Mind: Language and Human Nature* (New York: Harvester Wheatsheaf, 1993).

Jackson, Thomas Alfred, *Ireland Her Own: An Outline History of the Irish Struggle for National Freedom and Independence* (London: Lawrence & Wishart, 1971).

Jeffries, J.M.N, *The Balfour Declaration* (Beirut: Institute for Palestine Studies, 1967).

Johnston, Roy H.W., *Century of Endeavour: A Biographical and Autobiographical View of the Twentieth Century in Ireland,* rev. edn. (Carlow: Tyndall Publications/Dublin: The Lilliput Press, 2006).

Koestler, Arthur, *Darkness at Noon* (London: Penguin Modern Classics, 1964).

Koestler, Arthur, *The Thirteenth Tribe: The Khazar Empire and its Heritage* (London: Hutchinson, 1976).

Koestler, Arthur in Richard Crossman, ed., *The God That Failed: A Confession* (New York: Harper & Brothers, 1949).

Le Roy Ladurie, Emmanuel, *Montaillou: Cathars and Catholics in a French Village 1294– 1324* [Orig. pub. 1975] (London: Penguin, 2002).

Lamaze, Fernand, *L'Accouchement Sans Douleur: Un Guide Indispensable* (Paris: Librairie Artheme Fayard, 1957).

di Lampedusa, Giuseppe Tomasi, *The Leopard* (London: Collins, 1960).

Lenin, Vladimir Ilyich, *Imperialism: The Highest Stage of Capitalism* (London: Lawrence & Wishart, 1948).

Liebreich, Karen, *Fallen Order: Intrigue, Heresy and Scandal in the Rome of Galileo and Caravaggio* (London: Atlantic Books, 2004).

McCourt, Frank, *Angela's Ashes: A Memoir of Childhood* (London: HarperCollins, 1996).

MacDiarmid, Hugh, ed., *The Golden Treasury of Scottish Poetry* (London: Macmillan, 1948).

MacSwiney Brugha, Maire, *History's Daughter: A Memoir from the Only Child of Terence MacSwiney* (Dublin: The O'Brien Press, 2006).

Marx, Karl, *Grundrisse: Foundations of the Critique of Political Economy (Rough Draft)* (Transl. London: Pelican, 1973).

Marx, Karl and Engels, Friedrich, *Manifesto of the Communist Party* (London: Modern Books, 1929).

Morris, Frederick, *The Morris Report: The Tribunal of Inquiry into Complaints concerning some Gardai of the Donegal Division* (Dublin: Government Publications, 2004).

Morton, A.L., *A People's History of England* (London: Gollancz, 1938).

O'Brien, Edna, *The Country Girls* (London: Penguin, 1963).

O'Connor, Éimear, *Seán Keating: Art, Politics and Building the Irish Nation* (Dublin: Irish Academic Press, 2013).

Quinn, Ruairí, *Straight Left: A Journey in Politics* (Dublin: Hodder Headline, 2005).

Rabin, Yitzhak, *The Rabin Memoirs* (London: Weidenfeld & Nicholson, 1979).

Raferty, Mary and O'Sullivan, Eoin, *Suffer the Little Children: The Inside Story of Ireland's Industrial Schools* (Dublin: New Island, 1999).

Roberts, Monty, *The Man Who Listens to Horses* (London: Arrow, 1997).

Russell, Bertrand, *A History of Western Philosophy* (London: Unwin, 1984).

Ryan, Seán, *The Ryan Report: The Report of the Commission to Inquire into Child Abuse* (Dublin: Government Publications, 2009).


Sagan, Carl, *Cosmos* (New York: Random House, 1980).

Schumacher, E.F., *Small is Beautiful: A Study of Economics as if People Mattered* (London: Blond & Briggs, 1975).

Shaw, George Bernard, *John Bull's Other Island* (London: Constable, 1904).

Siggins, Lorna, *Once Upon a Time in the West: The Corrib Gas Controversy* (Dublin: Transworld Ireland, 2010).

Smith, Adam, *The Wealth of Nations* (London: Penguin Classics, 1982).

Smith, Adam, *The Theory of Moral Sentiments* (London: Penguin Classics, 2010).

Stein, Leonard, ed., *The Persecution of the Jews in Germany* (London: Joint Foreign Committee of the Board of Deputies of British Jews with the Anglo-Jewish Association, 1933).


Thompson, D'Arcy Wentworth, *On Growth and Form* (London: University Press, 1917).

Troy, Úna [Elizabeth Connor], *We Are Seven* (London: Heinemann, 1955).


Weber, Eugen, *Peasants into Frenchmen: The Modernization of Rural France* (Stanford, CT: Stanford University Press, 1976).

White, Trevor, *The Dubliner Diaries* (Dublin: The Lilliput Press, 2010).

Wilkinson, Richard and Pickett, Kate, *The Spirit Level: Why More Equal Societies Almost Always Do Better* (London: Allen Lane, 2005).

# Index